JAPAN'S ECONOMIC POLICY

By the same author

BRITISH INDUSTRY AND ECONOMIC POLICY
THE INDUSTRIAL DEVELOPMENT OF BIRMINGHAM AND
  THE BLACK COUNTRY
BRITISH INDUSTRIES AND THEIR ORGANISATION
THE STRUCTURE OF INDUSTRY IN BRITAIN
MONOPOLY AND RESTRICTIVE PRACTICES
A SHORT ECONOMIC HISTORY OF MODERN JAPAN
JAPAN'S ECONOMIC EXPANSION

Japan's Economic Policy

G. C. ALLEN

Emeritus Professor of Political Economy, University of London

First published 1980 by
THE MACMILLAN PRESS LTD
London and Basingstoke
Associated companies in Delhi
Dublin Hong Kong Johannesburg Lagos
Melbourne New York Singapore Tokyo

Printed in Hong Kong

British Library Cataloguing in Publication Data

Allen, George Cyril
  Japan's economic policy
  1. Japan – Economic conditions – 1868–
  I. Title
  330.9'52'03   HC462
  ISBN 0–333–26165–8

In memoriam
Eleanorae
conjugis amantissimae

Contents

Preface

My acquaintance with Japan began in 1922 when I took up a teaching appointment at the Nagoya *Koto Shogyo Gakko*, the precursor of the present Department of Economics at Nagoya University. At the outset my curiosity was aroused by certain distinctive features in the country's financial organisation and policy. This explains why the earliest of the papers in this collection are studies of Japan's foreign exchange, banking and monetary system in relation to her economic development. In the 1930s the centre of my interest shifted to her industrial organisation and to her progress as a producer and exporter of a widening range of manufactured goods. I retained this interest and later extended it to include the complex of factors responsible for her exceptionally rapid growth throughout the modern period, and especially for her industrial expansion after the Second World War. Aspects of this subject are reviewed in several chapters. One cannot proceed far in the study of this economy without becoming aware of the important role of the state in economic development. The role is not easy to understand. In Japan the public sector is small by international standards, and private enterprise and the market economy have flourished since the war. Yet the government, in recent times as in the past, has exerted a strong and pervasive influence on private decision-making and on the whole course of development. This theme is pursued in several of the papers and is central to some. Hence the title that I have given to this collection.

With two exceptions, the chapters reproduce the papers and articles in the form in which they were originally published, although I have not hesitated to make minor changes in the text in the interests of clarity, or when excisions were called for in order to avoid the tedious repetition of facts or arguments.

Such repetitions as remain are, I hope, justified by the differences in the context in which they occur. The first exception is Chapter 2 which is the result of conflating two papers, one published in the *Economic Journal* in 1925 and the other in *Economic History* in 1933. The second exception is Chapter 6. This consists, in both substance and form, of a long paper published in the *Annals of Public and Cooperative Economy* in 1968, but it also includes some paragraphs from an essay that appeared in the *Economic Review* of Hitotsubashi University in 1970. In the introductory chapter I have distinguished the main themes of the several papers and have called attention to the links between them. I have also ventured to carry a few of the arguments beyond the limits to which they were originally confined.

I express my thanks to the following for permission to republish the articles and papers of which the book is composed: the editors of *International Affairs*, the *Oxford Review of Education, Lloyds Bank Review*, the *Economic Review* of Hitotsubashi University, and the *Economic History Review* (for an article in *Economic History*); the editorial committee of the *Three Banks Review*; the Cambridge University Press (for two articles in the *Economic Journal*); the Director of the International Centre of Research and Information on Public and Cooperative Economy (for an article in the *Annals of Public and Cooperative Economy*); the Manchester Statistical Society (for the report of an address published in its *Proceedings*), and the British Association for Japanese Studies (for an address delivered at one of its conferences and afterwards published in its *Proceedings*). Acknowledgements in detail are given in the references to the individual papers.

I wish to record my indebtedness to my wife (to whose memory the two volumes of my collected papers are dedicated) for all the help, linguistic, literary and secretarial, that she gave me over many years.

November 1978

G. C. Allen

1 Introduction

For almost a century the Japanese economy has grown at an exceptionally fast rate by international standards: in the interwar period the annual average rate was about 4.5 per cent, well over twice the rate in Western Europe.[1] At that time the outside world paid little heed to this achievement, largely because Japan, having started from a low level of income and technical accomplishment, still lagged behind the leading countries. Even when certain Western industries, for example, the manufacture of textiles, pottery and some miscellaneous consumption goods, felt the impact of her competition in international markets, her success was commonly ascribed to her low wages. Her advances in productive efficiency were generally ignored. Up to the eve of the Second World War it seemed inconceivable that Japan could hope to match Europeans and Americans in the higher reaches of industrial enterprise. To quote Sir George Sansom's comment on this attitude: there long remained in the minds of Westerners the presumption that 'only they themselves had the secret of manipulating levers and valves'.[2] An enquiry undertaken by the Royal Institute of International Affairs in 1935 came to conclusions that expressed the general view at the time: 'Japan remains primarily a peasant and agrarian State', so it was declared.[3] Her industrial strength was confined to a few labour intensive industries, notably textiles, which drew their ill paid labour force from the overpopulated countryside. While she might well be able to enlarge her production of light manufactured articles, her prospects in the metallurgical industries or as a manufacturer of heavy and complex engineering goods were inauspicious.

Whether this prediction would have been generally accepted by European technicians with experience in Japanese firms during the middle 1930s is open to question. It is true that their

1

counterparts a decade earlier were dubious about the ability of Japanese producers to rise above mediocrity in the industries characteristic of the advanced countries, metals, engineering and chemicals. By the 1930s, however, their technical capacity shown in a wide range of industries had won the respect of their European colleagues. Still, these were a small minority. In general, the Western world, on the eve of the war, was content to accept the comfortable verdict that Japan, for all her apparent progress, had 'feet of clay'[4]. And, even in the years just after the war, what were regarded as reasonably well-informed business and official circles, in Britain at any rate, were pessimistic about Japan's economic prospects, as Chapter 11 shows.

Until well into the 1950s the outlook was unpromising. Industrial production did not approach its prewar level until the economy felt the impact of the American demand for supplies on the outbreak of the Korean War. Although output rose quite fast after 1952, Japan's competitive position in international trade remained weak in most classes of manufactures for much of the decade. There were exceptions. The cotton and rayon industries were quickly re-equipped and soon became formidable rivals once more to their Western counterparts. Japan also showed distinctive excellence in the manufacture of a number of new light manufactures (cameras, binoculars and sewing machines). Yet the latter class of goods could never hope to rank as staple exports, while her trade in textiles was threatened by the growth of domestic textile industries in some of the Asian and South American countries she had formerly supplied. Her heavy industries, metals, machinery and chemicals, were much larger than in 1937, but in the early 1950s they were handicapped by the presence of obsolete or inferior plant installed during the years of war. Her costs in these industries were high because of her technical backwardness, the lack of cheap coal and the loss of her former sources of raw materials in East Asia. In international trade in their products she was considered a 'marginal' supplier, finding markets only when Western competitors were short of capacity. Her export trade as a whole did not regain its prewar volume until 1959.

In the early and middle 1950s her forlorn present concealed from outside view the pace of her reconstruction. Her investment, chiefly in industrial plant, reached 25 per cent of GNP in 1952 and rose steeply (proportionately as well as absolutely) in subsequent years. The new equipment closed the technical gap between her and her Western rivals in one industry after another. Nor were her exertions limited to technical improvements. They extended also to the reconstruction of her financial and mercantile organisation (see, Chapter 7 below). So the pace of her recovery accelerated throughout the decade. The short cyclical recessions of 1954 and 1958, far from halting her secular advance, had a therapeutic effect by eliminating inefficiencies and compressing costs, thus preparing the way for future expansion. Yet it was not until the early 1960s that the small group of highly developed countries realised that a newcomer had joined their ranks. Even then there was widespread doubt whether Japan could stay the pace. Every recession gave rise to confident assertions that her days of rapid expansion were over, and that the influences responsible for her postwar achievements had spent their force.

Chapters 2, 3 and 4 consist of papers written during the interwar period and relate to the time when Japan, despite her progress, was still regarded as an 'underdeveloped' country. The financial difficulties analysed in Chapter 2 were closely linked with the expansionist financial policy that she had pursued from the early days of the modern era. Her leaders were preoccupied with the task of reconciling that policy with the maintenance of financial stability—the avoidance of inflation and of recurrent deficits in the balance of payments. In the days of the international gold standard, the problem presented itself in the form of constant threats to the gold parity of the yen. The chapter describes the expedients employed to meet these threats and traces the changing nature of the problem from the early years of the present century to the 1930s. Contemporary advocates of expansionist monetary policies may appeal to Japan's early experience in support of their views, but the identity between her policy at the time she adhered to the gold standard and the expansionist policies of the postwar years is more apparent than real. Japan's monetary expansionism was then kept in check by the discipline of a fixed exchange rate, a discipline which governments now repudiate.

At the time the first part of this chapter was written, economists, interested as many were in problems of the undervaluation or overvaluation of the exchange value of currencies, were much given to calculating purchasing power parities in trying to measure the extent of the divergencies. This technique, despite its theoretical blemishes, passed the pragmatic test in providing a plausible explanation of what had happened to Japan's finances and trade in the early and middle 1920s, as is shown here.

The latter part of this chapter, including the postscript, is directed to the study of the effects of the deflationary policy of 1929–31 and of the subsequent reflation. With hindsight, judgement on the relative merits of these policies is less certain than it appeared to contemporaries. Both made a contribution to Japan's industrial development; but both also had social and political consequences that make it impossible to reach a clear verdict on their respective advantages and defects. The resilience of the Japanese economy at this time, the mobility of resources, and the flexibility of wages, costs and prices in response to external pressure, won the approbation of many Western economists troubled by the increasing rigidity of their own systems. Few probed deeply into the causes of the resilience. Its roots during the 1930s, as is demonstrated in this chapter and elsewhere in the book, were to be found in the overpopulation of the countryside which was the source of cheap labour for the growing secondary and tertiary industries.

The detailed study of the cotton industry in Chapter 3 shows how a particular branch of manufacture adjusted itself to the economic pressures and stimuli described in the last part of the previous chapter. Cotton was Japan's chief large-scale manufacturing industry before the Second World War. It contributed substantially to the success in the export markets during the 1930s, and it provided a conspicuous example of the capacity of Japanese industry to adapt its structure, organisation and technique to changing circumstances. The quality stressed by British cotton spinners and manufacturers who suffered from Japan's advance as a competitor was not her growing efficiency, but the pliability of her wage-rates. It was left to disinterested observers to call attention to what they considered her superior organisation. Neither explanation of Japan's competitive success is wholly correct. The low and declining wage level among her cotton operatives certainly played its part, but the rise in productivity was the decisive factor. On the other hand, the contention that the form of organisation adopted by the Japanese industry was superior to that found in Lancashire is ill-founded. The combination of the spinning and weaving processes in the same mill, to which Japan's low production costs were often ascribed, was shown, on investigation, to possess commanding advantages only for certain classes of goods—those for which demand during the 1930s was growing comparatively slowly. The most rapidly expanding sector of the Japanese industry was structurally very similar to the British cotton industry. Again, the integration of producing and merchanting was sometimes acclaimed as a source of Japanese efficiency, but it was, in fact, the outcome of circumstances peculiar to that country and was not generally superior to the horizontal specialisation characteristic of the British industry. Thus, the paper calls attention to the danger of broad generalisations concerning the optimum method of conducting any complex industry. At the same time, it indicates, in the context of a particular branch of manufacture, some of the ways by which Japan's progress as a producer and international trader during the 1930s was achieved.

Chapter 4 deals with the great business houses, the *Zaibatsu*, (literally, 'money-groups') that have been called the 'spearhead of Japan's economic advance'. If in some respects these concerns resembled the large, multiproduct conglomerates found in the Western world, in other respects they were unique. Their origins, their sources and channels of authority, and the personal and interfirm relationships within each group, bore the stamp of Japan's distinctive social organisation. In the pre-eminent position that they occupied both in finance and in manufacturing industry, transport and trade, they filled a special category among the world's business enterprises. This paper was written at a time when the *Zaibatsu* were under attack from the *Gumbatsu* (the military clique), then intent upon the pursuit of imperialist ambitions in Asia, and their response to this pressure may help to illuminate some of the obscure features of Japan's policy. During the postwar Occupation (1945–52), these great concerns were broken up, but their constituents survived and they emerged again in a new guise to take a leading part in their country's reconstruction and subsequent expansion. The success of the *Zaibatsu* in accommodating themselves to the postwar needs of the economy and to the changed temper of the people affords a striking example of the skill of the Japanese in institutional adaptation.

During the 1950s the author, together with a colleague,

undertook a historical study of Western enterprise in the Far East and South East Asia.[5] The paper that appears as Chapter 5 expounds some of the results of their enquiries, chiefly those that relate to China and Japan. The contrasts between the part played by Western entrepreneurs and investors in the two countries form the main theme of the chapter. But there are wider implications. Those who dismiss Western enterprise in East or South East Asia simply as an example of the exploitation of the native peoples fail to do justice to its contribution to economic growth. The nature of the contribution, and its extent, differed profoundly according to the political constitution of the several countries, the attitude of government to the business ventures of foreigners, and to the presence, or absence, of technical and commercial expertise, (or the spirit of enterprise) among the local population. Towards the end of the chapter the author discusses whether the experiences he recounts are in any way relevant to contemporary problems in underdeveloped countries, especially in connection with the functions of Western enterprise.

The part of the state in economic development has been considered in several chapters, including Chapter 5 where comparisons are drawn between four Asian countries. Chapter 6 examines in some detail the economic activities of the Japanese government and its relations with the private sector. These are subjects about which there is much misunderstanding in the West; even among Japanese themselves wide differences of opinion exist about the significance of the state's participation in economic processes. On the one hand, some foreign journalists, conscious of the strong and consistent purpose that appears to inform the country's economic policy, have conjured up the vision of a monolithic, state-directed economy which they have called 'Japan Incorporated'.[6] According to this view, the government and the bureaucracy initiate the policies which a docile private sector then proceeds to carry out. On the other hand, there are those who consider that, at any rate since the Second World War, the government's main contribution to development has been the creation of an economic environment in which private enterprise can flourish. Some even go so far as to suggest that the political party that has been in office almost without interruption for thirty years has been the faithful and obedient servant of its paymaster, big business.

The truth, so it is argued, lies between these two extreme views. The civil servants participate in the making of decisions about industrial investment and development, but, while they influence the plans of private firms, they are in no position to dictate policies to them. To suppose that they are able, or that they expect, to do so, is to misunderstand the process of decision-making in Japan. The Japanese dislike confrontation as well as the resolution of differences by the majority principle. They prefer that decisions should emerge out of discussions leading to a consensus. It is true that both the state and private enterprise have usually found themselves in harmony during the last thirty years and have often acted in close association. But this accord is the outcome of the overriding policy that Japan has pursued, a policy that has found favour with the general public as well as with the country's leaders. Japan has directed her energies, without reservation, to fostering rapid economic growth. For the realisation of that purpose, she has allocated an exceptionally high proportion of her resources to manufacturing industries, especially to those that yield returns quickly in the form of marketable goods. This coincidence between the aims of the state and the interests of private industry has contributed conspicuously to economic success. In this respect, Japan offers a sharp contrast with Britain where, for much of the postwar period, government and private industry have been on bad terms, and where industrial growth, despite the lip-service paid to it by politicians, has occupied a lowly place in the nation's scale of preferences. One might say, without much exaggeration, that whereas in Japan the state seeks to influence, or to guide, the decisions of private firms, British industry (to use Schumpeter's term) has been 'state-broken' and, in consequence, has lost much of its vitality.

The extent of common agreement in Japan should not be exaggerated. The absence of dissension about general aims has not precluded sharp differences of opinion on details or means. The location policy of the early 1960s failed through the opposition of industrialists and the lack of accord among politicians. Wrangles between officials and businessmen have frustrated plans for particular industries. Yet as long as government and industry were at one in according priority to economic growth, rapid progress could be expected, if not assured. The experiences of the 1930s and 1940s gave warning to the postwar generation of how the country's economic strength might be wasted through conflicts over the national purpose.

The last part of Chapter 6 contains a description of the cooperative movement. A footnote should be added to call attention to aspects of that movement that are seldom mentioned. Japanese civil servants of the administrative class commonly retire at a very early age (often in their late forties), some of them, when the time arrives, becoming directors or executives of private firms. The officials of the Ministry of Finance obtain jobs in banks or insurance companies, and those from the Ministry of Trade and Industry enter industrial firms. Many, to an increasing extent, find a resting place (or a sphere of activity) in the public corporations. It need hardly be said that the officials of the Ministry of Agriculture seldom spend their retirement as peasant farmers; those who do not go into politics frequently find remunerative occupation as directors of the rural cooperative societies, a fine example of what the Japanese term *Amakudari* ('Descent from Heaven'). This process is referred to, in a different context, in Chapter 10.

The widely held notion that the Japanese economy is the result of successful 'planning' is refuted by the history of the succession of official plans devised since the war. The papers incorporated in Chapters 6 and 8 show that the Economic Planning Agency consistently underestimated Japan's rate of growth in all its predictions up to the time these papers were written. Its error persisted into the quinquennium 1967–71. Indeed, in that period the rate of growth, which had been expected to remain at about 8 per cent a year (considerably lower than the postwar annual average up to the middle 1960s), reached an annual average of over 12 per cent. It is sobering to recall that when at last the Agency had persuaded itself to take a favourable view of Japan's prospects, it was again put out of countenance. Its plan for 1973–77 forecast an average rate of 8 to 9 per cent, while other predictions were even more optimistic. The Boston Consulting Group, whose report was published in 1974, put the rate at 10 per cent between 1972 and 1980, and the Japan Economic Research Centre was equally confident of continued, rapid progress. In the event, the quinquennium had hardly begun when the 'oil shock' in the autumn of 1973 shattered all those hopes and plunged Japan, like the rest of the world, into a prolonged recession. Between 1974 and 1977 the annual average rate of growth was only 3 to 4 per cent.

The papers that appear as Chapters 7, 8 and 9 were written in 1962, 1967 and 1970 respectively. The chief object of all three was to analyse the causes of Japan's economic progress, especially during the postwar period. The reader may find some interest in observing changes of emphasis in the author's analysis during the time the papers were written. Chapter 9, which examines postwar growth against a historical background, stresses the part that a consistent, expansionary ambition has played in the country's economic achievements.

One of the chief conclusions to emerge from a study of the last twenty-five years is that the progress has been achieved through the convergence of numerous causes, some contrived, some accidental. This is probably true of any great outburst of national energy, economic, political or artistic. It is the object of several chapters in this book to identify them, and, where possible, to give some indication of their relative importance.

The compulsions that were the legacy of Japan's defeat in war meant that she was left with no course of action except that of concentration on economic recovery and expansion, in cooperation with her victors, although the restriction of her choice to a single, practicable objective was not, of course, a *sufficient* condition of progress. Since the men formerly in charge of her affairs were discredited, or had been 'purged' by the Allies, she had immediately to find new leaders. Enterprising business executives and officials, no longer frustrated by the restraints imposed by the military oligarchy, breathed a new air of freedom and responded with enthusiasm to the opportunities now before them. The country's morale and its social cohesion had survived defeat, and so the execution of national policy was seldom impeded by factional dissension.

Leadership has been the crucial factor in Japan's accomplishments throughout the modern era. In her most successful periods, vested interests and doctrinaire principles have yielded readily to the demands of efficient administration. For example, the great business families, from early times, ensured their own vigorous survival by the adoption, often by marriage, of young *Banto* (managers) of outstanding talent.[7] When Mitsui set about rebuilding its empire after the postwar Dissolution, the accumulation of material assets was deemed far less important than the recruitment of men of high quality. When Daiichi Bussan (the postwar successor to Mitsui Bussan) set out to extend the range of its interests, its first consideration was the 'acquiring of new ability'. Thus the merger with Nippon Kikai Boeki, a machinery firm, meant the assumption of responsibility for a deficit of from one to one-and-a-half billion yen, but this financial burden was accepted because Mitsui knew that success in its machinery department depended on its recruiting engineering experts, and NKB had '300 to 400 college graduates with technical competence.'[8] It was they who made the venture worth while.

Many observers of Japan's industrial scene have described, usually with admiration, her methods of management, particularly the *Ringi-sei* (literally 'circular discussion' system) which is designed to involve a high proportion of a firm's employees in decision-making.[9] Where this system works well, it ensures that the firm's policies receive the assent of staff of different grades before they are put into effect, and that every participant understands what is required of him. Although the process of discussion is time-consuming, the execution of the policy is rapid, once a decision has been reached. Like all systems, *Ringi-sei* has its limitations. For instance, it affords ample opportunities for the timid to evade personal responsibility, nor is it universally favoured throughout the Japanese business world. But, on balance, one may conclude that it has made a major contribution to efficiency and that it has done much to promote harmony in the country's industrial relations.

Another factor that has operated from early in her modern career has been Japan's readiness to discard the uneconomic and out-of-date in order to divert resources into new and promising lines of production. One of the best examples of this quality of resilience was her decision in the late 1950s to run down her high-cost coal industry and to base her future industrial expansion on imports of fuel, especially oil. To some critics in 1973 this decision seemed to have been imprudent. Yet, in the interval, Japan had built up her industrial capacity on cheap imported oil and, by the time of the 'oil shock', she was in good shape to cope with the problems to which it gave rise. Recovery from that crisis and subsequent developments have fully vindicated those who took the decision. It remains to be seen whether Japan will now show the same ready acceptance of change by letting slip her increasingly uneconomic labour-intensive industries and transferring her resources to other uses. Anxieties about oil are likely to stay with her.

The pace and range of Japan's industrial progress after 1950 would have been unattainable without the ample supplies of labour that became available for work in her new manufacturing industries. These supplies depended, in part, on the very considerable increase in numbers in the active age groups during the postwar years, and in part on the transference of rural workers to urban employments. In the latter respect, Japan's experience resembles that of European countries with large agricultural populations; for both France and Germany owe part of their industrial progress since the war to the migration of persons from low-productivity employment on the land to high-productivity employment in the capital-intensive industries. Britain, of course, had made this transference in the nineteenth century, hence her industrial lead. In Japan's case, as Chapter 8 shows, even when the surplus of labour from the land was approaching exhaustion, additional recruits for the new industries were found in the small firms that still make up a large sector of the economy.

Some economists have been content to explain Japan's rate of growth mainly in terms of her high investment which has been facilitated by her level of personal saving. Without that investment it would, of course, have been impossible to equip the technologically advanced, capital-intensive industries into which much of the country's resources has been directed since the war. But the relation between growth and investment is intricate. As argued in Chaper 9, growth is as much the cause as the result of investment. Further, Japan's high rate of personal saving, though related to certain features of her social system and to her methods of wage-payment, was made possible by the rapid advance in family incomes that attended increased productivity.

Economic performance depends not only on the *quantity* of investment but also on its *quality*. Japan has wasted few of her resources in bolstering up declining, uncompetitive undertakings (except in agriculture and, to some extent, in mining), or in promoting ventures that confer prestige but are indefensible on economic grounds. In the development of her new industries she has been well served by her large supply of well-trained technicians of all grades. Their presence in ample numbers enabled her to assimilate the 'knowhow' imported from the West in the first phase of her reconstruction and, in recent years, to work out new devices herself and to apply the results of her own scientific research. The indispensable contribution of her educational system to her economic achievements is analysed in Chapter 10.

Western observers have been impressed with her success in maintaining social and political stability despite technical and economic changes which disturbed the old ways of life. Some of them prophesied that, as Japan became richer, her people would lose their capacity for hard work and cooperative effort, and that her genial industrial relations would dissolve into acerbity. So far, this prediction has not been justified by events. No doubt her social system has deep roots, but part of the explanation may be found in conditions of recent origin, notably the trend towards greater equality in the distribution of personal incomes. As was explained in Chapter 2, economic development in the Meiji era was financed to a large extent by the heavy fiscal burdens imposed on the peasantry. With the growth of industry, the sources of public revenue changed, but the incomes of the farmers (who made up nearly half of the occupied population until the Second World War) remained low when compared with those in other sectors. Among the industrial workers also there were flagrant discrepancies in incomes. These probably widened during the 1930s, thus sharpening the distinctions characteristic of the 'dual economy'. The business class, especially men holding high office in the large concerns, were richly rewarded. The authors of a recent study of Japanese business history have produced some striking evidence of the enormous salaries of business executives in the early years of the century and in later times.[10]

The reforms introduced by the Americans during the Occupation period, together with the postwar inflation, destroyed former accumulations of capital and opened the way for a more equal distribution of income. After the middle 1950s rapid industrial growth, and the massive transference of workers from the land to the cities, put an end to the condition of chronic labour surplus in agriculture and raised the farmers' standard of living as high as that of the townsfolk. Those left on the land gave less and less of their time to cultivation, and in 1977 the average farming family obtained about 70 per cent of its income from non-agricultural occupations. The drying up of the stream of recruits from the countryside meant that, by the 1960s, both small-scale industry and the formerly lowly paid service trades had to increase wages beyond all the expectations of a few years before. So the discrepancies associated with the 'dual economy' became less conspicuous. It is likely, moreover, that the labour laws passed during the period of the Occupation also had a beneficial effect on the wages of groups of workers previously in a weak bargaining position.

One might have supposed, however, that other forces present in the postwar economy would have been powerful enough to offset these egalitarian trends. Japan has invested an exceptionally large proportion of her national income during the last twenty-five years. Much of this investment has been directed into private industrial equipment, a trend encouraged by the taxation system which has discriminated in favour of profits and investment. Japan is, in fact, a country where, by international standards, the share of the national product that goes to labour is very low, while that taken by investment is exceptionally high. Yet according to the report of the OECD on *Income Distribution*, it appears that her post-tax personal incomes are more equally distributed than in any Western country, except Holland, Norway and Sweden.[11] In this respect she and Britain rank close together. The statistical evidence seems to be justified by observation.

The paradox is not easy to explain. The answer is probably to be found in a complex of conditions, including the destruction just after the war of accumulated wealth formerly in the hands of a very few families, followed by the 'reforms', (especially the land reform), the absence of large underprivileged groups, such as racial minorities, the practice, common to most companies, of applying most of their profits to reinvestment rather than to dividend payments, and, finally, the high level of employment maintained since the war and the elimination of the once impoverished peasantry. Whatever the reasons, the results of the unusual association of relatively equal personal-income distribution and relatively biased functional distribution has almost certainly contributed to economic progress. The first condition helps to explain the comparative absence of social strains and unrest in a period of unparalleled economic and technological change. Social harmony cannot be assured simply by an egalitarian distribution of income. On the other hand, it is improbable that a steep rise in all personal incomes would itself suffice to preserve that harmony if the benefits of progress were allocated in a way popularly regarded as unfair. As it has turned out, it seems that there has been quite a widespread recognition that all groups in society, though of course not all individuals, have shared equitably in the fruits of the country's prosperity. Hence the general support for the policy of fast industrial growth. At the same time, the strongly biased functional distribution of the national expenditure, notably the large share invested in manufacturing industry, has made possible the rapid and almost continuous increase in productivity that lies behind the long series of industrial successes and the rise in the national income as a whole. In achieving this happy coincidence, which has enabled her to enjoy the best of both worlds, Japan may have been favoured by fortune; but two causes that cannot be considered accidental have made a major contribution to her accomplishment; first, the policy of giving priority to private industrial investment and, second, the propensity of the whole population towards a high rate of saving which has permitted the huge investment to be financed without inflation or penal taxation. Whether the postwar trend towards the more equal distribution of incomes will persist is doubtful. A serpent in the egalitarian paradise can be detected in the form of widening gaps in the distribution of *wealth*. Statistical evidence for measuring this tendency is lacking. But the steep rise in land and property values, and the marked appreciation in the price of industrial securities during the last decade must have conferred great benefits on the relatively few who own them. This increased concentration of wealth is likely to affect the distribution of incomes in the future.

The failure of certain parts of Japan's infrastructure, her housing, state-provided amenities, and social welfare services in general, to keep pace with her industrial advance is discussed in Chapter 8. On might have expected that this failure would have been a source of social unrest. By the late 1960s the Japanese had certainly become acutely aware of these deficiencies, but their dissatisfaction stopped far short of opposition to the established order. By the middle of the next decade, in response to public demand, some of the shortcomings had been put right. In certain types of welfare (for example, in the provision of medical services) Japan now compares favourably with countries that boast of being 'welfare states'. On the other hand, her standard of housing is still inferior to that in several countries which she has left far behind industrially, and the ratio of her public expenditure on welfare to the national income is low, 11 per cent in 1977, compared with 15 per cent in Britain and 30 per cent in Sweden.[12] These statistical comparisons, however, are difficult to interpret. For one thing, the age distribution of the population varies from country to country, and in Japan the proportion of persons in the older age groups is smaller than in Western Europe. Again, the Japanese are said to prefer to have much of their social welfare provided through the family, or through their employers, rather than through a centralised, bureaucratic administration financed by taxation. Finally, since unemployment has been low when compared with that suffered by Western Europe and the United States, payments in unemployment benefit have been small.

The outside world has not lacked information about the pollution of the atmosphere, rivers and seas that has attended Japan's industrial advance, nor about the congestion that has been caused by the concentration of population in a few huge conurbations. The Japanese, having ignored these evils during the years when everything was being sacrificed for industrial growth, began in the early 1970s to mount a determined assault against them. Rigid controls have been imposed over the sources of pollution, such as the exhaust systems of motor vehicles. Manufacturing firms have been obliged to incur heavy expenditure for dealing with waste products that may contaminate the environment, and it has been said that anti-pollution measures constitute the leading 'growth industry' of the 1970s. The attack on urban congestion has been less successful, despite Prime Minister Tanaka's ambitious but ill-fated plan for 'remodelling the Japanese archipelago'. Still, it is clear that a policy of growth irrespective of the social cost no longer commends itself to the Japanese public.

Industrial progress, like human happiness, seldom continues long in one stay, and Japan's future, after her many years as a favourite of fortune, has naturally become a subject for speculation. A period of comparative stagnation, after decades of exceptional growth, has led some observers to conclude that the great days are over and that an era of slow development lies ahead. What lends credence to this contention is the disparate movements during the last few years of industrial production and the national income, as well as the low growth rate itself. During the 1950s and 1960s when the economy was being driven forward under the impetus of heavy investment in manufacturing, the growth of industrial production much exceeded that of GNP as a whole. Between 1953 and 1973 GNP, in real terms, rose at an annual average rate of 9.7 per cent, whereas for industrial production the rate was 12.5 per cent. After the 'oil shock' industrial production declined and, despite a recovery in 1966 and 1977, in the latter year it was still below the level reached in 1973. On the other hand, the national income (real), after a slight fall, continued its secular rise (though at a much lower rate than before the 'oil shock') and in 1977 it was about 16 per cent greater than five years earlier. This divergence between the indices of industrial production and GNP is, of course, common to most economies during periods of recession, and it may be argued that it will disappear as recovery proceeds. In the previous recessions, however, there was no such striking contrast, and the recent divergence may be significant because growth in the last twenty-five years has been so closely associated with the expansion of manufacturing industry.

Since agricultural production has hardly changed over the period, the discrepancy can only have arisen because the service trades continued to expand, while manufacturing industry actually declined. If this were to mark the beginning of a new trend in the allocation of resources, the rate of economic growth would certainly be affected, since increases of productivity in the service trades as a whole are hardly likely to match those that occurred in manufacturing industry when it was surging forward under the thrust of high investment in the new technology. It would certainly be very rash to base conclusions about future trends on the experience of such a short period. The doubtful statistical evidence, however, finds support in what is known about the probable course of investment policy. In the years ahead much more of the new capital than in the past will probably be directed to the infrastructure, social welfare, fuel research, armaments, and enterprise overseas (part of which will be required to safeguard supplies of raw materials). These forms of capital are unlikely to yield their returns as quickly as investment in equipment for private manufacturing industry has done. So, it is reasonable to suppose that the secular rate of growth in future will be much lower than in the 1960s. Another influence may work in the same direction. In the next decade Japan will be obliged to make massive structural changes in manufacturing industry itself. With the growth in other Asian countries of manufacturing enterprise (not only in textiles and the simpler forms of labour-intensive goods, but also in ships and motor vehicles), her competitive position in some markets is likely to be assailed, and she will come under pressure to shift her resources to new fields of activity. Her capacity for structural adaptation will be put to as hard a test as ever in the past, and the costs of transference themselves may limit the rate of growth. In these speculations, however, if must be remembered, first, that what is considered a low rate of growth for Japan is an unattainably high rate for most Western countries and, second, that the world has, so far, consistently underestimated her economic strength and her resilience in the face of challenge.

When economists have surveyed the causes to which Japan's progress can be ascribed, they have not found it difficult to agree on a list. But opinions naturally differ about the *relative* importance of the several factors, and some economists, in obedience to the honourable tradition that measurement is always preferable to qualitative statements, have tried to assign weights to them. The author is dubious about the value of such attempts at precision. Japan's achievements since the Second World War are attributable to the fortunate convergence of a complex of causes, social, political and economic. Many of those causes have interacted with one another, and how any one of them would have operated in isolation can only be guessed at: the contributions of the individual notes of which these chords have been composed are not all susceptible to measurement. If this were not so, then it would be easy for others to imitate the methods that have brought success to Japan. For instance, it does not follow that the trade union structure and the system of industrial relations which, all agree, have done much to promote her industrial success, would yield similar results if taken up by a country with different social and political traditions. Similarly, the success or failure of a technical device or method of production depends in large measure on the industrial climate of the country that adopts it.

In Chapters 7 and 8 the relation between Japan's economic growth and her export trade is discussed. Since the papers of which those chapters are composed were written, however, events have taken a new turn which has brought her into conflict with some of her trading partners. This is no place to examine the criticisms sparked off by the rise in her competitive strength in foreign markets; but as one of those criticisms is based on a proposition of wide application, a brief examination of the problem is called for.

During the 1960s Japan's exports rose at twice the rate of increase in world trade, with the result that from 1968 onwards she earned a very large surplus on current account. The 'oil shock' of 1973 put an end to this surplus and for two years she was heavily in deficit. Between 1976 and 1978, however, her current account showed large and growing surpluses brought about entirely by the huge increase in her exports of manufactures unaccompanied by any corresponding increase in imports. The export surpluses of the last ten years were mainly the consequence of the decline in her manufacturing costs relative to those of her competitors, in other words, to a rise in her comparative efficiency in a fairly wide range of export industries. The yen, as a result, became increasingly undervalued on the exchanges, and only in the summer of 1978 was it allowed to rise to its (probable) equilibrium level. The author is not inclined to speculate on what lies ahead, for his own views are not exempt from the scepticism with which he regards all long-range economic predictions. But the episode has given rise to a controversy that deserves note.

The succession of surpluses was taken by many of Japan's critics in the Western world as evidence of her neglect of her duties as a member of the international trading community and of her ruthless pursuance of a self-regarding policy.[13] In so far as the criticism applies to her deliberately holding the yen at a rate of exchange much lower than the equilibrium rate, it is justified. But the attack has been pressed further. It has been claimed that Japan's trading partners have the right to require her to increase her rate of growth substantially so as to aid the weaker economies. This demand raises an important issue of policy. One certainly cannot conduct a satisfactory international economic system on the principle that the strong do what they can and the weak submit, hallowed though it be by illustrious precedents. Yet, one may properly ask: how far are a country's trading partners justified, when they are in difficulties, in demanding that it should mould its economic policy in order to benefit them? To particularise, can it be suggested that it is Japan's duty to take fiscal and monetary measures to raise her rate of growth (already higher than in other industrial countries) when such action might well lead to inflation damaging to her much prized social stability? Is it reasonable to ask her, for the benefit of others, to redirect her investment from manufacturing industry to other sectors to a greater extent than she herself would choose? Her institutions and her choice of ends since the war have been conducive to economic success. Is she to be required to modify her institutions and her scale of values, which seem to be well attuned to progress in an era of advancing technology and rapid economic change, in order to rescue less well-conducted countries from their difficulties? Should it not be for the latter, if they wish to match Japan's triumphs, to change their own institutions and purposes? The answers to these questions are not abundantly clear. An international community must observe certain rules of conduct, a principle enshrined in many international treaties during the last thirty years. The problem is to distinguish between the acts of national policy in the determination of which the outside world can reasonably claim a say, and those that must be left to the national government.

2 Financial Policy and Economic Development, 1897 - 1937[1]

From the early years of Japan's modernisation her leaders showed a firm grasp of the functions of a well-wrought financial system in economic development. The architect of the Japanese system was Count (afterwards Prince) Matsukata who presided over the country's finances during the last two decades of the nineteenth century. The survey in this chapter, which begins at the time when his work was almost complete, follows the course of financial events and policies from the adoption of the gold standard in 1897 to the 'China Incident' of 1937. The aim is not, of course, to present a comprehensive history of Japan's banking and monetary system but to analyse what can be identified as the most significant features of the financial policy from the standpoint of its contribution to economic development.

At the beginning of the Meiji era (1868), and for long afterwards, Japan was by Western standards a poor country, with most of its resources allocated to peasant agriculture. In its task of creating a modern state, the government had to solve two problems. The first was the provision of capital for a modern infrastructure and manufacturing industries. Railways, factories and equipment of many kinds had to be constructed quickly in a community that had hitherto used most of its resources for the satisfaction of its immediate needs. The diversion of these resources from the production of consumption goods to that of capital goods was achieved by several means. Funds raised by taxation were invested by the state in new industries or were given as subsidies to existing enterprises regarded as worthy of encouragement. The state used its credit to raise loans both at home and abroad which were applied in the same way. Once an industrial and commercial class familiar with Western ways had emerged, the state encouraged investment

20

by the provision of credit facilities through a group of semi-official banks, by subsidies, by imposing protective duties (after 1902), and by framing its taxation system so that it pressed lightly on the profit-earner. In the decade before the First World War these stimuli were administered with great effect. The successful issue of the Sino-Japanese War in 1895 and of the Russo-Japanese War in 1905 made the policy much easier to pursue than formerly; for the consequent rise in political prestige enabled Japan to obtain fiscal autonomy after the first of those wars and to borrow abroad at low rates after the second. During the early years of the present century, the protection granted to Japanese industries was steadily increased, the subsidisation of certain industries and of the mercantile marine was made part of a permanent policy, and the government itself invested heavily in a number of enterprises, notably the Yawata iron and steel works, and in railway development. In consequence, the period 1904–13 constituted an era of very rapid economic expansion.

The Japanese government of the time, however, was by no means concerned solely with economic objectives. The creation of an economic system such as might promote the maximisation of the national income was far from being its only, or even its chief, aim. It was also concerned with political security. For this reason it had taken Japan into war against China and Russia. For this reason it had embarked after 1895 on the development of the resources of Formosa, and after 1905 on colonial expansion in Korea. Political domination of these regions, however, did not satisfy the government. Japan wished also to develop colonial resources so as to provide herself with the raw materials she lacked, raw materials considered necessary to her political security. For instance, although the development of rice production in Korea, according to a Japanese economist, 'was originally undertaken as a colonial policy based on human love'[2], its prosecution was certainly pressed forward in later years because the domestic rice supply of Japan was becoming insufficient to satisfy the needs of the growing population. Economic penetration in parts of Asia outside the Empire was undertaken with the same ends in view. The efforts to develop the coal and iron resources of Manchuria and of the Yangtse valley were part of the policy of rendering Japan, which lacks coking coal and adequate supplies of ore, less dependent on foreign metallurgical industries, a policy which led also to the establishment of the government's iron and steel works, mentioned above.

The pursuance of these political objectives had important effects on the country's economic life. After the Russian War, Japan's military and naval expenditure continued to increase; while economic penetration in Asia involved the government in heavy expenses and required the establishment of official financial institutions, such as the colonial banks and the Oriental Development Company. These diverted much Japanese capital to enterprises which would not otherwise have attracted investors. It is improbable, for example, that the Formosan sugar industry would have grown as fast and as large as it did without official subsidies and preferential treatment in the home market.[3] The pursuance of this policy strained the state's finances. The additional taxation that had been imposed at the time of the Russo-Japanese War as a temporary measure was maintained; nevertheless, large loans had to be raised at home and abroad to finance the political and economic expansion. Japan's national debt (excluding certain special debts incurred at this time, such as the state's railway and steel works debts) rose from 445 million yen in 1903 to over 2000 million yen in 1912;[4] of this latter amount nearly three-quarters consisted of foreign debt. To some observers the country's financial position was disquieting. The expansionist policy had probably raised the productive powers of the nation to a level which they could not have attained in the same space of time under a *laissez-faire* régime. But it is obvious that a policy which involves the very rapid development of economic resources under the stimulus of governmental financial assistance is likely to lead to instability if the state should be unable to maintain its bounties, and Japan's capacity for doing this was being weakened by her heavy expenditure in the pursuit of strategic objectives.

The expansionist policy gave rise to especially serious problems in her foreign trade and payments. Japan had an urgent need for imports not only of industrial equipment, but also of raw materials for her developing manufactures, since her home supplies of most of them were scanty. To finance these imports in the quantities required by her furious economic growth, a substantial export trade had to be built up; for the policy of foreign borrowing could be regarded only as a temporary expedient. Consequently, the government did its utmost to foster exports. As early as 1880, a special bank, the Yokohama Specie Bank, had been established by the state to finance foreign trade, and this bank still handles about half of the exchange business of the country.[5] It has always had very close connections with the Bank of Japan, from which it has borrowed extensively for its operations; the Central Bank is authorised to advance loans up to a certain amount to the exchange Bank at a specially low rate of interest.[6] Thus, the merchant or industrialist engaged in the export trade was encouraged at the expense of those dealing with the home market.

Subsidies to shipping and foreign trading companies, the provision of low railway rates on goods destined for export, and the organisation of export guilds and other institutions for the development of foreign markets, all formed part of the government's scheme. Nevertheless, despite a steep increase in exports between 1900 and 1914, the balance of payments gave rise to anxiety just before the War.[7] By then, Japan's annual payments abroad had become not only heavy, but also very inelastic, because of the necessity for providing interest on her large foreign loans, her military and naval expenditure abroad, and the substantial imports of equipment and materials for industrial development. A reduction of these imports, of course, would have meant an abandonment of the government's political and economic objectives. The export trade, on the other hand, was liable to wide fluctuations. This trade was highly specialised. In 1913 raw silk, silk fabrics and cotton goods accounted for 55 per cent of the total. Moreover, the exports were concentrated on a few markets. Nearly all the raw silk, easily the largest export, went to the United States, and cotton goods and other manufactures were sent mainly to China. In 1913, 64 per cent of the exports went to these countries.[8] The reliance on two markets was a vulnerable feature of the trade, especially as the demand for raw silk was liable to be affected by alternations of prosperity and depression in America.[9] Thus, while the amount of Japan's annual payments was relatively inflexible, her receipts were variable. At times the resulting financial strain was very great, particularly because the Central Bank was not in a position to attract short-term funds to Japan in times of crisis.

The exchange difficulties were mitigated by the large foreign balances which Japan had begun to accumulate shortly after her adoption of the gold standard in 1897. In origin, these balances were the fruits of Japan's victory in the Sino-Japanese War of 1894–95. China, as a result of her defeat, found herself obliged to pay an indemnity of 230 million taels to the victor and her government decided to raise the necessary funds by issuing public bonds in Europe. At this time, however, Japan 'had the prospect before her of making large disbursements for several years in Europe; while at the same time the price of silver was undergoing great depreciation, so that the government of Japan was strongly inclined towards the adoption of the gold standard. In view of these two sets of facts, it occurred to Count Matsukata, the Minister of Finance at that time, that it would be to the advantage of both governments if the indemnity were received in English money'.[10] Accordingly, negotiations were opened with the Chinese government, as a result of which it was agreed that the equivalent of the indemnity in English money (£38,000,000) should be paid to the Japanese government in London. This was done by means of a series of instalments. In the course of time, part of the sum was brought home to Japan in specie and served to strengthen the gold reserves of the Bank of Japan, but a part of it was kept with an agency of the Central Bank in London and served as a nucleus of the foreign exchange fund. The maintenance of this fund subsequently became a conspicuous feature of the Japanese currency system.

It does not appear that the establishment of the exchange fund was the result of any far-sighted financial policy, or that it was regarded at first as anything but a temporary expedient. The practice owed its origin merely to the circumstances connected with the payment of the indemnity. It would have been difficult in any case to have transmitted such a large sum to Japan immediately without disturbing the exchanges, but the disadvantage of doing so was enhanced by the fact that Japan was about to embark on a policy of military and naval expansion which would certainly involve heavy expenditure abroad.

The government took advantage of the interval between the receipts and disbursements of the various instalments to utilise various parts of the indemnity fund. Sometimes a portion was employed to relieve the stringency of the money market at home; at other times portions of the fund were invested in a temporary way in the Treasury Bills of both British and Indian governments; . . . or at times when there was tendency for our specie to leave the country, a portion of the fund was employed as a provision fund for foreign exchange with the object of preventing the exodus of specie.[11]

The policy became firmly established after the Russo-Japanese War. A large part of the proceeds of foreign loans raised at that time was held in London. Thus, while the Bank of Japan's specie reserve held in the country amounted to only thirty-seven million yen on 31 December 1905, the balance in London on the same date was 442 million yen.[12]

The reasons which led Japan to convert into a permanent policy what had originally been a temporary expedient to meet the special circumstances produced by war become clear from an examination of her banking system, particularly the functions and responsibilities of the Bank of Japan. The Bank, which acted in very close conjunction with the Minister of Finance, had (and still has) a monopoly of the country's note-issue. According to the law of its establishment, the Bank had to hold, as cover, gold and silver coin and bullion equivalent in value to the notes issued, although it was provided that notes to the value of 120 million yen could be issued against certain specified securities. The notes, in the absence of a highly developed cheque currency, formed the country's most important means of payment; and though they were nominally convertible into gold on demand, gold coins did not circulate to any considerable extent. From the time of the Russo-Japanese War, moreover, the foreign balances had been counted as part of the specie reserve for the note-issue. So, Japan, prior to 1914, was, in fact, operating a gold exchange standard system.

In its relation to the money market the Central Bank was in a somewhat peculiar position.[13] Although it frequently rendered financial assistance to the government and to the official banks, it was not a banker's bank, and it had very little control over the activities of the numerous private financial institutions, which then numbered about two thousand. Very few of those banks kept their reserves with the Bank of Japan or cooperated with it, and, in consequence, it was unable to coordinate the banking activities of the country and to enforce a common policy. The reserve against the note-issue was divorced from the banking reserve, and the Bank Rate was quite powerless to affect the policy of the other banks. Such being the case, the Central Bank was unable to check the undue extension of credit on their part, and yet in the crises which followed the resulting booms (as in the years 1907–8 and 1920–21) it found itself obliged to lend freely to them in order to prevent a general financial collapse. Thus, though it could not determine their policy, it had to come to their aid when that policy had landed them in difficulties, whatever its own inclinations.

The provision of this aid meant, periodically, large increases in the note-issue. There was no legal obstacle to such increases, for in times of crisis the Bank was permitted to raise its security issue beyond the normal statutory limit on payment of a tax. In practice, however, if Japan had operated a pure gold standard, the fluctuations in the economy would have involved from time to time large imports and exports of gold. Because of Japan's distance from the world's financial centres, these movements would have been embarrassing. A note-issue backed to a large extent by holdings of foreign currency was obviously more suited to the financial condition of the country than an unadulterated gold standard currency. Further, the Japanese exchanges were especially liable to severe fluctuations, partly because of the government's large periodical payments abroad as interest on Japan's foreign debt or for the purchase of those Western manufactures which her naval, military and industrial expansion necessitated, and partly because her chief export, raw silk, was one for which the demand fluctuated widely in the world markets. The seasonal strain, too, was severe, for Japan was still mainly an exporter of raw materials and agricultural produce, exports of which were naturally concentrated in the latter part of the year. Thus it would have been exceptionally difficult for Japan, in the absence of special measures, to prevent heavy gold exports on occasion. The Central Bank, as we have seen, was in no position to protect its reserves by means of the mechanism of the Bank Rate.

As a result of the adoption of this system of regulating the exchanges, the balance of indebtedness between Japan and the rest of the world was settled, if adverse to Japan, not by gold

TABLE 1

Date	Gold reserves in Japan	Balance in London[14]
31 December 1905	37 million yen	442 million yen
31 December 1907	45 million yen	401 million yen
31 December 1910	135 million yen	337 million yen
31 December 1911	133 million yen	231 million yen
31 December 1912	136 million yen	215 million yen
31 December 1913	130 million yen	246 million yen
31 December 1914	129 million yen	213 million yen

exports but by sales of credits held in London, and the reduction of the exchange fund at that centre was offset by a cancellation of notes paid into the Bank of Japan when the exchange was purchased. Table 1 below shows that between 1905 and 1910 the foreign balances were in decline. This came about almost entirely through the transference in 1908 of specie from London to the home reserves in order to relieve the financial stringency that followed the panic of that year. Between 1910 and 1914, however, while the gold reserve in Japan remained unchanged, the foreign balances fell steeply and continuously despite the floating of several foreign loans to replenish them. Had this process continued Japan would have been obliged either to restore equilibrium by deflating, or to have cut the links between the yen and gold. The former policy would have led to industrial depression; the latter would have meant reduced imports and a loss of credit in the international money markets. In either case the result would have been a slowing down in the rate of economic expansion.

A former Minister of Finance, in commenting upon the state of Japanese finances at that time, declared: 'Japan is inherently an excess importer'.[15]. He presumably meant that the debit balance of Japan on income account was likely to persist as long as the existing expansionist policy was pursued. The Minister's diagnosis (with hindsight) went deeper than that of contemporary bankers who ascribed the difficulty simply to the practice of issuing notes against the foreign balances and demanded that only the specie held at home should be counted as a currency reserve. They were confusing symptoms with causes. The real problem that presented itself to the policy-makers was how could Japan maintain equilibrium in her balance of payments and at the same time press on with her schemes of economic and territorial expansion?

The outbreak of the First World War temporarily obscured the issue; for it not only permitted the expansionist policy to be pursued still more vigorously, but it also solved for a time the exchange and currency problems associated with the policy. After the middle of 1915 an urgent demand for Japanese goods and shipping services arose both from the Allied Powers and also from other countries deprived of their normal means of supply of manufactured goods. Consequently, the rate of industrial advance was accelerated and exports of manufactured goods grew very quickly. As far as can be calculated, the quantum of commodity exports increased by over 50 per cent between 1913 and 1919; in value they more than trebled, and a large favourable trade balance resulted. As invisible exports, chiefly in the form of receipts from shipping services, also increased, Japan's surplus on her current account during the four years of war was massive, and by 1919 she had been transformed from a debtor to a creditor country. Yet so far committed had the government become to the encouragement of exports, that even during this period the policy of affording special assistance to them was maintained. Japan no doubt hoped that her footing in markets from which competitors had been temporarily removed could be made permanent.

The large export surplus for which the demands of the Allied Powers were in part responsible had far-reaching financial consequences. For a time the greater part of Japan's foreign trade continued to be financed through London; but from 1916 onwards her balance of indebtedness was settled by specie shipments from the United States. As a result, the gold reserves held in Japan increased from 129 million yen in December 1914 to 228 million yen in December 1916. Meanwhile, the previous downward trend in the foreign balances was reversed; from 213 million yen in December 1914 they rose to 487 million yen in December 1916. The flow of specie into Japan continued until September 1917 when the United States placed an embargo on the export of gold. From that time onward net payments to the credit of Japan accumulated in New York. The balances rose from 487 million yen in December 1916 to 1355 million yen in December 1919.

The financial machinery of Japan was scarcely equal to dealing with the unfamiliar problems with which it was confronted;

the Yokohama Specie Bank, being unable to transmit the proceeds of its export bills to Japan, found difficulty in maintaining advances to exporters. So the Bank of Japan and the government purchased the balances standing to the credit of the exchange bank in New York, and so provided funds for financing the expanding export trade. Indeed, since the funds of the ordinary banks were, in the absence of a discount market, unavailable for exchange purposes, the Central Bank's chief function during the First World War was the support of the exchange bank. Its huge loans for this purpose led to a large increase in its note-issue and precipitated an inflationary boom. The Bank of Japan's index number of wholesale prices which stood at 95 in 1914 (1913=100) rose to 239 in 1919; these are annual averages. The end of the boom in 1920 found Japan far more highly industrialised than in 1914, a creditor instead of a debtor country, and with short-term balances abroad that amounted to well over 1300 million yen.[17]

The financial authorities realised that these balances constituted a danger to stability, and they made some effort to fund the short-term debt. But conditions were unfavourable for the execution of such a policy. The bonds issued abroad by Japan in the years before the War had risen in price and little was done to redeem them; their amount was practically the same at the end of the war as at the beginning. Japan certainly lent substantial sums to the Allies—1140 million yen by September 1918—but as these loans were mainly in the form of short-term debt, they did not help in solving the long-term financial problem. By December 1921 the amount outstanding of foreign loans issued in Japan was only 454 million yen, of which the greater part consisted of advances to the Czarist government and the notorious Nishihara loans to North China. Indeed, the only long-term loans of importance made by Japan during the War were to debtors who defaulted.

The spring of 1920 marked a turning point. The index number of wholesale prices reached its maximum in March, but then the boom broke with a collapse of the silk market. Prices fell rapidly and continuously until the spring of 1921 after which the decline slowed down. Industrial production also fell.

It seemed at first to contemporary observers that the postwar depression in Japan was following a similar course to that in other countries. But, in fact, there were some striking differences.It soon became evident that deflation was not being carried as far in Japan as in the United States and Great Britain. A comparison of the movements of the wholesale price index of the Bank of Japan and that of the United States' Bureau of Labour shows a much wider divergence between them after the end of 1920 than can be explained by differences in their composition. The same is true if the comparison is made between the wholesale prices of Britain and Japan. An early indication of the Japanese government's reluctance to face the consequences of ruthless deflation came in 1920 when the state gave financial support to a silk valorisation scheme. In the next year the Rice Control Act was passed with the object of relieving distress among the farmers by operations designed to stabilise the price of rice.[18] These, and other similar schemes, were responsible for a marked increase in public expenditure which rose from 1172 million yen in 1919–20 to 1430 million yen in 1922–23. The additional expenditure was covered by borrowing from the Bank of Japan.[19]

Since deflation was arrested at an early stage, the decline in industrial production was soon reversed. Although a few industries, such as shipbuilding suffered from a prolonged depression, on the whole recovery was quick, and after the end of 1921 expansion was resumed. The postwar slump thus proved to be a brief interlude between two long periods of substantial growth. This conclusion is borne out by figures of industrial production. In the years between 1922 and 1926 there was no important industry in which the quantity of production was not far above that of the prewar years. In most of them the trend was consistently upwards (except during 1920–21) throughout the period 1914–26. Japan had shown that she was not prepared to accommodate her financial policy to that of the United States and Britain to the extend of abandoning her traditional expansionist ambitions.

It may be argued that the course she followed at this time was less the result of deliberate policy than of the undeveloped character of her banking and monetary system, and the distribution of economic power. The Bank of Japan, as already shown, was able to exert little control over the numerous commercial banks some of which confined their operations to particular localities. The large expansion in Japan's industrial production and trade during the war had been made possible only by lavish extensions of credit by those banks. When the boom broke they found themselves with many of their assets frozen and with no sources of liquidity available. Had the government, in an effort to keep Japanese prices in line with those of the United States and Britain, sought to press deflation further, it is probable that the effect on both banks and their industrial clients would have been devastating. It had, therefore, every reason to hold its hand. It is also probable that the concentration of economic power in the *Zaibatsu* influenced financial policy. These great business houses were predominant not only in many branches of manufacturing industry and trade, but also in banking and finance. There was, therefore, not the same clearcut division between financial and industrial interests as in Britain. Some of the largest commercial banks belonged to Mitsui and Mitsubishi which also owned many of the leading manufacturing and trading companies. These concerns were capable of pursuing a credit policy independent of the Central Bank and it is probable that their influence was thrown against any policy that might intensify the industrial depression.

Although the Japanese monetary authorities were unwilling, or unable, to carry the postwar deflation as far as their chief trading partners, they were committed to maintaining the exchange value of the yen. This inconsistency was the source of many troubles during the 1920s. To understand how this was so we must discuss briefly the course of the yen exchange rate. During the last years of the War, when the settlement of Japan's export surplus by gold shipments was impossible, the yen rose high above dollar parity. With the end of the postwar boom Japan's balance of trade became once more adverse, and the yen lost its premium. It might have been expected that when, after 1921, Japanese prices began to diverge from American and British prices, the yen–dollar and yen–sterling rates of exchange would have fallen further. But this did not happen. Although the government was unable, or unwilling, to bring Japanese prices into line with those of her trading partners, it refused to allow a depreciation in the exchange value of its currency.

The prewar problem had thus re-emerged. Could Japan maintain exchange parity and at the same time press forward with her expansionist policy? Yet the problem seemed of little urgency in the early postwar years because of the huge foreign balances accumulated between 1915 and 1920. The government and the Central Bank now resold their balances to the exchange banks to enable them to meet their import bills, and the yen was maintained for several years at within 3 per cent of dollar parity. The result was that, from 1921 until the end of 1923, the yen was overvalued on the exchanges by about 20 per cent, according to an estimate based on the purchasing-power-parity of the currencies concerned. The consequences were to be seen in the return of a large import surplus and a decline in the foreign balances. This phase of Japanese financial history may be compared with events in Britain between the spring of 1925 and September 1931. This country, which, after the restoration of the gold standard, failed to bring its internal prices into line with those of its chief trading partners, was able to maintain the overvalued pound at par by attracting short funds to London, until the withdrawal of these funds during the financial crisis of 1931 drove the country off the gold standard. Similarly, Japan kept the exchange value of her currency at an artificially high level by drawing on her foreign balances until September 1923, when the Kwanto earthquake, which necessitated the purchase of large quantities of reconstruction materials, so reduced these balances that further support of the exchange became impracticable. By April 1924 the exchange had fallen to under 40 dollars to the 100 yen (par being 49·85), and until the end of 1925 the yen remained about 20 per cent depreciated.

The earthquake led to a further period of inflationary finance. The rapid reconstruction of Tokyo and Yokohama was considered essential, and firms whose assets had been adversely affected by the disaster had to be assisted. Easy credit conditions necessarily accompanied this policy; and in order to relieve financial institutions whose assets had become frozen as a result of the earthquake, and to accelerate the work of reconstruction, the Bank of Japan was authorised to discount specified bills ('earthquake bills') under a government guarantee against loss up to the limit of 100 million yen. The increased governmental expenditure resulting from the earthquake was borne partly by the disposal of most of its remaining foreign balances, but mainly by borrowing both at home and abroad. The national debt (excluding the special debts) was about 75 per cent greater in 1926 than in 1918. At the same time, local and colonial government indebtedness much increased, and public utility companies all over Japan raised large sums at home and abroad for public works.[20] Prices rose sharply in 1924 and 1925 and there was a boom in most branches of industry. Thus, just as the government's policy had served to check deflation after 1920, so, after 1923, it led to a further period of inflation.

The financial authorities were disquieted by the prospects. A long series of unbalanced budgets seemed to be threatening the yen with the disaster that has overtaken other currencies in the postwar decade. In 1926 the government, influenced by the British return to the gold standard in the previous year, tried to stop the inflation so that it might follow suit. Economies were effected in administration, new taxes were imposed and, as a preliminary to a return to gold, the government set out to liquidate the outstanding earthquake bills.[21] The immediate effect of this new policy was to give rise to speculation in the yen on the part of operators in Shanghai and New York, and from a low level of $41 in November 1925 the exchange rose to just under par in the early months of 1927. This rise in the exchange disorganised the exporting industries, particularly the raw silk producers, and a severe financial crisis followed in the spring of 1927. The crisis was the inevitable result of the attempt to check the boom. For a long period Japan had been stimulated by inflationary finance, and a reversal of the policy was bound to have disturbing effects.

The genesis of the crisis deserves detailed attention. In April 1927 the government proposed to compensate the Bank of Japan for losses incurred in discounting earthquake bills by delivery to it of government bonds. Bonds were also to be lent to the ordinary banks for the same purpose. Parliamentary discussion of these proposals revealed the extent to which banking assets were frozen, causing a crisis, which developed into a panic. There was a run on the banks, which responded by attempting to call in loans. Ultimately thirty-six banks, including the Bank of Formosa, a semi-official bank, which was deeply involved in the Suzuki sugar interests, and the Peers' Bank, suspended payment. A moratorium had to be proclaimed, and the state guaranteed advances by the Central Bank to the amount of 700 million yen. The panic was arrested by these measures; but by this time the government whose policy had produced the crisis had lost office, and its attempt to restore the gold standard was abandoned by its successor. It is true that the crisis brought about a fall in prices and some liquidation of frozen credit conditions; but the state could not carry through the drastic measures necessary to implement a return to gold.

The crisis involved the extensive readjustment of industry to the new price conditions; but it does not appear to have given more than a temporary check to expansion. However, this proceeded at a lower rate than during the previous period. Although there was a rapid growth in certain new industries, some of the older staples, such as mining and cotton manufacture, grew more slowly, and there does not appear to have been any increase in industrial employment between 1927 and 1929. Meanwhile, the failure of the deflationary policy of 1926–27 was followed by a further period of heavy borrowing by central and local governments. The consequence of a decade of budgetary deficits was the doubling of the national debt and a tenfold increase in the debt of the local authorities. It was not until the summer of 1929, when the Minseito party came into office with a programme of deflation and economy, that a serious attempt to secure budgetary equilibrium was made.

Throughout the postwar period, in addition to the stimulus of cheap credit provided by the government and its financial institutions, Japanese industry continued to receive official subsidies and an even greater measure of protection against competing imports than before the First World War. Throughout this period, too, economic penetration in Asia was pushed forward. This is not the place to examine the penetration in detail, or to assess the net advantages which have accrued to Japan as a result of it. But this at least can be said. Although the development of continental resources has led to a substantial interchange of raw materials and manufactured goods between Japan and the regions in which she had acquired 'special interests', yet there have been grave disadvantages associated with her policy. State finances have been burdened by many unremunerative loans made for the purpose of extending Japanese control. The iron ore resources of Manchuria and China proper, in the development of which much Japanese capital has been invested, have proved insufficient for the needs of the iron and steel producers, and Japan has been forced to look further afield for her ores, to the Malay Peninsula and to north-western Australia.[22] Ironically enough, the development of the coalmines belonging to the South Manchuria Railway has been retarded since 1926 by limitations imposed on coal imports into Japan for the benefit of domestic coal-owners. It has even been suggested that imports of Korean rice, the production of which the government has been at great pains to encourage, should be restricted so as to protect the Japanese peasants. Thus, a conflict has arisen between what are conceived to be the interests of the state and the interests of particular groups.

There was, however, little sign of any such conflict in the figures for the country's international trade. When adjusted for changes in the value of money, Japan's exports, which at the end of the First World War were at least 50 per cent greater than in 1912–14, in 1927–29 were 100 per cent greater.[23] As might be expected, the fluctuations in the exchange prevented the rise from being continuous. Thus, owing to the overvaluation of the yen in 1921–23 the recovery of the export trade after the postwar slump was slow, and it was during the post-earthquake boom and the period of the low exchange that the most rapid advance of the decade was made. During the next three years there was little further increase; but in 1929 another upward movement occurred. In spite of this growth in commodity exports, and in spite of a rise in invisible receipts, the balance of payments on income account was adverse for every year between 1920 and 1928 (inclusive). From the figures given by H.G. Moulton and Junichi Ko, it would appear that the aggregate deficiency of the period 1920–28 amounted to 1700 million yen.[24] As before the First World War, the expansionist financial policy and an adverse balance of payments were inevitably associated. The rigidity of the Japanese demand for foreign currencies was, in one respect, even greater in postwar than in prewar days. With the rise in population the home production of foodstuffs was becoming increasingly insufficient for domestic requirements. Whereas before the War Japan imported only about 5 per cent of her rice consumption, during the 1920s her annual imports amounted to between 15 and 20 per cent of the consumption, although her own production also had greatly increased.[25]

Meanwhile, certain of the leading characteristics of the export trade were accentuated. Before the War about 55 per cent of the value of exports consisted of raw silk, silk tissues, cotton yarns and fabrics; by 1928–29 this proportion had risen to 66 per cent. Thus the export trade became even more highly specialised than formerly. The concentration of the trade on a few markets also increased. The United States and China, which took 64 per cent of the exports before the War, in 1928–29 took 68 per cent. British India's proportion rose from 3 per cent to 10 per cent. Clearly the economic advance of Japan, her ability to import the commodities necessary for her expansion, depended on her capacity for selling increasing quantities of silk to America and of cottons and other manufactures to China and India. The growth in the American market for silk was especially impressive in the postwar period; this growth accounts for the increase in the proportion of silk in the total export trade from 29 per cent in 1913 to 40 per cent in 1928–29. In a large measure, therefore, the rise in Japan's export trade, and thus her capacity for economic expansion after the War, was closely bound up with 'American prosperity'.

Apart from the danger arising from this degree of dependence on a single commodity and a single market, there were features of the trade which made it especially vulnerable. Both the cocoons and much of the reeled silk were produced by the peasantry. As this class was suffering from the diminishing returns to arable farming, it devoted itself more and more to satisfying the American demand for silk. But partly because production in Japan grew even faster than the demand, and partly owing to the competition of artificial silk and Chinese silk, the price of raw silk fell much more than general prices after 1923.[26] As the real cost of production of raw silk was not then susceptible to any considerable reduction, it is clear that the great expansion of the silk export trade took place only because the peasants were willing to produce an increasing quantity at a lower price per unit. Obviously this process could not continue indefinitely. The impoverishment of the peasants even before 1929 had already produced grave social problems, and any contraction of the American demand was bound to have damaging effects on their wellbeing.

The rise in the exports of cotton goods during the 1920s was almost as great as that of raw silk. At the end of the decade, however, there were fears that the favourable circumstances that attended the expansion might not persist. Between 1914 and 1919, in the absence of established competitors, Japan was able to make headway in China and India. When the War was over, the fall in silver persuaded Asian consumers to turn from Lancashire's goods to the cheaper fabrics which Japan was able to produce. In the critical years 1925–29 she benefited by a depreciated exchange, while her chief competitor was suffering from the effects of an overvalued currency. The boycotts of British goods in India also gave additonal opportunities to Japanese exporters. There is, of course, ample evidence to show that, apart from these fortuitous stimuli, Japan had real advantages as a producer of cotton goods.[27] But, although her position was in many respects very different from that of Great Britain at the time when she was building up her great cotton export trade, the British experience was not irrelevant to Japan's future in this branch of international trade. Lancashire was driven out of one market after another as local manufactures grew up. She was able for a long period to maintain her prosperity by shifting to new markets as old ones were lost, but in the end she found herself faced by formidable competition in every part of the world. There were lessons for Japan. Throughout the 1920s the tendency towards self-sufficiency in cotton manufactures was causing a contraction of world trade in these goods. So Japan was confronted with a task of securing an increasing share of a diminishing total trade. She was successful up to 1929; but at that time it seemed that attempts to extend the trade still further might be frustrated.

Tariffs were rising in her chief markets, India and China; her trade was liable to be affected by Chinese boycotts; and already she was being forced out of the lower grades of production by the cheaper costs of Asian competitors. If Japan were obliged to concentrate on the finer goods, it was by no means certain that she would find the organisation of her cotton trade so advantageous in competition with Lancashire as it had proved so long as she was concerned mainly with coarse and medium fabrics. An adequate discussion of Japan's prospects as a cotton goods exporter in 1930–32 would take us beyond the scope of this paper. But there then seemed little justification for the assumption that because Japanese cotton exports grew very fast during the last decade, therefore, this rise was likely to be resumed at the same rate when the world slump was over. So, the conclusion is that the economic development of the postwar period and the ability of the government to pursue its expansionist policy depended largely on 'American prosperity' on the one hand, and on the partly fortuitous events which gave Japan exceptional opportunities in Asian cotton markets on the other hand. In the absence of these favourable circumstances, the government would have been forced to modify its economic policy. Moreover, it is clear that the country's commercial position was liable to be severely shaken by any change in either of her two great markets.

Let us now return to Japan's financial history. The Minseito government, which came into office in the summer of 1929, immediately put into operation its programme of reducing public expenditure and returning to gold. The moving spirit behind this policy was J. Inouye, the nearest approach to an orthodox liberal financier that Japan has produced. He was a man of wide experience and considerable ability. He had for years been conducting a campaign in favour of deflation and a removal of the gold embargo. By this time he had convinced the industrial interests that the fluctuations of the exchange were more harmful to them than would be the adjustments needed to restore the gold standard. His policy, known as the 'No Loan' policy, was launched under what appeared to be favourable circumstances. Trade was improving in 1929; the continuance of 'American prosperity' was causing an exceptionally rapid expansion in the demand for raw silk; the increased demand for Japanese cotton goods on the part of India was assisting the other great export; the general improvement in foreign commerce was raising receipts from the mercantile marine; and a series of good harvests was reducing rice imports to insignificant dimensions. In 1929 the balance of payments appears to have been favourable to Japan for the first time since 1919. Further, although the foreign balances had become small, the ratio of the Bank of Japan's gold reserve to its note-issue was 65 per cent and to its note-issue and deposits combined, 49 per cent. There seemed, therefore, ample security against speculative withdrawals of funds once the yen had reached par. The announcement of the new government's policy led to a rise in the exchange from its low level of 43 dollars in June 1929, and the embargo was removed in January 1930.

No more unfortunate moment could have been chosen for the operation of the new policy. Even had the world boom continued, the rise in the exchange value of the yen and the fall in domestic prices would have placed a strain on the economic system, especially as financial relations had been for such a long period in a process of consolidation at a level of prices well above that of the world. But the steep decline in world prices which coincided with the return to the gold standard enhanced the difficulties of adjustment. Japan, having insulated herself against world price movements throughout the postwar decade, committed herself to following them at a moment of drastic decline. The Japanese wholesale price index fell between June 1929 and December 1930 by forty-six points, or 27 per cent, a much greater decline than that of the corresponding indices of the United States or England. Japanese financial authorities assumed that this fall in the price index was an indication that their country's price structure had adjusted itself to the new situation.[28] But they misjudged the scale of the correction required. It proved to be impossible for Japan to preserve a balance of payments without large shipments of gold, and the Bank lost 260 million yen, about a quarter of its gold reserve, during the year.

The chief source of the country's difficulties was the collapse of 'American prosperity'. During 1930 raw silk prices declined by 50 per cent, and silk exports amounted to only 53 per cent in value (although 82 per cent in weight) of those of 1929. The fall in silk prices brought acute distress to the peasantry and obliged the government to modify its financial policy, just as the crisis of 1927 had done. In the spring of 1930 it launched a scheme of silk valorisation which involved it in heavy losses, since, in spite of this effort, the price per bale fell from 1250 yen in April 1930, to 750 yen in August 1932.[29] Furthermore, it was obliged to increase its expenditure on public works and to make large loans to distressed classes. These additional expenses, together with the fall in receipts from taxation, forced the government to abandon its 'No Loan' policy. Although the collapse of the American market was the chief cause of the trouble, Japanese sales of manufactured goods in Asia were also affected, though somewhat less seriously, by the world slump. Exports of cotton tissues declined by 34 per cent in value and 12 per cent in quantity. In 1930 the value of the export trade as a whole was 32 per cent lower than in the previous year, a decline far greater than that in world trade.[30]

In 1931 the situation quickly deteriorated. The government was obliged to resort extensively to borrowing to meet its expenses, which grew as resistance to deflation became stronger. The export trade in manufactured goods, which had been less seriously affected than the demand for raw silk in 1930, now began to suffer from the higher Indian tariffs on the one hand, and Chinese boycotts, a protest against economic and political penetration, on the other hand. The series of good harvests was broken, and in 1931 Japan was obliged to import unusually large quantities of rice. Under the stress of these adverse conditions, the gold reserve continued to decline.

The Minseito government, however, was determined to preserve the yen. In order to carry deflation further, it proposed to reduce a number of its subsidies, a policy which aroused the opposition of the industrialists. Then, in the summer of 1931, Inouye pressed for a lowering of military and naval expenditure, as this alone could enable him to effect a substantial reduction in his budgetary deficit. The proposal antagonised the military and naval leaders, whose influence at the same time was growing as a result of the deterioration in the economic situation. During the period of prosperity the old military leaders in Japan had been losing their power; but the depression, by discrediting the constitutional and commercial elements in the state, was causing a reversion of popular opinion. It was, indeed, the collapse of 'American prosperity' which was indirectly responsible for undermining constitutional advance in Japan and again placing the Sat-Cho combination in control.[31] The final blow to the Minseito government was given by the British abandonment of the gold standard. Immediately, manufactured exports and the mercantile marine began to suffer from renewed British competition; while the financial position of the country was weakened by the depreciation of its funds in London.[32] At the same time, the government, unable to restrain the military party from its Manchurian adventure, found its finances still more strained. A flight from the yen began and the gold reserve dwindled until, towards the end of the year, it was less than half the amount of January 1930. In December the government fell, and the embargo on gold exports was immediately reimposed. Two months later what were regarded as Inouye's economic consequences provoked a 'patriotic' association to assassinate him. Thus the second attempt on the part of Japan to return to gold during the postwar period ended in disaster.

POSTSCRIPT

In 1932 the verdict on Japan's financial policy in the decade after the First World War was generally unfavourable. It was considered by most economists and financial experts that she had allowed the large foreign exchange holdings which she had accumulated between 1914 and 1920 to seduce her, in the early postwar years, into postponing the harsh measures necessary to counter inflationary pressures and to establish financial stability. The result was that when, at last, under the persuasion of foreign example, she tried to return to gold, the task was beyond her powers. Moreover, the timing of the attempt proved to be ill-judged. As to the condition of the public finances at the end of the postwar decade, a passage from Professor Andréadès' work on the subject may be quoted:

> Le déficit était devenu un élément permanent tant du budget de l'État que des budgets locaux, administrés avec encore plus d'imprévoyance. Jusqu'en 1928 on y avait fait face par des emprunts; de 1920 à 1929 on avait émis en moyenne des titres nouveaux d'une valeur annuelle de 271 million yens. On avait abouti ainsi à doubler la dette publique en dix ans, tandis que la dette locale décuplait en seize années; . . . Pour rétablir l'équilibre budgétaire on ne pouvait pas d'avantage songer à une augmentation de l'impôt, puisque ainsi que nous l'avons vu, celui-ci avait été maintenu a son niveau des temps de guerre et l'avait même, pour ce que est des finances locales, dépassé.[33]

Thus far the course of Japan's financial experience as originally set out in the papers of which this chapter is composed. But the story would lose half its interest if it were not supplemented with an account of what followed. To the period of 'orthodox' finance associated with Finance Minister Inouye there succeeded a period of reflation. The mechanism of this policy was contrived by K. Takahashi who became Finance Minister on Inouye's fall. Government expenditure financed largely by borrowing was much increased and easy credit conditions instituted by the monetary authorities. The fiduciary note-issue of the Bank of Japan was raised from 120 million yen to 1000 million yen and the note-issue itself rose from 1331 million yen at the end of 1931 to 1790 million yen five years later. Meanwhile, the exchange value of the yen was allowed in the course of 1932 to fall from dollar parity (49·85 dollars = 100 yen) to under 20. After the devaluation of the dollar in 1933, the rate rose to about 30, a level at which it became stabilised. The decline in wholesale prices was at once reversed, in contrast to world prices which continued to fall until 1933. However, between 1933 and 1936, the rise of prices in Japan was moderate, and in that period inflationary pressures were under control.

There can be no doubt that Takahashi's policy was remarkably successful in inducing economic recovery. The index of industrial production, which had fallen from 100 in 1929 to 92 in 1931, rose rapidly to 151 in 1936 and 171 in 1937. This growth occurred in a period in which American industrial production failed to regain its predepression level and British industrial production rose by less than a quarter. Japan's success at this time owed much to her structural adaptability. Although some of her older industries, notably cotton manufacture, continued to grow in absolute terms, the expansion was associated mainly with the advance of new trades, or of trades previously of little significance in Japan. In 1929 the rayon industry was in an early stage of development in Japan. By 1937 she was the world's largest producer of continuous filament and a leading producer of staple fibre. There was also a marked expansion in many of her industries producing miscellaneous consumption goods (toys, rubber shoes, hosiery and metal smallware), but the most striking advance occurred in the capital goods industries, metals, engineering goods and chemicals. In 1929 these groups accounted for less than 25 per cent of factory employment; and in 1937 for 43 per cent. The range of output within these groups was also much extended.

Japan's recovery and progress as an international trader were even more remarkable than the rise in her output. During a period when international trade as a whole was stagnating, the volume of her exports grew by three-quarters. Again, this growth had been made possible by the resilience of her economy. Whereas before the depression two-fifths of Japan's exports consisted of a semiproduct (raw silk), by 1937 the proportion had fallen to 15 per cent. The place of silk had been taken by a wide variety of finished manufactures.

The rise in exports, however, was only one factor in economic recovery. The direction of much of the new investment associated with the revival was determined by large-scale rearmament and the development of strategic industries in Manchuria. The Japanese term for describing the economy of the Takahashi period, *junsenji keizai* (literally, 'quasi-wartime economy'), was said by an American commentator on the period to be the 'equivalent in modern economic terminology . . . of full employment induced by deficit financing'. Takahashi had, in fact, been practising a Keynesian policy several years before the publication of *The General Theory of Employment, Interest and Money*. But the impulse behind the policy was supplied largely by the ambitions of the military clique whose influence in government had been immensely strengthened by economic hardships of the years of depression, especially those endured by the peasantry. This association between reflation and military ambition was in the end to pervert the policy. Takahashi aimed at carrying reflation to the point at which the country's underemployed resources were brought into use; up to that point, he realised, reflation would be largely self-financing. But the military, who were concerned solely with securing the resources necessary to fulfil their strategic designs, recognised no such limit. When, in 1936, Takahashi considered that his policy had been carried far enough and that a further increase in demand would lead to inflation (since 'bottlenecks' in the supply of resources would be encountered), he came into bitter conflict with the military. Hence the revolt of February 1936, the murder of Takahashi and several of his ministerial colleagues, and the further strengthening of the military grip on government.

The balance of righteousness in the dispute between the deflationists of 1927–31 and the reflationists of 1932–36 is not as easy to reach as the modern fashion in economic ideas would suggest. It is true that the social pressures that arose from deflation, especially in the rural population, did much to kindle the revolt against parliamentary government and to augment the influence of the military clique. On the other hand, the harsh economic discipline of the deflationary years, by eliminating inefficiency in industry and by stimulating the adoption of cost-reducing devices, laid the foundations for the growth that followed. Reflation called the underemployed resources into productive use, stimulated investment and extended the industrial base. But, by making lavish provision for the militarists' appetite, it led, perhaps inevitably, to war.

In judging these policies, therefore, one must bring into account their social and political consequences. At the same time, their economic effectiveness cannot be understood without reference to the country's social conditions. The steep reduction in industrial costs achieved in the deflationary period was dependent on the responsiveness of the economy to downward pressures. Markets for the most part were highly competitive, and prices fell quickly as demand declined. The workers, for their part, were in no position to resist reductions in wages. There can be no doubt that among the peasantry and the numerous small industrial producers real incomes definitely fell in the depression.

What seems, at first sight, more surprising is that wages and other incomes responded so slowly to the reflation of the Takahashi period. According to a reliable estimate, the real wage index in the first half of 1937 was, on average, about 10 per cent below that of the autumn of 1931.[34] This average conceals wide divergences from industry to industry. For example, real wages, especially women's wages, in textiles and in several of the older industries (including those responsible for a large share of the exports) remained low throughout the period of economic recovery, while the wages of skilled men employed in the metal and engineering industries rose conspicuously. The condition of the workers in the former group was responsible for the charge that the expansion of the export trade had been achieved by 'social dumping'. There is no reason to suppose that the government deliberately pursued any such policy. The failure of certain wages to rise when recovery set in can be explained simply by reference to the oversupply of labour available for employment in textiles, small-scale industries and the service trades. All these recruited much of their labour from peasant families impoverished by the collapse of agricultural prices. Moreover, in industries that were rationalised and reequipped during the depression, the demand for labour in subsequent years did not increase in proportion to the rise in production.

It may seem difficult to reconcile the failure of the workers to improve their living standards with the massive increase in production that occurred. The answer is not difficult to find.

During the 1930s resources were concentrated increasingly on the capital goods industries, especially those connected with rearmament. Heavy investment in the strategic industries of Manchuria also absorbed a share of the enlarged production. Finally, the worsening of the terms of trade—by 40 per cent between 1931 and 1937—meant that much of the additional production had to be exported simply to enable Japan to acquire the imports needed for developing her industry and her 'quasi-wartime' economy. Thus little or nothing of the enlarged production was left over for an improvement in the standards of consumption of the growing population.

As to the technique by which the reflation was financed, most of the increased public expenditure after 1932 was met by borrowing; in 1936–37 (fiscal year) about 27 per cent of the expenditure was so covered. The bond issues were taken up by institutional lenders, chiefly the commercial and savings banks. These banks seem to have extended into the new era the cautious credit policy towards their business customers that they had practised during the deflation. They were thus left with ample resources for investing in the new issues of government bonds. After the fall of Takahashi, however, and especially after Japan launched her campaign in North China (July 1937), public expenditure bounded ahead and borrowing with it. The resources of the commercial banks were quite insufficient to enable them to absorb the bulk of the bonds issued after that time; so these had to be taken up increasingly by the Central Bank. It was now that the note-issue (the money supply) began to expand very fast, while prices also started to rise at a rate much higher (up to the spring of 1939) than in the outside world. Japan was moving steadily towards a centrally controlled war economy in which the financial mechanism was to play a subordinate role in the allocation of real resources.

3 The Concentration of Economic Control[1]

Contemporary accounts of the present economic system of Japan leave the reader with two apparently inconsistent interpretations of her industrial and financial structure. On the one hand, we are informed that her major industries are operated on a large scale, in plants with up-to-date equipment by huge vertically integrated concerns, and that coordination has been achieved among merchants, manufacturers, financiers and officials to such an extent as to make possible the formulation of a common policy with regard to both production and foreign trade. Indeed, it is sometimes said that Japan has attained the modern stage of 'monopoly-capitalism' without passing through a period of economic liberalism with which Western countries were familiar in the nineteenth century. On the other hand, there are observers who state that outside the heavy industries the major part of Japan's manufacturing activity is conducted in small workshops, and that most of her industries have successfully resisted governmental attempts to rationalise them. The implication is, of course, that modern capitalistic methods have penetrated only a small part of her economic life. Evidence may be found in support of each of these interpretations, although the second certainly comes nearer to the truth. What is not generally realised, however, is that both the concentration of financial power and the existence of large integrated concerns in some branches of economic life, and also the predominance of small workshops and primitive methods of production in other branches, are symptoms of the immaturity of the economic system. Japan, with a dense population which is still rapidly increasing, and with scanty natural and capital resources, necessarily selects, when technical conditions make this possible, industries and processes of manufacture which require abundant labour and

46

little capital and natural resources. But in certain industries which are considered to be essential parts of the economy of a Great Power, the advantages of highly capitalistic methods are overwhelming; for technical reasons these industries must be conducted in large establishments, if at all. The state could only introduce these industries by granting privileges of various kinds to the few groups that possessed capital and experience of large-scale operations, and it still looks to them to initiate, under its protection, any new enterprise which is believed to be necessary in the interests of national power. It is, then, the scarcity of capital and entrepreneurial ability in a country with high political ambitions that led to the appearance of a few huge concerns with a wide range of interests in the midst of a multitude of very small producers.

These concerns are popularly known in Japan as the *Zaibatsu* or money-cliques.[2] Of these, four are outstanding—namely, Mitsui, Mitsubishi, Sumitomo and Yasuda, in that order of importance. The term *Zaibatsu* is also applied loosely to other large business groups, like Okura, Asano, Kuhara, Ogawa-Tanaka, Kawasaki, Shibusawa, Furukawa and Mori;[3] but, although these have some features in common with the *Zaibatsu* proper, there are important differences which warrant their being placed in a separate class. A brief reference to the early history of each of the great *Zaibatsu* will show how the foundations of their present position were laid. The Mitsuis, whose enterprises began in the seventeenth century, were financiers and traders even in Tokugawa times, and large-scale organisation has been familiar to them for centuries. For example, for many decades before the Restoration (1868) they were operating a trading enterprise from which the modern Mitsukoshi Departmental Store has developed.[4] In the troubles that preceded the Restoration both the *Shogun* and the supporters of the Emperor appealed to the rich merchants for donations, and most of these merchants responded to the appeals of both parties. Mitsui, however, correctly estimated the outcome of the struggle and gave wholehearted support to the Emperor's party. The result was that when this triumphed, the firm was entrusted with the government's financial business, and so laid the basis of its modern financial supremacy.[5] Marquis Kaoru Inouye, the great statesman of the Meiji period, worked in close association with Mitsui. In return for help given to the new government in times of financial stress, Inouye gave Mitsui substantial privileges. For instance, state properties, acquired from the *Shogun* and the clan governments, were sold to Mitsui at low prices, and formed the beginnings of their present great industrial interests. The famous Mitsuike coal-mine was acquired by the firm in this way. Governmental purchases and sales of materials in foreign countries were made through Mitsui, which reorganised its trading concern in 1876 and then began to play an active part in the import of cotton and the export of raw silk. When the period of territorial expansion began, Mitsui, together with other *Zaibatsu*, was given privileges which enabled it to develop colonial enterprises. Since the creation of constitutional government Mitsui has been closely associated with the Seiyukai, one of the two chief political parties, and its officials have from time to time held important offices of state.

Mitsubishi has quite a different origin. Its founder, a *samurai* named Yataro Iwasaki, in the later years of the Shogunate was engaged in managing a trading enterprise established by his feudal superior, the Lord Tosa. When feudalism was abolished in 1872, this business, then on the verge of insolvency, passed into Iwasaki's hands, together with its chief assets consisting of eleven ships. Shortly afterwards, political troubles occurred in Formosa, and Iwasaki was entrusted with the task of carrying troops and supplies, while his merchant fleet was supplemented by thirty steamers bought by the government from abroad. From this time the firm, now known as Mitsubishi Shokai, went ahead rapidly. The government was anxious to extend Japan's mercantile marine, and through the influence of Count Okuma, a friend of Iwasaki's, financial assistance was granted by the state to enable him to buy more ships.[6] In this way the great Nippon Yusen Kaisha was built up. In 1884 Mitsubishi leased the Nagasaki Dockyard from the government, and so began its shipbuilding enterprise. About the same time Yataro's brother Yanosuke began to develop the mining business to supply steamers with coal; later a bank was purchased and a marine insurance business started. In 1890 Mitsubishi, under pressure from the government, which was then in financial difficulties, bought from it a tract of waste land near the Imperial Palace in Tokyo. This land has since become one of the most valuable sites in the city, for the famous Marunouchi business quarter is located there; and from this purchase date the real-estate interests of the firm. Mitsubishi's political affiliations have been with the Minseito, formerly called the Kenseikai, the second of the chief political parties. Kato, who was Prime Minister in 1924, and Shidehara, who was Foreign Minister from 1929 to 1931, were closely connected with the Iwasaki family.

Sumitomo's interests are supposed to be about one-third of those of Mitsubishi, although, like Mitsui, it is an old firm and dates back to the sixteenth century. In feudal days its main activities consisted of copper-mining and copper-refining, and it also conducted a trade in rice. From copper-mining there developed in the modern era its great interests in all the non-ferrous metal trades, in chemicals, steel production and coal-mining; while out of its rice trade there emerged its banking and trust business.[7] Because of the location of its headquarters at Osaka this firm has not had such close connections with the government as have Mitsui and Mitsubishi; although it is concerned with supplying government departments and semi-official enterprises with materials. Yasuda, the smallest of the four *Zaibatsu*, was an important firm of money-lenders in Tokogawa times. Its rise to its present position coincided with the development of banking business in Japan after the 1890s. It furnished the government with large loans at the time of the Russo-Japanese War, and it acquired substantial interests in the colonies and Manchukuo. Yasuda's political influence has been exerted mainly through the military societies rather than by the contacts with political parties. What is especially significant is that the rise of the *Zaibatsu* has depended upon privileges extended to them by the government and upon their ability to provide the state with financial and other resources in times of stress. They have all benefited from colonial development, and in each of the great wars in which Japan has been engaged they have earned large profits, both from the provision of loans and from supplying war materials. In other words, they have been the necessary instruments of national policy and have reaped a considerable share of the rewards attending the success of that policy. In times of depression and financial panic they have enlarged their sphere of interests through acquiring the property of firms in financial difficulties. In the course of Japan's economic development many old concerns have been struck down, and their properties have usually passed under *Zaibatsu* control.[8]

What distinguishes the four *Zaibatsu* today from other large firms is not merely the magnitude of their interests, nor even their close associations with the government, but rather the fact that they are pre-eminent at once in finance and also in industry and commerce.[9] In Japan the association of financial institutions and industrial and commercial undertakings under a single control confers an important competitive advantage which cannot be enjoyed by firms which operate in only one of these fields. This is largely because there is no considerable section of the public willing to invest in industrial securities. The bulk of the public's savings is placed with the Post Office, on fixed deposit at the banks, or entrusted to insurance companies and to the trust companies which have made remarkable progress during the last ten years. Some important industrial concerns have, of course, been built up from small beginnings through the reinvestment of profits. But large-scale enterprises in need of outside investment-capital have to obtain it mainly by selling their securities to banks and other financial institutions; while their working capital is provided for the most part by bank loans against promissory notes. The small producers, who in the aggregate are responsible for the larger proportion of the output of consumable goods, are financed by merchants, who, in turn, obtain the bulk of their resources from the banks. Those who control the financial institutions can, therefore, play a dominant part in the development of industry. An industrialist who has no bank under his control through which the supply of savings may be directed into his own manufacturing undertakings, is liable to fall into a position of dependence upon some financial group which, because of its associated industrial enterprises, may be in fact a rival. It is significant that the firm of Okura, with substantial interests in the heavy industries in Japan itself, Manchukuo and North China, has been forced recently to seek a liaison with Yasuda because of its need for capital.[10] Now, of the six 'ordinary' banks of outstanding importance in Japan, one is controlled by each of the *Zaibatsu*, and these four banks, together with their subsidiaries, possess over one-third of the total deposits of the ordinary banks. The trust companies controlled by these *Zaibatsu* possess nearly 70 per cent of all trust deposits, and their insurance companies about 20 per cent of the amount insured for life. Most of the premiums paid in connection with marine and fire insurance pass through the hands of the *Zaibatsu*. Through their investments in the securities of industrial companies or through loans made to them, the *Zaibatsu* financial institutions are able to control smaller banks, electric-light and power companies, gas companies and private railways in addition to many manufacturing enterprises.[11]

The power of the *Zaibatsu* is not limited to the control which they can secure through the medium of their great financial concerns. A mass of industrial and commercial undertakings have been established by them, or acquired from their original founders, and are now administered directly as part of their enterprise. These include some of the leading firms in every line of industry. There are numerous other undertakings which, though not directly controlled by the *Zaibatsu*, are brought into close association with them because they hold blocks of shares or have appointed many of the directors. The *Zaibatsu* also have large investments in many important enterprises not within their sphere of control. This applies to concerns that are managed by the state as well as to private undertakings.[2]

Their range of interests extends to all the modern industries of Japan and to some of the traditional trades also. Shipping, shipbuilding, foreign trade, warehousing, colonial enterprise, engineering, metal manufacture, mining, textiles, and sugar-refining and flour-milling all fall within their sphere. Although each concern ranges over a wide field, there are some differences of emphasis. Thus, Mitsui's foreign trading activities are far more important than those of the other three, while its mining properties are also very extensive. Mitsubishi is concerned predominantly with real-estate, shipping, shipbuilding and engineering. Sumitomo's main strength lies in the heavy industries, especially non-ferrous metals, and it trades only to a slight extent in products other than those turned out by its own plants. Yasuda's interests, apart from banking, are largely in colonial enterprise.

A glance at a few of the leading trades will show the extent to which the concentration of control over industry and trade has been achieved. For this purpose we may confine ourselves to Mitsui, Mitsubishi and Sumitomo. These three control about half the copper production and nearly the same proportion of the coal output, and Mitsui Bussan (the trading company of Mitsui) alone deals in about one-third of the coal marketed in Japan. More than half the tonnage of merchant ships is owned by them. Of the steamers being built in 1936, 55 per cent of the gross tonnage was being constructed in yards belonging to Mitsui and Mitsubishi.[13] The Oji Company controlled by Mitsui has about 75 per cent of the capacity of the paper industry and Mitsubishi owns the greater part of the remainder. These two firms possess 70 per cent of the flour-milling capacity and practically all the sugar-refining mills. Much of the chemical industry is in their hands, including the bulk of the ammonium-sulphate production. Mitsubishi dominates the aircraft industry, and through its control over the Asahi Glass Company monopolises the sheet-glass output. About half of the goods in warehouses are in those owned by the three *Zaibatsu*, who also conduct about one-third of the foreign trade. Mitsui Bussan alone is responsible for nearly one-fifth of this trade; it imports a quarter of the raw wool used in Japan, and about the same proportion of the raw-silk exports passes through its hands. Toyo Menkwa, another Mitsui concern, until recently handled one-third of the raw cotton imports and one-fifth of the exports of cotton textiles. Most of the enterprises which have been founded to develop the raw material resources of the colonies, Manchukuo, China and the South Sea countries have been established by the *Zaibatsu*; for instance, much of the Manchurian soya-bean trade is conducted by them or their subsidiaries. The cotton-spinning industry is less dependent upon the *Zaibatsu* than are the other large-scale trades. Yet even here Mitsui has interests in Kanegafuchi Boseki, and Mitsubishi in Fuji Gasu Boseki, which are among the six largest companies in the country; while Mitsui, through its subsidiary, Toyo Menkwa, has control over several smaller concerns. Mitsubishi manages much of the canned-fish trade, one of the three main brewery companies in Japan and one of the two large foreign-style confectionery manufacturing companies. The *Zaibatsu* are predominant in the heavy engineering industry. Their interests extend to woollen textiles, rayon, cement and petrol-refining and petrol-dealing.[14] In all the new industries as they have appeared the *Zaibatsu* have usually taken the initiative. At present Sumitomo is developing the aluminium industry, and Mitsui the hydrogenation process. The *Zaibatsu* have been associated with several foreign concerns in the direction of particular industries and have acquired many foreign patent rights. For example, Mitsui is linked with Babcock and Wilcox in the control of the boiler-making works of Toyo Babcock. As already indicated, the close association of these firms with the state has led them to invest heavily in official or semi-official enterprises, such as the South Manchuria Railway Company and the special banks.

The influence of the *Zaibatsu* extends far beyond the confines of the concerns which they directly or indirectly control. This extension is brought about by several methods. Two of these methods have already been referred to. First, through their control over the credit machinery of the country they are able to dictate policy to their debtors to no small extent. Secondly, their trading companies handle the goods both of the large manufacturers and also of the multitude of small producers and local factors and merchants who depend on them for working capital. Both Mitsui Bussan and Mitsubishi Shoji[15] have long made a practice of advancing funds to small-scale producers, offering them technical advice, and providing machinery on credit. Sometimes this financial control is exerted directly, and sometimes through local merchants, who obtain supplies from the small-scale producers. Mitsui has acquired in this way a share of the trade in such agricultural products as eggs, milk and fruit. Thus, although much of Japan's manufacturing activity has not been affected technically by modern methods, yet the control exercised by large capital interests has penetrated deeply into the country's life. Since each of the great trading companies has behind it a powerful bank, it is clear that large resources are available for this type of business.

A third method by which *Zaibatsu* influence is extended is through various cartels and associations. When the possession of plants entitles a *Zaibatsu* to share in a cartel's deliberations, it can often determine the policy of a whole industry, and when, through its export business, it becomes a member of an Export Guild, dealing with a particular product, it can secure a generous share of quota allocations. Thus, the coal, chemical and many other trades are almost entirely dominated by the *Zaibatsu*, even though they do not possess the major part of the capacity of those industries. Where selling syndicates have been formed in recent years, Mitsui Bussan and Mitsubishi Shoji have frequently been appointed as sales agents. In carrying out governmental schemes for national control over certain industries, they have often been given important functions, as in the fuel-oil trade. Finally, through the influence which the *Zaibatsu* can exert over the government, either by the establishment of connections with the leading bureaucrats or by their control over one or other of the political parties, they can win considerable advantages for themselves through the general direction which they can give to policy, as well as through the securing of subsidies, fiscal protection for their enterprises, and government contracts. Moreover, the power which they exercise in one field is used to develop their business in others. For instance, it is said that a *Zaibatsu* sometimes uses its influence as a banker to induce outside traders and manufacturers to give their custom to its shipping lines or stevedoring companies.

These great concerns—and this is true of all large Japanese firms—are family businesses. Control is centred upon a partnership (Mitsui Gomei, Mitsubishi Goshi, Sumitomo Goshi and Yasuda Hozensha), the capital of which is owned entirely by members of a family or group of families with a common ancestor. For instance, Mitsui *Zaibatsu* has long consisted of eleven families who are descended from the founder of the firm. The partnership exercises its control through the holding of shares in other companies and through the appointment of directors and managers, and it is responsible for all the main decisions of policy. Thus, any proposal to branch out into some new line of business would be discussed by the partnership council. This does not mean, however, that the family members themselves always take an active part in administration. In the House of Mitsui actual control was vested in officials even before the Restoration. This was according to the famous *Banto Seiji* or manager-system, and the success of Mitsui can be attributed largely to the series of able *Banto* (managers), who have been in its service since the beginning of the Meiji era. These *Banto* have been drawn from various classes of the community. At present the cream of the Universities and the higher technical and commercial schools is recruited by Mitsui and by the other *Zaibatsu*.[16]

Each great *Banto* has trained a number of subordinates of promise who have ultimately succeeded him, or have been placed in charge of some new branch of business. They are not so much employees of Mitsui as fellow-clansmen who devote themselves to the service of their overlord, and in this respect the organisation of the concern is characteristic of the social, political, military and economic life of present-day Japan. Thus, a *Banto* who had been placed in charge of a firm where he enjoyed considerable freedom from central control would be expected in an emergency to come to the aid of the parent concern. It would, moreover, be almost out of the question for a *Zaibatsu* to allow one of its subsidiaries to become bankrupt; the loss would be borne by the parent concern. The *Banto* watch each other with a critical eye, promoting those who have shown ability and relegating to obscurity even those of high position who have made mistakes. Yet the dismissal of a *Banto* scarcely ever occurs. It is in Mitsui that the *Banto* system is most fully developed, but among the other *Zaibatsu* the same type of organisation has appeared. It is true that the Iwasaki family for long retained a great deal of personal control over Mitsubishi; but now that the founders have gone the separation of ownership and control has been realised in this firm also. Until very recently the members of the Yasuda family kept in their own hands the direction of their businesses. But even they are now withdrawing from active participation.[7]

In the ordinary conduct of business a high degree of decentralisation is permitted, especially in Mitsui, although subject to the qualifications already mentioned. While one branch of the concern would naturally obtain its supplies through an affiliated company, other things being equal, yet it would not do so as a general rule if it could get better terms from outsiders. In other words, each concern is supposed to stand on its own feet and to work for its own profit. The method of remunerating officials employed by Mitsui gives an indication of the policy that is followed. Their salaries, which are relatively low, mark merely the rank or grade of the recipient. But besides his salary the official receives a semi-annual bonus, varying with the prosperity of the branch of Mitsui in which he is engaged. In a prosperous branch his bonus is likely to be considerably more than his salary; in other branches his bonus may be very small. This system of payment appears to be peculiar to Mitsui. In Yasuda, Mitsubishi and Sumitomo bonuses in the directly controlled concerns do not vary with their individual profits, although of course in the subsidiaries the situation is different.

Figure 1 below shows the range of Mitsui's interests and the methods by which control is secured. It will be observed that the firm makes much use of the holding company device. The

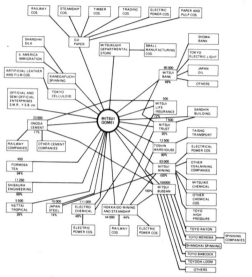

Figure 1   The House of Mitsui

The companies to the right of the chart are the six main Mitsui concerns and their subsidiaries. The companies to the bottom left are those which are completely controlled by Mitsui Gomei, and the capital of which is provided chiefly by Mitsui Gomei or the main subsidiaries. The companies to the top left of the chart are those in which Mitsui has substantial interests or exercises considerable influence over policy, although it does not directly control them. The figures above the name of each company show the paid-up capital in thousand yen, and the figure below indicates the proportion of the capital held by Mitsui Gomei or the main subsidiaries. The chart does not include by any means all the Mitsui companies or interests, but is intended to give a representative picture of the concern's scope. ·

assets of Mitsui Gomei consist of the securities in other companies. Of these, there are six major companies capitalised wholly or mainly by Mitsui and under the direct control of the partnership – Mitsui Bank, Mitsui Bussan, Mitsui Mining, Mitsui Trust, Toshin Warehouse and Mitsui Life Insurance. Each of these concerns in turn controls through security holdings or other financial connections and through the appointment of directors a large number of other companies, which include some of the most important in Japan in their several lines of business. For instance, the companies controlled by Mitsui Bussan are engaged in the following industries: rayon, flour-milling, cotton-merchanting, engineering, electrical apparatus, loom, condensed milk, marine and fire insurance and oil-refining; these subsidiaries also have interests in other concerns. Apart from these six great companies, Mitsui Gomei also controls large firms such as the Shibaura Engineering Company and, in conjunction with other Mitsui concerns, the Hokkaido Mining and Steamship Company, Japan Steel Works, Electrochemical Industry Company, each of which has several subsidiaries. All these are part and parcel of Mitsui.[19] There are other very important companies in which the House has only small capital holdings but a considerable influence over policy. The largest of these is the Oji Paper Company, with a paid-up capital of 112 million yen. This firm owns numerous subsidiaries engaged in pulp-production, electricity-generation, railway and steamship transport and forestry at home and abroad.[20] Another concern, originally established by Mitsui, but now bound to it by a looser connection, is the Kanegafuchi Spinning Company. Figures similar to Figure 1 above could be drawn to illustrate the interests of the other *Zaibatsu*, although, of course, their range is less extensive.

A word must be said about the mutual relations of the Zaibatsu. Although each concern has a different emphasis, their interests conflict in many spheres of activity—mining, banking, trust and insurance business, chemical production and foreign trade. They are jealous of each other's power, and, as we have seen, the rivalry of the two largest concerns extends even to the political sphere. As a general rule, one *Zaibatsu* refrains from lending any financial assistance to enterprises in which a subsidiary company of some other *Zaibastu* is concerned. Nevertheless, in the development of trust companies, which during the last ten years have played an important part in Japanese finance, the various *Zaibatsu* cooperated in the provision of capital for each other's concerns. Further, in the establishment of semi-official enterprises, or those considered to be of national importance, the *Zaibatsu* have often subscribed capital jointly. Thus, when the Japan Iron and Steel Company (Nippon Seitetsu) was formed a few years ago to rationalise the iron and steel trade, they all invested in it. They have cooperated with the Industrial Bank of Japan in taking up the debentures of the electricity-generating companies; most of them hold shares in the South Manchuria Railway Company, the semi-official banks, the Japan Air Transport Company, oil-mining enterprises in Saghalien and many other concerns in Korea, Formosa and Manchukuo.[21] Indeed, their participation is essential in the development of colonial regions and in the working out of a policy of power.

Of late years the *Zaibatsu* have been subjected to much public criticism, and this has led them to modify considerably their business methods. The reasons for these attacks deserve explanation. As long as the *Zaibatsu* confined their interests to large-scale industry, the financing of new enterprises, colonial development and the administration of concerns of national importance, they did not come into serious conflict with that part of Japan's economy which is associated with small-scale manufacture and trade and with agriculture. But partly through the ambitions of able officials who wished to extend their sphere of control, and partly through certain developments in Japan's economic situation, the activities of the *Zaibatsu* began to encroach on fields hitherto outside their scope. After the First World War there was a pronounced movement towards the consolidation of banking. This is to be attributed in some measure to the deliberate policy of the government which was anxious to eliminate the recurrent financial panics—the concomitant of a system composed of numerous small and recklessly managed banks—and also to the gradual disappearance of the minor banks by amalgamation or bankruptcy. As a result, a banking system has been created which is much less prone than formerly to succumb to panic, but the smaller merchants and manufacturers who were the chief customers of the minor banks have suffered from this change. To an increasing extent they have been forced, resentfully, within the financial orbit of the *Zaibatsu*. The trading activities of these concerns, moreover, have increased during the last decade; Mitsui Bussan has much enlarged its range. Small merchants have found themselves driven out of markets and small manufacturers have been reduced to dependence on the great trading companies. It is said that groups of small merchants originally opened up the trade with the South Seas countries, but that this trade has since been absorbed by Mitsui Bussan.[22] A few years ago this concern also began to trade in agricultural and marine products, such as eggs and seaweed, formerly conducted entirely by local merchants. The intense depression of the period 1929–32 drove many of these small concerns out of business, leaving Mitsui Bussan supreme. There can be little doubt that Japan's foreign trade benefited by the intrusion of the *Zaibatsu* into these new lines; but this did not prevent the rise of a strong feeling of hostility against them. At the same time the growing influence of the political parties was objected to not merely by the Army and Navy, but also by the peasants and small traders, who saw in that development a further extension of the power of the great concerns that were known to control the politicians. Frequent political scandals fomented this discontent, while the economic distress, the consequence of the deflationary policy of the Minseito government in 1930–31 and of the fall in raw silk prices, was attributed to the *Zaibatsu* also. When Japan was driven off gold at the end of 1931, the Mitsui Bank and Mitsui Bussan were charged with having made large profits from speculating in the dollar exchange.

Popular disapproval was directed particularly against Mitsui. It was the largest of the *Zaibatsu*; its trading activities were far more extensive than those of the other concerns, and so affected a greater number of small businesses; and it was more efficient and perhaps more ruthless than the others. Sumitomo seems to have been most successful in escaping censure, largely because its interests were predominantly in the heavy industries and because its headquarters were at Osaka, remote from the political excitements of the capital. For some time before 1932 Mitsui's leading *Banto* had foreseen the danger attending their policy of expansion, and apparently they had decided to move more cautiously. But before this change had been put into effect, the storm of disapproval had grown, the Press was filled with virulent criticisms of the *Zaibatsu*, particularly of Mitsui. Finally, Takuma Dan, the chief *Banto*, was assassinated. Since then the *Zaibatsu* have been trying to demonstrate their conviction of sin. The managing director of Mitsui Bussan, who had been responsible for its successful forward policy, was relieved of his office and was given an obscure position in the firm. It was announced that Mitsui would withdraw from business in minor agricultural products. To meet the criticism that they were monopolising all the more profitable industries, Mitsui Gomei have sold large holdings of shares in some of their most important companies to the public, notably shares in the Oji Paper Company.[23] In 1932, three million yen were given to the nation for the relief of distress during trade depression, and a year later the Mitsui Requital Fund was established with an endowment of thirty million yen for the promotion of social welfare.[24] Mitsui and the other *Zaibatsu* have also tried to divert public attention from their business interests. At one time it was customary for new enterprises, when launched by Mitsui, to bear the house name; but an attempt is now being made to confer anonymity upon many of their enterprises. For instance, the Mitsui Tea Company has come to be known as the Nitto Tea Company.[25] After the February Incident of 1936, which was to a large extent the outcome of anti-capitalist feeling, the family members announced their intention of withdrawing from directorates and from all active participation in the business. A compulsory retiring age has also been instituted which will lead to the removal of several of leading *Banto* in the course of a few years. To placate the Army by showing that they are devoted to the national interests the *Zaibatsu* have established new enterprises that are considered to have strategic importance, such as plants for hydrogenation and for staple fibre production. They have recently provided most of the capital for a new bank instituted to finance small traders and industrialists who are members of manufacturers' and exporters' associations. They all exert themselves to prevent references to their families from appearing in the Press.

The public has scarcely been placated. The new policy is commonly known as the 'camouflage policy'.[26] It is pointed out that the selling of blocks of shares in certain firms does not mean the elimination of *Zaibatsu* control of them. The donations to the social services are held to demonstrate not their change of heart, but their capacity to pay. Indeed, it is doubtful if the *Zaibatsu* have done more than *reculer pour mieux sauter*. The smaller industrialists and the raw-silk producers and merchants who have to find export markets for their goods cannot dispense with the huge resources and world-wide organisation of Mitsui Bussan. The public may dislike these great concerns, but its savings will still be entrusted to their efficient financial institutions rather than to the less secure minor banks. Whatever government is in office must depend upon the *Zaibatsu* for the resources and expert knowledge needed to carry out its programmes of political and economic expansion. The Kwantung Army cannot develop Manchukuo without their help. The Admiralty and the War Office can only extend armaments by utilising the resources of the *Zaibatsu* factories. In a time of crisis the government must turn to them to furnish officials to act as heads of the semi-official banks and other public enterprises. It is significant that only recently, at a time when the Army has achieved a still further measure of control over the political machine, S. Ikeda, formerly president of the Mitsui Bank, and one of the *Banto* who were held responsible for the aggressive policy of Mitsui, should be called to the position of Governor of the Bank of Japan. The recently appointed head of the Yokohama Specie Bank is a relative of Iwasaki. No doubt the appearance of a more liberal régime in economics and politics and the reduction of expenditure on armaments and colonial development might weaken the grip of the *Zaibatsu* upon the economic life of Japan; but this cannot reasonably be expected for many years to come. As long as Japan persists in the course of development upon which she has been set ever since the Restoration, *Zaibatsu* power is not likely to diminish.

POSTSCRIPT

From the early 1930s the dominance of the *Zaibatsu* was challenged by new groups, commonly known as the *Shinko-Zaibatsu* ('new *Zaibatsu*'). These groups, of which the most important was Nissan,[27] came to the front with the growth of the war industries. After the outbreak of fighting with China, in July 1937, the government, obedient to the demands of the military clique, decided on a policy of massive industrial development in Manchuria. The old *Zaibatsu*, the obvious agents for executing the policy, were denied the key role because of the antagonism of the military. So a new concern, the Manchuria Industrial Development Company, was formed to take over the industrial properties of the South Manchuria Railway Company and to promote further development. In this concern Nissan held half the capital and the Manchukuo government the rest. Nissan was more acceptable to the Army than Mitsui or Mitsubishi because its shares were widely distributed and its directors were presumed to be the willing tools of military ambition. Yet the contrast with the old *Zaibatsu* was more apparent than real. Aikawa, who directed Nissan's affairs, had family connections with the leaders of Mitsubishi, while Mori, a new group in the chemical and electrical industries, had affiliations with Yasuda.[28] In the event, the rivalry between the old and new *Zaibatsu*, as between them and the *Gumbatsu* (Army clique), was shortlived. As Japan moved towards war with the Western Powers, both industrial groups were called upon to act as agents of the state in organising the economy for the conflict. It seems probable that, in Japan itself, the importance of the old *Zaibatsu* was enhanced between 1941 and 1945, for, by the end of the war, their dominance, as indicated by their share of industrial capacity and financial resources, was even larger than in their heyday.

After the war the *Shinko-Zaibatsu*, whose interests were predominantly in the munitions industries and in Manchurian undertakings, succumbed to the American policy of dissolution, although some of their constituent companies (for example, Hitachi) survived to thrive as leaders in the engineering industries. As for the old *Zaibatsu*, after dissolution the managers left in charge of the successor companies seem to have enjoyed their new-found freedom from central control and did not wish to press for a return to the former system of administration. Although, after the end of the Occupation, the groups were reconstituted, they never regained their former cohesion. The great *Zaibatsu* families had lost their wealth and had withdrawn from active participation in business affairs. The member-firms, no longer controlled by a central holding company, retained a large measure of independence. Some commentators on the postwar scene have been so deeply impressed with the magnitude of these changes as to deny that there is any identity between the prewar and the postwar *Zaibatsu*. It is, of course, true that their empires are much less closely knit than in the past, and that they now have to share their power with other large business groups. But if the ties that link the members of a particular *Zaibatsu* are loose and often difficult to detect, the very subtlety of the relationship may be a source of strength. At any rate, in their new guise, the *Zaibatsu* have played a leading part in Japan's postwar economic expansion.[29]

4 The Cotton Industry in the 1930s: Its Organisation and Efficiency[1]

Cotton-spinning was the first modern factory industry to achieve a place of importance in Japan's economy, and up to 1939 the cotton industry remained the outstanding example of her enterprise in large-scale manufacturing. The present paper, which was written in 1937, describes and analyses the changes in the industry's structure, organisation and efficiency between 1929 and 1935–37. This was a critical period in the country's economic history, and the experience of this industry epitomised, in many respects, that of her factory trades as a whole.

One of the salient characteristics of the cotton industry at the present time (1935–37) is the sharp distinction between the large firms engaged in both spinning and weaving, and the section composed of specialist weavers. A close examination of the industry, however, shows that within each of these sections many differences exist between the activities and nature of the various firms, and also that some important producing units are not accommodated within either of these two classes. So while the majority of the spinning companies also control weaving sheds, a considerable number of them are engaged solely in spinning. In 1929 there were seventeen specialist spinning companies with 553,000 spindles (or 8·4 per cent of the total). By 1935 there were twenty-six companies with 1,126,000 spindles (or 10.9 per cent of the total) in this group.[2] Most of these companies owned very small mills, but there were a few notable exceptions. In view of the alleged superiority of vertical integration over horizontal specialisation, it may seem surprising that the group of specialist spinning mills has actually grown relatively and absolutely during the last seven years. It is doubtless to be explained by the rapid development of the

63

cotton hosiery trade and of specialist weaving mills, to which I shall refer later on. The not insignificant place occupied by these spinners is indicative of the fact that the spinning branch of the industry cannot be treated as homogeneous; it consists of firms catering for a variety of markets and so faced with problems that differ from one to another.

Again, very great differences exist among the integrated firms in respect both of their size and also of their dependence upon the outside market for the disposal of their yarn. The size of the firms may be discussed in connection with the changes that have occurred in spinning capacity over our period. Table 5 on page 80 shows that the three largest companies possessed in 1929 about one-third of the ring-spindles in Japan itself, while the seven largest companies had 56 per cent. Between 1929 and 1935 one of these large companies (Godo) combined with Toyobo, thus creating the largest spinning company in Japan with one and a half million spindles, and in 1935, this company, together with the remaining five large companies, possessed 48 per cent of the spindles. Thus, while the spindle-age of the large company group had much increased, and while some concentration had taken place within it, that group as a whole had not maintained its relative importance, and the tendency of the decade before 1929 had, in fact, been reversed. This movement was, no doubt, to be expected in a period in which equipment and output were rapidly expanding.

If we look at the rest of the spinning industry a remarkable growth is seen to have occurred in the size of the firms. In 1929 no less than fifty-five companies out of a total of sixty-eight had less than 100,000 spindles, and these companies together owned over two million spindles or 30 per cent of the total. By 1935, while the number of companies had risen to seventy-two, only forty-four had less than 100,000 spindles. These possessed 1,514,000 spindles or only 14 per cent of the total. So the small companies are tending to disappear from the Japanese spinning industry; and the most marked change in our period has been the rise of companies of intermediate size. Excluding the seven largest companies, there were in 1929 only six companies with more than 100,000 spindles; these possessed 14·4 per cent of the total. In 1935 (excluding the same large company group now reduced to six) there were twenty-two companies with over 100,000 spindles, and these together owned 38 per cent of the total. The greatest development had taken place in the 100,000 – 200,000 group. In 1929 there were only four companies of this size with 7·7 per cent of the total spindles; in 1931 seventeen companies with 21·5 per cent of the total (see Table 6, page 81.) The growth in the number of firms of intermediate size has been due mainly to extensions of existing mills or the establishment of new ones, rather than to a process of amalgamation.

The changes of the period may be summed up as follows:

(1) There was a slight decline in the relative importance of the giant companies, in spite of a large absolute increase in their spindleage.

(2) Small firms have greatly diminished in number.

(3) Firms of intermediate size have increased in number and are now taking a much larger share of the trade than formerly.

Even more striking changes have occurred in the size of the mills as Table 7 on page 81 indicates. In 1929 only 8 per cent of the spindles were in mills with over 100,000 spindles; in 1935 this percentage had increased to 24. In 1929 half the capacity was found in mills with under 50,000 spindles; in 1935 the proportion had fallen to one-third. Even within this group there has been a tendency to enlargement; for the average number of spindles per mill in it rose from 24,000 to nearly 30,000 during this period. It is clear that the growth in the spinning branch of the Japanese cotton industry had taken place mainly through the increase in the size rather than in the number of its mills.

In spite of the increasing range of counts produced by the Japanese industry, there is not, as yet, a very clear distinction between the fine, medium and coarse spinners. On the whole, the small companies appear to concentrate on the coarser counts, (though there are some that spin medium and fine counts), while the largest concerns have a wide range. Some degree of specialisation, however, is exhibited by firms in this group. For instance, Toyobo, Dai Nippon and Kurashiki produce mainly low counts, averaging about twenty-fours, and use a high proportion of Indian cotton in their mixtures; Kanebo is chiefly concerned with medium counts, and the bulk of the cotton used is American; Fuji Gasu and Nisshin are still higher up the scale and use a large proportion of Egyptian cotton; but it is difficult to say whether this kind of specialisation is increasing or not.

In the manufacturing (weaving) activities of the spinning–weaving firms we find a high degree of concentration. In 1929 the seven giant firms had 50·3 per cent of all the looms owned by spinning–weaving companies, while twenty-two companies owned four-fifths of the total. In 1935 the six largest concerns had 53·4 per cent of the total, and four-fifths of the looms were in the hands of eighteen companies. There has thus been some concentration in this branch of activity. But the most interesting feature revealed by an examination of the figures is the wide differences in the ratio of looms to spindles in these concerns, differences, moreover, which are by no means tending to disappear. In the three largest firms the ratio does not differ greatly; but the rest exhibit striking contrasts. Nisshin has a ratio of 1:80; Fuji Gasu 1:166; and Kurashiki 1:278; and equally remarkable disparities can be found in other firms. Now if vertical integration makes possible more economical production than horizontal specialisation, one would expect to find a balance existing between looms and spindles in each of the firms, or at any rate a tendency towards an optimum relationship. Nothing of the kind can be discovered. The explanation seems to be that each of the great firms represents to a large degree merely a financial fusion of mills that are, from a technical, managerial and marketing standpoint, separate units catering for different markets.

A glance at the history of the Japanese cotton industry shows how this situation has come about. In the early post-Restoration period (*i.e.*, after 1868) Japan imported yarn to supply the multitude of domestic weavers situated mainly in country districts. The first spinning mills were set up to replace this imported yarn. Later, large mills were established at Osaka and other coastal towns to produce yarn for export. When this trade diminished large spinners with no domestic market close at hand added weaving sheds to their mills and began to produce fabrics for export. For example, the Nagasaki Cotton Spinning Company began its career as a producer of yarn for export to Hong Kong; but the decline of this trade forced it into the production of piece goods for export, and its name was changed to the Nagasaki Cotton Spinning and Weaving Company. Yet, while the export spinners were forced into 'forward integration', opportunities for specialist spinning mills, situated in centres where many weavers were to be found, continued to increase. Japan is a country in which financial power is highly concentrated. It was natural, therefore, that the big spinning–weaving firms with great resources should play their part in establishing new spinning mills in weaving centres, and that in times of financial stress the smaller mills should pass under their control. The kind of grouping that is now found has depended on the date when the companies were established, the extent of their financial resources, and the degree to which it has seemed advisable at different times to extend the sphere of control.

Outside the spinning–weaving concerns, upon which attention is usually concentrated, a very large number of specialist weaving concerns exists. At the end of 1934 there were 377,000 looms in Japan, and these were distributed as follows: (The figures for 1929 are given for comparison).[3]

TABLE 2

	1934	1929
Specialist weavers:		
Hand looms	56,000	86,000
Narrow power looms	80,000	106,000
Wide power looms	150,000	93,000
Spinning–weaving concerns:		
Wide power looms	91,000	78,000
	Total 377,000	363,000

The totals have, in fact, little meaning, for it is clear that the term 'loom' is applied in this table to very different kinds of equipment that vary from one another in productive capacity. This point receives further emphasis when it is realised that, while the looms owned by the spinning–weaving concerns are mainly automatic looms, the rest of the wide power looms are of the ordinary type. The table does bring out, however, the substantial decrease that has occurred since 1929 in the number of handlooms and narrow power looms, as contrasted with the increase in the number of wide power looms. It also suggests that the branch of the weaving industry that is in the hands of specialists has itself several subdivisions with different characteristics. Nearly four-fifths of the hand looms are to be found in sheds with from one to nine looms, and these are engaged on producing narrow cloth for Japanese use. Many of them are still found in the homes of farmers where weaving is a subsidiary occupation of the female members of the families. But this part of the industry, which is bound up with their household system of manufacture, is dwindling. The narrow power looms some ten years ago formed the bulk of the equipment of the small weaving sheds with from ten to forty-nine looms, and at that time well over half the looms of the larger specialist weavers (those with fifty looms and over) were of that type. Since then their numbers have rapidly diminished, especially after 1929, and at the present time even in the small factory group (ten to forty-nine looms) the wide looms predominate; in the larger specialist mills they form about two-thirds of the equipment. A marked change has taken place, not merely in the equipment used by the specialist weavers, but also in the importance of different types of weaving sheds. Those with under ten looms have declined progressively; the number of looms in the ten to forty-nine group has scarcely been maintained; but since 1929 a very substantial increase has taken place in the relative importance of the larger weaving mills in this branch of the trade.[4]

This analysis of the equipment helps us to understand how it is that units of very different sizes can exist in Japanese industry. In fact, the various weaving sheds are catering for different kinds of markets. This is obvious enough so far as the small and very small sheds equipped with narrow power or hand looms are concerned; they are turning out fabrics for the manufacture of Japanese-style clothing. But an equally sharp distinction can be drawn between the types of cloth upon which the sheds of the combined spinning–weaving concerns and those of the specialist weavers using wide looms are respectively engaged. The former concentrate to a large extent upon standardised fabrics for which their organisation and equipment are well suited. Thus, of their total output in 1933, 58 per cent (in quantity) consisted of shirtings, and over 14 per cent of sheetings; that is to say, nearly three-quarters of their total output was of these two classes.[5] In the specialist weaving mills, however, no such concentration on particular fabrics can be observed. Their most important product (drills and jeans) accounts for only one-fifth of their output of wide cloth,[6] which is made up largely of fancy goods and of fabrics less suited than those upon which the spinning–

weaving mills are engaged to mass-production methods. It is true that some of the great firms, like Kanebo, are pioneers in the introduction of new styles of fabrics and fancy goods; but the relative importance of this class of goods is evidently quite small in the spinning–weaving mills.

Let us consider the changes that have occurred since 1929 in the share of the piece-goods output enjoyed by combined and specialist weavers respectively. We have already seen that the production of narrow cloth has been dwindling. It now amounts only to about three-quarters (in quantity) of the output of the predepression period; and in value wide cloth accounts for 85 per cent of the total output of cotton textiles.[7] How is this production distributed between specialist and combined firms respectively? The British Cotton Mission reported that in 1929 the members of the Japan Cotton Spinners' Association produced between 55 and 60 per cent of the wide cloth output (in quantity). In spite of the large absolute increase in the output of these firms, their production of the total diminished to under 50 per cent in 1932 and to 44 per cent in 1935.[8] In value the proportion would be lower, since the specialist mills are producing on average higher quality fabrics. Well over two-thirds of the piece-goods output of the spinning–weaving mills is exported, compared with two-fifths of that of the specialist mills. The share of the total exports taken by the latter group, after falling during the depression, has now risen again, and in 1933 (the last year for which I have figures) they were responsible for 45 per cent of the total exports (in square yards) and for over 50 per cent of their total value.[9] As Japan is forced by competition and trade restrictions in her large markets to diversify her exports, it seems probable that the share of the specialist weavers will increase, since the integrated organisation of the great spinning–weaving concerns is directed to the production of standardised fabrics and confers no advantage in other lines. The bulk of the exports of the specialist weavers are provided by the larger sheds.

Thus Japanese cotton weaving is in the hands of several distinct groups of firms, each faced with the task of serving particular markets. A closer analysis than I have been able to make would doubtless reveal further important subdivisions. The small weavers with hand looms or narrow power looms are dealing with a market that has little in common with the markets served by the great weaving sheds of the combined firms, or even those of the larger specialist weavers. The former are producing fabrics of narrow width and of varying qualities solely for home use, and the diversified character of their market preserves them from the competition of mass producers. Although this branch of the industry may be declining, yet so long as the Japanese retain their traditional habits of dress it is likely to retain a place of some importance in the industry. The larger specialist weavers are concerned with a wide variety of fabrics, and so are supplying different demands from those catered for by the spinning–weaving mills which concentrate on a few standardised lines, chiefly for export. In the future the relative importance of these two types will largely depend on the kind of piece-goods for which the growth of demand is most rapid. These considerations ought to be borne in mind when the structure of the Japanese industry is being compared with that of Lancashire.

It is often said that the integration of spinning and weaving gives the Japanese a considerable advantage over competitors with a horizontal form of organisation. On the other hand, apologists for Lancashire sometimes point to the fact that the cotton industry in this country was vertically organised during the greater part of the nineteenth century, and that horizontal specialisation became the typical form only during the thirty years before the First World War. In other words, they assert that the present structure of the Japanese industry is due to its immaturity. When confronted by this argument the Japanese reply that the combined spinning–weaving concern has a more important place in their industry at present than it had twenty years ago.

I do not think that the problem can be usefully discussed in these terms. An appreciation of the relative advantages of rival types of organisation requires a study of the purposes which each is required to serve, of the conditions attending the supply of the factors of production, and of markets. From what has been said above it would appear that in Japan the integration of spinning and weaving has been found to possess advantages only in the production of particular kinds of piece-goods, standardised fabrics for which a mass demand exists. In these lines the advantages of integration are considerable. The chief of these appears to lie in the economies to be derived from specialisation. The spinning section of a combined mill usually concentrates upon a narrow range of counts and sends the bulk of its production to the adjoining weaving shed, which is specialising on one or two fabrics. To give an example from one of the medium-sized mills I visited: the spinning section, in which there were about 50,000 high draft spindles, was concerned with only three counts of yarn, and four-fifths of the output went to the weaving sheds in another part of the same building. Here there were 840 automatic looms which were concentrating on two kinds of fabric. The same company has nine other combined mills, each of which was specialising in much the same way, and its 6000 automatic looms were concerned with only twenty kinds of cloth; this was a firm engaged in the upper end of the trade. In one of the Toyobo mills, producing coarse fabrics, a shed of 1800 looms was concerned with only three qualities of cloth. Apart from the obvious economies attending this specialisation of plant, the mill owners claim that the close proximity of spinning and weaving enables any faults observed in the yarn in the course of manufacturing to be reported at once to the spinning mill, while 'better methods of cotton mixing and spinning are sometimes discovered which would perhaps be overlooked if cotton yarns were being manufactured as the final object of production.'[10] These advantages are, no doubt, very important in Japan, where the industry is not as highly localised as in Lancashire. Further, the juxtaposition of spinning and weaving obviates processes like rewinding and packing which are necessary if the yarn has to be disposed of to independent weavers. In addition to the advantages attached to this type of technical unit, the large firms with numerous mills under their control appear to be able to reap economies through centralised buying of cotton—a point to which I shall return, and quite small specialist spinning mills under their control may, of course, share in these economies.

As we have seen, however, the advantages to be reaped by the concentration of numerous mills under a common general ownership are evidently not sufficiently great to prevent a considerable development of independent spinning mills. And, in the same way, the advantages of combining spinning and weaving in the same mill are decisive only for a narrow range of goods and are outweighed by other factors over the greater part of the industry. Indeed, it may not be rash to suggest that the development of the combined spinning–weaving mill may be reaching its limit. The growth of restrictions on Japanese cotton imports into the main markets is reducing the profitability of the trade in grey standardised goods, and the industry has been forced to turn is attention to finished goods and to a wider variety of weaves to satisfy a growing diversity of markets. The Japanese government's own policy seems likely to strengthen this tendency. With the object of forestalling import restrictions in foreign markets the government is trying to curtail the competition among Japanese producers and so to raise prices. It has become so sensitive to the foreign view that by supplying cheap fabrics Japan has done a disservice to the world, that it is encouraging the production of higher quality and higher-priced goods. For social and political reasons, moreover, in order to allay discontent among the smaller and medium-sized industrialists and merchants who are very critical of the activities of the great firms, the government, through its laws concerning export and manufacturers' associations, is trying to support the small mills. All these restrictive devices must reduce the profitability of mass-production plants. The managing director of one of the large firms told me that a year or two ago he would not have accepted an order for less than three hundred pieces, but that at present he would take orders for any quantity. He believed that if this tendency were to persist Japan's cotton industry would probably assume a structure similar to that of Lancashire. A further indication of this trend is given by the fact that the big concerns have been investing to an increasing extent in other branches of textiles—wool and rayon.

I mention briefly the changes that have shown themselves recently in the relations of the main producing branches of the industry and the merchant firms. It is often said that the Japanese cotton industry owes some of its efficiency to the close association of the producing and the merchanting sections of the trade, for this enables a common policy to be worked out. Has this view any basis of truth? In the first place, it must be remembered that the specialist weavers, who are responsible for three-fifths of the wide cotton cloth (including nearly half the exports) and for all the narrow cloth, have no close connections of the kind here described. This branch of the industry has much the same relation to the merchants as its counterpart in England. The weavers buy their yarn through yarn agents and sell their piece-goods destined for foreign markets sometimes to local merchants who resell to exporters and sometimes direct to large or small exporters. These merchants send out the grey cloth for bleaching, dyeing and finishing. The great spinning–weaving firms are, of course, in closer touch with the big merchants who carry on both an import and an export trade. The latter sell the raw cotton to the spinners and contract to take the piece-goods. Since their interests are closely linked, it often pays them to assist one another in times of difficulty. If there is a glut of piece-goods and yarn, the exporters may help the producers to clear their stocks at little profit to themselves, because they know that their own sales of cotton and their own export business will be handicapped until the market has been relieved. And the merchants may, at such times, bring pressure to bear on the spinners to curtail production. But there is no common policy or programme worked out by merchants and spinners in conjunction. Very frequently their interests conflict seriously, especially recently in the administration of the export quotas.

Part of the misconception about the close association of merchants and spinners in Japan probably arises from the knowledge that Mitsui holds large interests both in Kanebo and in Toyo Menkwa, the largest merchant house. But, in fact, these are little more than financial interests, for Mitsui has long followed the policy of compelling each of its concerns to stand on its own feet. Thus, while Kanebo might give preference to Toyo Menkwa if no better terms were forthcoming from some other source, it would not do so if this involved it in higher costs; nor would Toyo Menkwa give Kanebo any preference in order to handle its business. The closer links which have, in fact, been forged recently between the merchanting and producing sections have owed nothing to a desire for a common policy. They are, however, worthy of notice. During the last five years the 'big three' among the cotton merchants have diminished in importance. This decline has occurred through the establishment of numerous small firms of importers and exporters, many of them controlled by foreigners, especially Indians. Since the fall of the yen these have found it profitable to operate an export business from Japan instead of an import business in India. On the other hand, the big Japanese houses have found that the cost of maintaining staffs abroad has much increased. The contraction of their business and the narrow margins of profits have led them to enter the field of production. Toyo Menkwa, for instance, now controls a number of spinning mills with a total spindleage of 700,000. A few of these mills owned by the merchants are in Shanghai, and were installed to produce yarn previously supplied by Japan for the China market. Some, including one Indian mill, were taken over as bad debts in 1930–31, and others were newly established or acquired as a means of providing more profitable investment than that now afforded by merchanting. These mills, though small, are said to be very efficient. Integration has also been brought about for other reasons. A short time ago Toyobo acquired a large interest in Gosho, one of the three great merchant houses. But this step was taken, not with the object of reaping advantages from carrying on producing and merchanting under single control. It occurred because Gosho was threatened with insolvency, and because Toyobo, the largest purchaser of raw cotton, was anxious to see that the area of competition in the cotton market was not significantly reduced, as would have happened if one of the three great importers had disappeared.

Japanese spinners are said to be able to buy cotton of the same grades at lower prices than their British rivals. For instance, a firm dealing with both Lancashire and Japan estimated the difference at 5 per cent in 1936. Various reasons are put forward to explain this discrepancy. Some emphasise the purchase by Japan of large quantities of particular growths ahead of requirements, while Lancashire is said to select more carefully and to buy in small lots. Others point to the fact that the big merchants have used their financial resources to buy cotton in years of glut, and so have been able to meet the spinners' demands at low prices afterwards. The latter explanation seems to leave out of account the cost of carrying the cotton over the period, which must be borne by someone, and also the losses attending unsuccessful speculation of this kind. Here one may find a clue to the problem. The great producing firms have established a strong buying position *vis-à-vis* the merchants, and they have apparently managed to reap most of the advantages of successful speculation, while throwing on to the shoulders of the merchants the losses incurred in less fortunate times. It is said that during the last twenty-five years the merchant houses have lost from 100 to 150 million yen of capital through bankruptcy or through the writing down of shares.[11] In addition, the huge losses which attended the depreciation of cotton in the slump of 1930–31 were borne by the Yokohama Specie Bank. The unprofitableness of this trade, which is now affecting even the largest merchants, is the reason why they are withdrawing their resources from it and are investing in industrial plants. Thus, to some extent, the low prices at which spinners have been able to buy cotton have been to the detriment of the other sectors of the Japanese economy, and are not entirely the result of efficiency in the conduct of the trade.

I now pass to a discussion, inevitably brief, of the changes that have occurred in the efficiency of spinning and weaving. The published figures indicate that a remarkable increase in output per operative has taken place since 1929 in both of the main producing branches of the industry.

TABLE 3

	Output per operative engaged in spinning mills of members of Japan Cotton Spinners' Association	*Output per operative engaged in weaving mills of members of Japan Cotton Spinners' Association*
1929	7000 lbs	36,100 yards
1931	8400 lbs	48,800 yards
1935	9300 lbs	49,500 yards

It should be observed that these averages are obtained by dividing the total annual output of yarn or cloth by the average number of operatives per day engaged in spinning mills and weaving mills respectively. While the figures of yarn output cover practically the whole of the spinning industry, the figures of piece-goods output apply only to that produced in the mills owned by members of the Japan Cotton Spinners' Association, that is to say, to about two-fifths of the wide cloth output of Japan.

How can this increase be explained? Let us first turn to spinning. Between 1913 and 1928 there was apparently only a slight improvement in efficiency as measured by output per head, but since then the changes have been even more remarkable than the figures suggest, because of the greater concern of the industry with medium and fine counts. At first sight it would seem that no part of the increase can be attributed to a speeding up of the machinery; for figures show the average output per ring spindle to be slightly less in 1935 than in 1929. This conclusion must be rejected, however, because we must take account of the increasing fineness of the yarn as well as of the reduction, brought about by legislation, of the time the spindles were worked. Yet mill owners declare that only a small proportion of the increase can be attributed to speeding up, and we must look elsewhere for the significant changes responsible for the economies in labour.

The date when this improvement began is significant. In 1929 a Factory Law became effective which abolished night work in the industry, and involved also a reduction in the hours of work per shift. The leading companies had, of course, anticipated this change, and many of them carried out a reorganisation of their mills in preparation for it. About the same time there began an intense depression in Japanese industry. Apart from the effects of the world slump, the cotton trade was also badly hit at this time by the deflationary policy adopted by Japan after her return to gold in January 1930. The response of the industry was exactly in accordance with the suppositions of the orthodox trade-cycle theorists. There was a widespread improvement in productive methods and in management; some of the less efficient mills disappeared or passed under the control of other companies and were reorganised; and there was a weeding out of inefficient workers. Nearly all operations were affected; but by far the most important change consisted of the widespread adoption of high draft spinning, which enabled the whole process to be much shortened; for instance, the roving operation has been generally eliminated. It is this change to high draft which is responsible for most of the economies in labour.[12] No figures showing the number of high draft spindles are available; but, from information supplied to me from authoritative sources, it would seem that the bulk of the working spindles, which amount to over eight million out of a total of ten-and-a-half million, are now newly installed high draft spindles or remodelled high draft spindles. The introduction of this equipment on a significant scale began in 1929, and it has continued down to the present time. In the six large companies it is estimated that at present four-fifths of their total spindleage is high draft. Apart from these savings, costs have been reduced by the substitution of female for male labour. In 1929 male workers accounted for 22 per cent of the labour force; by 1935 the percentage had fallen to 12. To some extent the fall in the number of men employed may have been brought about by an improvement in the equipment and layout of the mixing and blowing sections of the mills. But there has been much actual replacement of men by girls. Thus, in 1929, men were usually employed on the drawing frames, but now in most mills the work is done by girls. The improvement in internal transport, particularly by the widespread adoption of an overhead carrier system, has also enabled this substitution to take place. Again, power charges have been diminished during the last two or three years by the introduction of individual drives, and the efficiency of the workers is said to have responded noticeably to the great improvements that have occurred in lighting and in temperature and humidity control. Table 4 below throws some light on labour costs in spinning.[13]

In weaving the figures show that while output per loom was about the same in 1935 as in 1929, there was an increase in the number of looms per worker from 1·6 to 2·2. (The term worker here, of course, includes all operatives engaged in the weaving sheds, whatever their occupation). Output per worker has expanded from 36,100 yards to 49,500 yards. It appears that the improvement in weaving occurred rather earlier than in spinning. It began in 1925, and was very rapid between 1927 and 1931, and since that year has continued at a lower rate. The main cause of the improvement has undoubtedly been the general adoption of automatic looms. Published figures seem to under-estimate the extent to which these have been brought into use in Japan. According to reliable information the bulk of the looms installed in the spinning–weaving mills are now automatic, and in the large mills this type is almost universally employed; ordinary looms are used only for specialities. The Mitsubishi Economic Research Bureau goes so far as to say that the proportion of automatic looms to the total looms in the combined mills is higher than the proportion of high draft rings to the total spindleage.

In the specialist weaving mills the equipment in use is very different. In these, which are responsible for the greater part of the output of piece-goods, automatic looms are seldom encountered, and in the chief branches not used at all. Reliable data are difficult to obtain for this section of the industry, but it is evident that there has been a considerable improvement during the last decade in output per worker, except in the very small mills that employ only hand looms. The rise in efficiency is most noticeable in the mills with fifty looms and over. The increase in output per worker is to be associated with the change in the equipment of these mills. Hand looms have almost disappeared from the medium and large mills; narrow looms have greatly diminished in number; and much new equipment in the form of wide looms has been installed. During the last three or four years economies have been effected in some branches of weaving as a result of the development of *Kogyo Kumiai* [14] among them. These associations provide joint equipment and services for their members, and in some places they have helped to reduce substantially the costs of subsidiary processes and of transport.

I have not referred specifically to the lowering of unit costs that has been effected throughout the industry as a result of the rise in the scale of operations since 1929; but considerable economies in the power and management charges and in other overhead costs have been brought about as a result of the increase in the size of the plants. Further, I have been unable in this short paper to discuss the fall in money wages which also made a contribution to the decline in total costs. This fall was very steep during the depression and it persisted well into the period of recovery.

STATISTICAL TABLES

TABLE 4

Year	Average count	Production per spindle per day.*	Daily wages per 10,000 spindles	No. of male workers per 10,000 spindles	Average daily wage per male mill hand	No. of female workers per 10,000 spindles	Average daily wage per female mill hand
		Momme	Yen		Yen		Yen
1929 (December)	23s	88·00	323·9	56·9	1·59	206	1·14
1934 (December)	24·5s	81·2	153·05	23·4	1·36	162	·75
1935 (November)	25·3s	77·2	147·57	22·5	1·35	160·2	·73

* The first figure in this column is for the second half of 1928; the others are for the second half-years of 1934 and 1935.

TABLE 5
Equipment and yarn production of the large companies

Firms	1929 (Second half-year)				1935 (Second half-year)			
	Ring spindles (in thousands)	Mule spindles (in thousands)	Doubling spindles (in thousands)	Yarn output (in thousand bales)	Ring spindles (in thousands)	Mule spindles (in thousands)	Doubling spindles (in thousands)	Yarn output (in thousand bales)
Dai Nippon	705	4	193	149·5	919	4	200	180·9
Toyobo	780	—	109	198·4	} 1,476	—	222	292·7
Godo	436	—	64	107·1		—	111	143·4
Kanebo	633	4	93	119·2	928	4		
	2,554	4	459	574·2	3,323	4	533	617·0
Kurashiki	279	—	22	61·2	500	—	43	88·8
Fuji Gasu	478	26	91	75·6	649	26	95	69·0
Nisshin	418	5	83	62·4	498	5	79	52·9
Total	3,759	35	655	773·4	4,970	35	750	827·7
*Proportion of total capacity and output in hands of above firms	56%	—	81%	53%	48%	—	83%	48%

* Only firms that are members of the Japan Cotton Spinners' Association are taken into account. The 'Outsiders' possessed in 1929 2·4 per cent of all ring spindles in Japan and Korea; in 1935 the proportion was 3 per cent.

TABLE 6

Distribution of ring spindles according to size of firms

Size of firms	Percentage of total spindles		
	1929	1932	1935
Under 100,000 spindles	30.0 (55 firms)	23.6 (51 firms)	14.4 (44 firms)
100,000–200,000 spindles	7.7 (4 firms)	16.8 (11 firms)	21.5 (17 firms)
Over 200,000 spindles	62.3 (9 firms)	59.6	64.1 (11 firms)
('Big Six', together with Godo in 1929)	(55.5)	(50.6)	(47.2)

* All firms in Japan itself are included

TABLE 7

Distribution of ring spindles according to size of mills

Size of mills	1929 (Second half-year)			1935 (Second half-year)		
	Number of mills	Ring spindles (in thousands)	Percentage of total	Number of mills	Ring spindles (in thousands)	Percentage of total
Under 50,000 spindles	144	3,524	52	115	3,390	33
50,000–75,000 spindles	24	1,518	22	46	2,775	26
75,000–100,000 spindles	13	1,198	18	21	1,812	17
Over 100,000 spindles	4	532	8	21	2,552	24
Total	185	6,772	100	203	10,529	100

* All mills in Japan itself are included

TABLE 8

Size of plants and distribution of equipment in the specialist weaving industry in 1933

| Size of weaving sheds | Number of looms in each size group | | | |
	Total	*Hand looms*	*Narrow Power looms*	*Wide Power looms*
1–9 Looms	63,000	54,000	4000	5000
10–49 Looms	85,000	4000	35,000	46,000
50 Looms and over	129,000	1000	44,000	83,000
Total	277,000	59,000	83,000	134,000

5 Western Enterprise in the Far East [1]

The transference of initiative from individuals to governments has affected international economic relations no less than the internal economic structures. This applies with especially great force to the export of technical knowledge, capital, and entrepreneurship from the advanced countries of the West to the economically and technically backward countries of Asia and Africa. The role of the private Western firm in those regions is still important, but in the development of 'underdeveloped' countries—or at any rate in the plans for the development of such countries—the private firm is being overshadowed by governments and international agencies. Moreover, the propaganda against Western private capitalism (which has destroyed much of its self-confidence) has been most effective in those overseas countries where it enjoyed some of its greatest triumphs. In certain regions socialistic and nationalistic sentiments now combine to discredit it. Private enterprise has shown its traditional skill in accommodating itself to these new conditions, but in many of the Asian countries it now receives only a grudging welcome.

It may be contended that the future of economic development lies mainly with governments and international agencies and that henceforth private enterprise must content itself with a subordinate role in the economic life of Asian countries. Even so, there may be advantage in looking back to the last century, or century and a half, when private enterprise played almost everywhere the leading part in promoting economic change. It may even turn out that the experience of private enterprise in the Far East has lessons for those who seek to replace it. Governments and international bodies, although they have achievements to their credit in this respect since the war, have not had such uninterruptedly successful careers as economic developers as to suggest that they can afford to neglect the experience of their predecessors.

Entrepreneurship, or innovating activity, expresses itself in the creation of new wants as well as in the organisation of new supplies of goods to satisfy existing wants. If one is considering the disruptive, revolutionary effect of the impact of the West on the formerly conservative Asian societies, the part of private enterprise in the creation of new wants must be regarded as by no means the least important of its achievements. For even those Asians who are now critics of the former political and economic activities of Westerners in the East, are keenly alive to, and anxious to share in, the benefits of Western technology and Western methods of economic organisation. This awareness and this change in outlook have come about through contacts with the West for which private enterprise was largely responsible.

It would be misleading to suggest that Western enterprise in all countries was of the same pattern, or that its dynamic function had an identical form throughout Asia. On the contrary, the form varied with the political organisation of the countries in which the enterprise was found. In Indonesia and Malaya Western enterprise operated within a legal and political framework created by the colonial powers. There the Western businessmen looked to their own governments to provide security and the basic conditions for a well-ordered economic life; among those conditions a sound monetary system was regarded as of primary importance. In Java at times the Dutch authorities went much further than this; for they assumed in some sectors of the economy a high degree of economic initiative themselves. The point for emphasis, however, is that in both Indonesia and Malaya, and in some other Asian countries also, Western enterprise could conduct its activities within an imposed institutional and legal framework which was, in essentials, not dissimilar from that within which economic development had taken place in Europe.

In China and Japan, with which this paper is mainly concerned, the position was very different. In both these countries commercial intercourse with the West was started under Western compulsion, and in both of them Western enterprise was for a long period conducted under conditions created by the 'unequal treaties'. In Japan those conditions lasted until nearly the end of the nineteenth century; in China until the Second World

War. In most respects, however, there were more contrasts than similarities in the response of these two countries to the Western impact. While this applies to their response to Western civilisation as a whole, it is especially true of their attitude to Western technology and of the role assigned to Western enterprise in each of them. These contrasts are interesting to study.

When Western merchants first traded with China, they had to deal with an intensely conservative society ruled by bureaucrats to whom the very idea of progress was uncongenial. Western enterprise, in the most dynamic phase of its career, was thus confronted with a formidable obstacle, and this obstacle continued seriously to impede the business operations of the West, at least until the revolution of 1911. The whole history of Western relations with China was deeply affected by this attitude of the authorities to economic change.

At first the West was confined to trading through the Cohong at Canton. After 1842 foreigners were allowed to reside and to trade in a number of settlements and concessions on the China coast, and Hong Kong began to develop as a trading centre. After 1860 the foreigners obtained the right to travel and trade in the interior. From that time they were able to get into closer touch with their markets and their sources of supply, instead of confining themselves to dealings with Chinese merchants at the ports. A further stage was reached in 1895, when the Treaty of Shimonoseki was signed; for it then became legally possible for foreigners to set up large-scale manufacturing undertakings in the concessions. They also began to participate in mining enterprises in various parts of China, and they became actively engaged in the construction of railways. Yet throughout the whole of this period the Chinese government remained reluctant hosts to the Western entrepreneurs. It resisted at every step, not merely the enterprise of the Westerners, but Western civilisation itself, its technology, and its very idea of material progress.

I cannot in this paper concern myself with the deeper causes of this opposition, for I am here engaged solely in an analysis of an economic situation. Still less am I inclined to pass a moral judgement on whether the Chinese were right or wrong in resisting what the West regards (or regarded) as progress. All statements in this paper should be read in the light of this disclaimer.

At the beginning of the nineteenth century trade between China and the West took the form of the export of silk and tea and the import of silver. Then a three-cornered trade came into being—exports of manufactured goods and of services from Europe to India, exports of cotton and opium from India to China, and exports of silk and tea from China to Europe. In the last few decades of the nineteenth century, the exports became more diversified, while the imports included mineral oil, cotton fabrics, and other manufactured consumer-goods. In the present century, engineering products and various types of proprietary goods were added to the import list. All these new trades, both on the import side and on the export side, were begun on the initiative of the Western traders (joined towards the end of the century by the Japanese). Chinese merchants participated in the trades, but seldom in the capacity of innovators. Indeed, until very recent times they had only a passive part in the economic development of the country.

The Western merchants came to China in search of the profits of trade. But they could not confine themselves to buying and selling goods. They had to engage in a wide variety of commercial and financial activities, since none of the economic institutions or ancillary services that modern commerce requires existed in China. The Westerners had, therefore, to establish public utilities in the places in which they lived; they had to found municipal administrations; they had to set up port installations. They had to provide ships, not merely for the ocean-going trade, but for the efficient distribution of goods in China by river and coastal services. In Shanghai and Hong Kong they established yards where ships could be repaired and even built. When the age of steam arrived, the Westerners had to find sources of coal supply for bunkering the ships. The Chinese monetary system and banking practices were ill-adapted to the needs of modern commerce, and so the Western merchants had to introduce their own financial and banking methods. Some of the banks founded by them discharged *inter alia* functions which were similar to those carried out in other countries by central banks. They even became responsible for furnishing a considerable part of the currency. Finally, the merchants had to provide themselves with insurance facilities. All these economic institutions, industries, and services had to be introduced into China at the same time as efforts were being made to build up a flourishing international trade.

The Western merchants were drawn also into manufacturing industry, not so much because of prospective profits to be gained from industrial investments as such in China, but rather because supplies of merchandise of the right quality were not forthcoming unless the merchants made provision for the inspection of the materials and the processing of the goods for export. As in all preindustrial societies, uniformity of product was very hard to ensure, and quality tended to deteriorate when the older industries expanded under the influence of increased demands. Yet unless adulteration could be prevented and a reasonably uniform quality of supply assured, trade was liable to fall away. The foreign merchants were, therefore, forced to concern themselves with the actual conditions of production. Their participation became necessary not merely in large trades, such as silk reeling (where they founded power-driven filatures), but also in the miscellaneous group, such as straw hats, hairnets, braid, bristles, egg products, vegetable oil, brick tea, and many other goods which the Chinese supplied for export. In this way new techniques were introduced into China, and modern methods of organisation became familiar to the Chinese business community. From this type of enterprise, the Europeans passed towards the end of the nineteenth century—when they were joined by the Japanese—to the establishment of large-scale manufacturing industries. The most important of these were textiles, especially cotton textiles, where Western technique and capital could be profitably used in association with cheap Chinese labour. Then, as further development depended upon communications, the foreigners interested themselves in the building and operation of railways.

None of this development could have taken place unless the Western powers had been able to compel a reluctant Chinese government to give Western traders privileges so that they could conduct their affairs outside the jurisdiction of the native authorities. In the absence of these privileges the traders would have been exposed to arbitrary financial exactions on the part of the local and central governments, and their enterprises would probably have succumbed to the determined opposition of the conservative court and bureaucracy. The truth of this contention is underlined by the failure that overtook most of the modern enterprises started by the few progressive Chinese statesmen, or by Chinese businessmen, in the face of opposition from the ruling circles. Even when Chinese businessmen began to participate in modern industrial enterprise—as they did after the 1890s to an increasing extent—they usually set up their factories in the concessions. In many cases they associated themselves with Western partners. Only by so doing could they be assured of reasonable security for persons and property.

Even when China became ready to abandon her old ways, the country was distracted by two decades of civil war, and it was not until the late 1920s that the government was able to exercise any sustained economic initiative. Until then the foreigners provided the only effective innovating force in Chinese society. Through them, moreover, and through them alone, the Chinese began to learn modern techniques and to become familiar with Western equipment. The Chinese government for their part made no systematic attempt, as the Japanese did, to provide training in Western technology for their people.

Thus Western imperialism was not an unmixed evil from the standpoint of China's economic development. If it had not been for the concessions, and for the extraterritorial privileges which were accorded to the foreigners, material progress would scarcely have begun in China during the nineteenth century or the early years of the present century. In the absence of those privileges, the conditions necessary for foreign enterprise would have been lacking, and there was nothing to take its place. Chinese critics are accustomed to say that Western enterprise developed merely the coastal fringe to the neglect of the great hinterland. There is some truth in this charge; but it must be remembered that it was only on the coastal fringe, and in the areas over which foreign control was imposed, that throughout the greater part of the last century the conditions for economic growth were present. It is, therefore, reasonable to conclude that practically all the material progress in China between 1842 and 1930 was the result of Western and Japanese initiative, and was achieved under the shelter of foreign privilege.

Yet, when all this has been said, it remains true that the material progress of China was slow, to the disappointment of the Western pioneers. It seems that the 'error of optimism' was extremely common among Western firms in China, and that it long persisted to their own great cost. An early example is illuminating. Soon after the Treaty of Nanking an English merchant house sent out a large consignment of pianos to China in the belief that, now that the country was opened up, at least one million Chinese women would want to learn to play the piano! The optimistic mood persisted in spite of many bitter experiences. Nor was it rooted in folly. Here was a vast country with an enormous population, and a most industrious population at that. Western merchants might well suppose that the opportunities for trade were unbounded. Yet, although development did occur, the hopes were never fully realised. Even in 1929 (a relatively good year for comparison since it was before China had lost Manchuria), China's share of world trade was less than 2 per cent. This was only two-thirds of Japan's share, and only about one-sixth of the United Kingdom's share. The number of factory workers in China itself in 1937 was probably not more than one-and-a-quarter million.[2] Apart from the textile industry, large-scale industries were of minor importance in China itself, although of course in the 1930s there was a rapid industrial expansion in Manchuria under Japanese direction. Many trades that started with high promise and good prospects languished. Even in the silk trade, China was outclassed in the early years of the present century by Japan.

The causes of China's relative failure—of the slowness of her economic development—are worth considering. The explanation is not to be found solely in the political insecurity of the country, although that of course made a powerful contribution to stagnation. The following suggestion is offered. When underdeveloped countries and their traditional peasant industries are called upon to adapt themselves to the modern world economy, and to become suppliers for international trade, large-scale centralised organisation must usually be introduced into those industries from a source exterior to the peasant economy itself and its traditional merchanting bodies. In the silk and tea trades of Japan, for example, the initiative in this respect was taken by the Japanese government and the great Japanese merchant houses as well as by foreigners. In many of the trades of South East Asia it was taken by the foreign plantation companies. In China, however, these agencies were not available. The government was indifferent. The legal and institutional environment was too unfavourable to produce Chinese businessmen who could provide the organisation that was necessary. And the foreigners could not undertake the whole task, because their rights did not extend to the point at which they could impose regulations over scattered suppliers or refashion traditional social and trading relationships. To quote a passage from a recently published work in which I have collaborated:[3]

> In the absence of a native government interested in economic change and competent to promote it, the necessary reorganization could only have come from a more extensive foreign political control than in fact existed. As it was, many trades languished in the face of competition from industries in other countries which had been able to adapt themselves to the needs of foreign markets, and China's economic development was thus seriously impeded. Foreign enterprise in China could build on what it found, and could modify traditional arrangements in some degree; but it could not penetrate far enough to bring about a thorough-going transformation of the traditional economic structure.

The contrast with Japan was very striking. When the West forced open her gates, power passed into the hands of men who realised that the salvation of their country lay in the modernisation of the economy. The oligarchy in control was determined to take the lead in bringing about this transformation, and to create the conditions for industrialisation and the rise of a modern commercial community. New educational, legal, administrative, banking, and monetary systems were quickly built up on the initiative of the government. New systems of communication were soon established. Western-style manufacturing plants were set up, and Western technicians and managers were engaged by the state to introduce the expertise needed. In other words, the 'public overhead capital', which the Westerners themselves had to introduce into China, was in Japan mainly provided by the state as part of a deliberately conceived plan of modernisation.

The contrasted experience of Japan and China may not be irrelevant to the contemporary problem of the development of underdeveloped countries. That experience suggests that an economic and technical advance must be organised on a wide front. To introduce an alien form of organisation in trade or industry into an economically primitive society is a delicate operation. The adaptation of many institutions and services is necessary if particular innovations are not to wither. In other words, it is useless to pour foreign capital into some sector of a primitive economy if that economy has not been adequately prepared to receive it.

In Japan this work of preparation—of institutional adaptation—was performed by the state. This does not mean, however, that Japan came to possess a state-made economy; for when Western technique had been naturalised and 'public overhead capital' set up, the state withdrew from most of its industrial enterprises. From the 1880s onwards control in most sectors of the economy was left in private hands. It is true that economic initiative was concentrated in the small group of business houses, the *Zaibatsu*. But a high degree of concentration of control is probably necessary in any primitive society which is trying to modernise itself rapidly—that is, in any society which is shifting quickly from one plane to another. On the whole, the Japanese state regulated, but did not direct the economy in detail.

It is wrong to assume that the Western merchants' function in Japanese development was merely to provide 'know-how', while the Japanese undertook the entrepreneurial function. It is true that Western entrepreneurs did not play as important a part in the development of Japan as they did in that of China; but they were nevertheless indispensable, at any rate in the early days of modernisation. At that time the Japanese had little experience of the conduct of foreign trade, and the creation of trading relationships with the outside world was largely a task for Western business houses. Western mercantile, banking, and shipping enterprises predominated in the first few decades of the modern era, and it is estimated that even in 1900 about three-fifths of the Japanese foreign trade went through foreign merchant firms. The development of many of the chief trades in the nineteenth century—the silk trade and the tea trade—owed much to foreign enterprise. Through the activities of foreign merchants, the Japanese economy was exposed to the transforming influences of international trade, and these influences were in some ways as compelling as those that derived from official interventionist policy. Even in the 1930s—especially in the period just after the fall of the yen—the Western merchant firms played a leading part in the expansion of the Japanese export trade in miscellaneous goods.

In manufacturing industry foreigners had a comparatively minor role in Japan. Even there their enterprises were important in some lines of production, for example, in the rubber industry, where they were pioneers, and in the manufacture of motor cars. In the present century, moreover, several foreign firms established joint enterprises with the Japanese, notably in the electrical engineering industry, and their presence helped Japan to keep her technique up to date.

As to capital supply, whereas in China most capital for large-scale development and for the modern sector of the economy came from abroad—or from the profits of enterprises located in the concessions—in Japan most of the capital was provided by domestic saving. But there were two key periods in Japanese economic history in which foreign borrowing was important, between 1900 and 1914 and between 1923 and 1930. In the first of them, 1900–14, Japan was engaged on a great programme of political as well as of economic expansion. She fought against Russia. She began to exploit her newly won resources on the continent—in Korea and in the South Manchuria Railway zone, and she established a number of basic industries, notably the iron and steel industry. It is very doubtful if it would have been possible for her to develop at the pace she did during that period, if foreign capital had not been forthcoming. From 1923 to 1930 there was another influx of foreign capital. This assisted the reconstruction of the country after the great earthquake, and it also made possible a rapid increase of hydroelectric capacity which provided a basis for the industrial expansion of the 1930s. Unlike the Chinese government, the Japanese government acquired a good reputation as an international borrower, and consequently was able to raise money abroad, after the early period, on very satisfactory terms. Much of the foreign investment in China was direct investment—that is, the capital remained under the control of the firms which provided the money. In Japan investment was mainly in government securities or in the debentures of public utilities. Direct investment by foreign firms was relatively small. These contrasts between the types of foreign investment in the two countries, reflecting as they do the equally sharp contrasts in the economic behaviour of their peoples and governments, may not be without relevance to the current problem of international investment in underdeveloped countries.

It is easy to understand why economic development went much further in Japan than China. In Japan the enterprising native leaders saw that the conditions for economic progress were established, whereas in China the advance had to be made by foreigners in the teeth of official indifference or opposition, and often in conditions of insecurity. The contrast may be pointed by reference to a particular trade in which the two countries were competitors, namely the raw silk trade. The silk industry needs a wide dispersion of productive units, largely because the production of cocoons is essentially a small-scale peasant process. But it also requires centralised control at a few points in order that uniform quality can be ensured, for uniform quality is necessary if the product is to be used on power looms and knitting frames. Now in Japan the necessary centralised control was realised through the licensing of the egg raisers and by the growth of large filature firms, whose plants were scattered over the silk-raising districts and so were able to remain in close touch with the cocoon-producers. In China there was no authority to impose this sort of control. The government was indifferent, and foreign firms lacked the power to do all that was needed. The filatures tended to be concentrated in the ports for security reasons, and close contact between the filatures and the silk raisers was thus difficult to maintain. Even conditioning arrangements were not introduced until very late, and then on foreign initiative.

Similar deficiencies could be found in other Chinese industries. Consequently, China remained economically backward and the standard of life poor, not so much because foreigners 'exploited' the Chinese producers, but rather because Chinese productivity was low. In Japan the standard of life rose far above that in the rest of Asia because the Japanese successfully naturalised Western technique and organisation and so raised productivity.

A survey of the economic history of these countries prompts a reflection on the importance of leadership in economic development. It is useless to pour capital into underdeveloped countries if able entrepreneurs are lacking there, or if the legal and institutional environment is uncongenial to the activities of enterprising people. In Japan leadership was provided partly by a government controlled by a purposeful oligarchy, and partly by a small group of dynamic business houses. In the early days of the modern era the Western merchants also had a not insignificant role. In China economic leadership was exercised almost exclusively by private foreign enterprise operating from enclaves of extraterritorial privilege. To the extent that this foreign enterprise found freedom to operate, to that extent China's economic development was promoted. But the enclaves were limited, and in the vast regions outside them the conditions under which enterprise, either native or foreign, could flourish were absent.

The implications of what I have said may well be uncongenial to the current temper of Asia, for enthusiasm for private enterprise and for the conditions that make it work, is scarcely extravagant in that continent at the present time, while the example of economic leadership successfully provided by an oligarchical government may be an unwelcome one to liberals and democrats. I shall make no further comment, except to suggest that, although the past offers no sure prescription for success in the future, its lessons are not irrelevant to modern policies.

When today politicians and journalists in the successor-states of the former colonial empires look back on the history of European overseas enterprise, they are more sensible of the benefits that accrued to the Western merchants themselves than of the contribution of Western entrepreneurship and investment to the economic growth and welfare of their countries. At the present time policy (or propaganda) centres upon social improvement, the enhancement of the incomes of the impoverished peoples, an aim hardly conspicuous among those who, in the past, were responsible for economic development in East or South East Asia. *Their* presiding motives were of a different kind. The Japanese leaders were animated chiefly by considerations of national power, the Westerners throughout the region by ordinary commercial motives. Such social improvements as occurred came as a byproduct of economic growth. Nowadays, to men intent upon narrowing the wide gap between incomes in the developed and underdeveloped countries, this system of priorities seems to show a confusion of means with ends and is unacceptable. Economic development, it is urged, should be undertaken with the avowed object of improving welfare, a proposition resting on an assumption that would command wide support. Yet, it would be unfortunate if, in the enthusiastic pursuit of the right ends, governments and their advisers were to lose sight of the essential means for their attainment. If, as seems probable even in these days, private investment and private enterprise are still necessary instruments of economic advance in underdeveloped countries, then an important function of government in such countries should be to ensure that the conditions for their successful operations are present, however discordant these conditions may be with the current temper. Otherwise the most ambitious plans for economic advance may suffer the fate of Chang Chih-tung's attempt to found a centre of heavy industry near Hankow at the end of the nineteenth century,[4] and the peoples of Asia may learn that American generosity cannot solve all their economic problems. It may well be that, in the end (to paraphrase a famous passage from Adam Smith), we get fuller rice bowls not through the benevolence of our suppliers, but through their regard to their own interest—by talking to them not of our own necessities but of their advantages.

6 The State and Economic Development[1]

INTRODUCTION

The importance of the state's role in Japan's economic development during the modern era is more difficult to assess than is
commonly supposed. This is chiefly because generalisations
about it are likely to differ according to the perspective in which
the economy is viewed. In the early years of Meiji, when the *laissez-faire* prescription for economic management was applauded
and generally followed in Western countries, the widespread
economic functions exercised by the Japanese government, and
especially its part in the introduction of new manufacturing industries, seemed abnormal to the foreign observer and coloured
his judgement about the nature of the economy. Even in the
1930s, when economic liberalism was in retreat all over the
world, Japan, intent upon building up a *junsenji-keizai* ('quasi-
wartime economy'), could properly be grouped with those
countries in which state control had been most widely extended. Since the Second World War, however, comparisons of
Japanese practices with those of other countries may lead, at
first sight, to quite different conclusions. The Occupation
Authority in the years immediately after the war sought to create a liberal market economy and to restrict the government's
direct control over economic processes. Despite the modifications that have occurred since 1952, this policy has persisted.
Its fruits have been gathered during a period in which the economic functions of the state were being much enlarged in countries formerly regarded as the homes of private enterprise. The
result is that in present-day Japan the public sector is small
when judged by the standards that prevail elsewhere, and the
market economy, which in Western countries has been en-
feebled, appears to have gained a new lease of life.

A measure of the state's relative economic importance in some of the leading industrial countries is provided by Table 9 below which shows public expenditure in 1967 as a percentage of GNP at market prices.

TABLE 9

*Government expenditure as percentage of GNP in 1967**

Country	Current expenditure**	Total expenditure
UK	32·9	39·0
USA	28·3	31·4***
France	35·5	40·9
West Germany	33·7	40·0
Italy	31·9	36·0
Japan	14·8	20·6***

    *   Source: OECD National Accounts 1967
  **   Includes subsidies, debt interest and current transfers
***   Excludes gross capital transfers

If we supplement this statistical comparison by figures which show the disparity in the proportion of manpower employed in the public sector in different countries (for example 8 per cent in Japan and 22 per cent in the UK, excluding employment in the armed forces in each case), then we might seem to be justified in concluding that what was once a state-ordered system has now become one of the few surviving examples of a private enterprise economy.

This interpretation, however, though plausible, ceases upon deeper enquiry to command unqualified assent. In the first place, the figures quoted above provide quite insufficient evidence to support any confident assertions about the relations between private industry and the state, for those relations are not all susceptible of measurement. Secondly, the relative size of the public sector and the ratios of public expenditure to total national expenditure in different countries are to be explained largely by disparities in expenditure on defence and on social welfare. It may, of course, be objected that the vast expenditure of Western governments on defence and social welfare has itself made a powerful impact on relations between government and industry and has been closely associated with the advance in the economic role of the state. But this objection does not rule out the possibility that in Japan state intervention in the economy since the Second World War has taken other forms than those familiar in the West and may have been prompted by other causes. Indeed, one may reach the provisional conclusion that, while the economic importance of the government in economic development and the nature of its relations with private industry have varied widely from time to time during the last century, a thread of continuity can be detected which, for an understanding of Japan's development, is probably more significant than the oscillations.

Before an attempt is made to support these propositions by further evidence and argument, it is important to establish that many analogies with Japan in respect to the role of the state in industrial development can be found. Japan was exceptional only in her timing, in the fact that during the period in which the lead in her economic development was being taken by government, elsewhere the state was usually assigned a subordinate role. Japan set a precedent which other countries followed, not as acts of deliberate imitation but rather because similar circumstances called for similar solutions. Since the era of state entrepreneurship in early Meiji times many other countries with ambitions to achieve a 'takeoff' have relied on the state to assume the initiative. As in Japan, the reason for this choice was often the absence of experienced private entrepreneurs and of inherited institutions congenial to technological and commercial development. One may quote as examples Imperial Russia in the 1890s, China in the *kuan-tu-shang-pan* period ('official supervision and merchant management') between 1878 and 1894, India since her independence, and several other countries during the last twenty years. Doctrine has no doubt exerted a considerable influence on the choice of the instruments of growth, but until recent years not the chief influence outside the communist *bloc*. This introduction may serve as the preface to a brief historical survey and an examination, in some detail, of the contemporary scene.

THE EARLY PERIOD OF MODERNISATION

The Meiji Restoration of 1868 marked the downfall of the conservative forces in Japanese society and the establishment in the seats of power of leaders intent upon modernisation. Only by importing techniques and forms of organisation from Europe and America could Japan hope to confront the advanced countries of the world on equal terms. The creation of powerful defence forces was an immediate aim, but political security, it was recognised, must be based on sound economic foundations, and these, too, had to be laid down. Although the country already possessed a traditional skill in metals and textiles, a quite sophisticated financial and commercial system and many other desiderata of a nineteenth-century economy, she was backward in the application of science to her industries, and her long period of seclusion had left her without knowledge of overseas markets and commercial practices. The older merchants had gained their experience in providing for the needs of a feudal society and they could not easily adapt themselves to the new world. So, inevitably, the state took the lead.

The economic activities of the early Meiji government were far-reaching. It reorganised the whole administrative, financial and fiscal systems, introduced methods of education, both general and technical, modelled on those of Western countries, and established most of the services and institutions considered essential to a civilised country at that time. It began to construct a modern system of communications, including the first railway line, a steamship service and postal and telegraphic services, and it actively promoted the development of modern types of bank. But it did not content itself with intervention in the infrastructure and went far beyond what was generally regarded at that time as economic activities proper to government. In particular, it set about the establishment of new manufacturing industries. It had inherited a number of enterprises, including cotton mills, munitions works, shipyards and shipping services from the feudal governments, and these it reorganised and expanded. During the 1870s factories with modern equipment were set up by the government in a wide range of industries, and oceangoing ships were purchased. In 1880 a summary statement of government-owned industrial undertakings and properties enumerated three shipyards, fifty-one merchant ships, five munitions works, fifty-two other factories, ten mines, seventy-five miles of railway, and a telegraph system.[2] The government also gave financial assistance to private firms and sold to them on easy terms machinery which it had imported for the purpose. It engaged foreign technicians,

teachers, managers and skilled workmen to provide the expertise needed for operating the new sectors of the economy.[3] The
Japanese leaders realised that these foreign experts were indispensable to their country's progress and the government was
ready to bear the heavy expense of employing them; their salaries in the early seventies are said to have amounted to about 5
per cent of the total public expenditure.

Although the underlying motive of the government was to
bring the Japanese economy into line with that of advanced
Western countries, it would be an error to suppose that it acted
in accordance with a long-term, detailed plan. It would,
indeed, be foolish to read into the mind of the statesmen of a
hundred years ago the latest notions of economic policy. The
government of early Meiji had to face many problems that
required immediate solution, and in its economic policy it was
frequently obliged to resort to expedients to deal with sudden
crises. For instance, the measures taken to create new banks
and manufacturing concerns were influenced in part by the
necessity of finding employment for the *samurai*, the former
military class which had lost its privileges and functions and
which, unless usefully occupied, might well become a source of
insurrection. Writers on this period have pointed to various
other motives that led to the government's far-reaching activities, such as the achievement of military and administrative
unity, the provision of metal products and fuel for its own
needs, the prevention of unemployment among miners, the
exclusion of foreign capital and even the elimination of quarrels.
among private interests.[4] After the first few years of the new era
other motives became more prominent, such as the furnishing
of models for private enterprise and the establishment of
import-saving industries to check the drain from the specie
reserves. Whatever the presiding motives, there can be no doubt
about the fact of the government's pioneering activity. As was
stated by a contemporary: 'We find that every company or
manufactory deserving of notice in any way has been furnished
with capital by the government or has been endowed with
special privileges by the same power'.[5]

Few of its manufacturing enterprises were financially successful during the 1870s. So, since its initiative had been determined by the pressure of necessity and not by any doctrinaire
view of its proper functions, it had no hesitation about selling its

industrial properties to private firms when it found itself in financial difficulties. Most of its properties were, in fact, disposed of in this way shortly after 1880, and subsequently the development of industry was left mainly to private enterprise. This applied for some years to come even to the further expansion of the railway system.

METHODS OF STATE CONTROL

The withdrawal of the state from the direct ownership and control of manufacturing industry and some other forms of enterprise did not mean that henceforth it was content to follow a *laissez-faire* policy. On the contrary, its influence continued to be exerted, although its methods changed. Many of the government's properties (its factories, mines and shipping lines) were acquired by a small number of rapidly growing business houses, some of which had been prominent from early times, while others were newcomers. Before the end of the century there began to emerge a group of large concerns with widely ramifying interests, and these subsequently became known as the *Zaibatsu* (literally, money-groups). The four most prominent were Mitsui, Mitsubishi, Sumitomo and Yasuda (see also Chapter 3). These business houses became agents through whom the government operated in executing its economic policy. They undertook the development of industries regarded as of national importance, and they provided financial help for the government when it was in difficulties, as at the time of the Sino-Japanese and Russo-Japanese wars. From the outset they had close links with leading politicians. In return for their support the government gave them privileges and contracts. They became the spearhead of Japan's economic development and very effective instruments of official policy. The relationship was of some subtlety for, as they expanded, the *Zaibatsu* themselves were able to influence policy and they became rivals of other power groups, such as the *Gumbatsu* (military clique).

The *Zaibatsu* were by no means the only instrument used by the government for carrying out its policy. Towards the end of the century it created a new banking system which had the effect of strengthening its grip on the economy. A Central Bank was set up in 1882 and then followed the formation of a number of special banks each designed for a particular purpose. The Yokohama Specie Bank, founded in 1880, entered in 1887 upon its long career as the chief foreign exchange bank of the country. It was given the privilege of borrowing from the Bank of Japan at low rates of interest and it played a part of great significance in fostering the country's foreign trade. The next step was the formation of two banks for long-term lending, the Hypothec Bank, established in 1896 for making advances to public authorities, cooperative societies, fishery guilds, and agricultural landowners, and the Industrial Bank of Japan established in 1900 for financing large-scale industries and public utilities. About the same time the Hokkaido Development Bank was formed for financing the development of the northern island.

Part of the capital of these special banks was subscribed by the government and the imperial household. The Ministry of Finance appointed their chief officers, guaranteed their dividends and supervised their business. A large part of their resources was obtained by debenture issues which were taken up largely by the Treasury Deposits Bureau.[6] When Japan began her career as a colonial power the government established special banks to finance developments in Formosa and Korea. After the Russo-Japanese War two semi-official companies, the South Manchuria Railway Company and the Oriental Development Company became intimately concerned with key economic enterprises in Manchuria. Throughout the present century up to the Second World War these official or semi-official financial concerns, in association with the *Zaibatsu*, provided the chief means by which the government promoted industries of national importance and guided the country's foreign trade upon which internal development closely depended.

The government was not content to rely wholly on these instruments. From time to time it assisted new industries by subsidies and, after 1902, when it secured tariff autonomy, by protection. Among the most important subsidies were those granted to the shipping and shipbuilding industries from 1896 onwards, and those to the Formosan sugar industry after 1902. Moreover, its policy of disengaging itself from the direct management of industry was not unqualified. For instance, certain industries became government monopolies for purely fiscal reasons, notably the tobacco, salt and camphor industries. Then, after a period in which development had been left largely to private persons, in 1906 the main railway lines passed under government ownership and control. The importance of communications had early impressed itself on the minds of the Japanese leaders, and by its control of the railways the government provided itself with a powerful means of guiding economic development. From a fiscal point of view these nationalised undertakings were profitable. The net revenue from the state monopolies and enterprises contributed a high proportion of the total revenue of the central government. In 1910–11 the proportion was about 30 per cent and after then it declined only very slowly. In 1955 the proportion was about 23 per cent. From that time onwards, with the steep increase in the tax revenue, it fell rapidly, but it was still about 10 per cent in 1965.[7]

In manufacturing industry, despite the inclination to leave development to private enterprise, the government was not slow to step in whenever the progress of a strategically important industry seemed to require it. Thus, in addition to managing naval dockyards and munitions works, the government took the lead in setting up the first moden iron and steel works in the country. The Yawata Steel Works, which began production in 1901, remained for many years the chief producer of steel in Japan. On the other hand, the new public utilities (electricity generation and gas production) were left mainly to private enterprise, although local authorities operated tramways, docks and harbours, and other services.

On the eve of the First World War, despite the continued importance of the state's initiative in economic development, the size of the public sector in Japan itself was quite small. Of the total employment in factory industry in 1914 government plants were responsible for only 12 per cent. The list of publicly owned and operated enterprises then included the postal and telegraph services, certain munitions factories, the largest steel plant, the Mint, the trunk railways, the government printing office, and establishments connected with the salt, tobacco and camphor monopolies. The greater part of the forests belonged to the Imperial Household and the government held large investments in the South Manchuria Railway Company and other colonial development enterprises, and also part of the capital of the special banks.

Although the greater part of industry and the whole of agriculture and fishing were left in private ownership, the state was never reluctant to intervene at points where its influence might be effective in contributing to efficiency or in fostering the kind of development in official favour. For instance, from the middle of the Meiji era the government encouraged by legislation the establishment of various types of associations among manufacturers and traders, partly for the promotion of their common interests, and partly in order to construct useful channels of communication between itself and private firms. Some of these associations were given authority to inspect the quality of their members' products, particularly those intended for export. Until the 1930s, however, these associations were of comparatively little importance.

In agriculture and fishing, the effects of intervention were much more substantial. From 1897, when a Fishery Encouragement Act was passed, the government through the prefectural authorities supervised the methods of fishing, marketing, equipment and storage. Various types of associations composed of members of the fishing industry were established by law, including some with the responsibility of serving the export markets. From the beginning of the modern era, moreover, the government was active in its attempts to improve agricultural methods and to increase production. During the 1870s it established agricultural schools and experimental stations, and before the end of the century it had set a network of prefectural experimental stations as well as several national research institutions. It imported farm implements and livestock from the West, and it gave assistance, in the form of subsidies or low-interest loans, for improving methods of irrigation and drainage and for encouraging the use of fertilisers. The government's rice policy, both in Japan itself and in the colonies, had a powerful influence on the farmers' activities. The same was true of its policy towards other agricultural products, such as tea and raw silk. For these two industries its chief preoccupation was in connection with the preparation of the products for export. Administrative machinery designed to maintain quality in the tea-export trade had been set up in the 1870s and a licensing system for the producers of silk-worm eggs was also introduced. This was systematised by the Silkworm Eggs Inspection Law of 1898 which enforced the standards to be applied in the inspection of eggs and laid down that silk-raisers should obtain their eggs only from licensed dealers. Silk-conditioning houses were established at Yokohama and Kobe with the object of maintaining a high uniform quality in the exports.

The government's intervention in the silk industry helps to explain Japan's successful competition against China in world markets. The production of cocoons in both countries was conducted in peasant households and the silk was reeled domestically or in small filatures. Success in selling the product in foreign markets, however, depended upon ability to supply filament of uniform quality, a condition difficult to satisfy in an industry conducted by widely dispersed units. China, lacking a strong central administration, never achieved this result. But the Japanese government, by imposing control at certain key points, won the confidence of foreign purchasers.

STATE INTERVENTION IN THE INTERWAR PERIOD

In the decade after the First World War the direct intervention by the state in economic affairs diminished, and its influence was exerted to an increasing extent in association with the *Zaibatsu*, then rising to the height of their power. The government introduced measures to maintain farm incomes by price support schemes for rice and silk during the postwar depression (1920–21), and it was involved in heavy expenditure, financed in part by foreign loans, on reconstruction after the great earthquake of 1923. But, in general, this could be regarded as a 'liberal' period in Japan's economic history. By 1930 employment in government factories had fallen to only 4 per cent of total factory employment, and the share of the gross national product attributable to the government amounted only to between 15 and 18 per cent.[8]

The next decade brought far-reaching changes in the government's functions and a marked growth in the size of the public sector. The world depression that began in 1929 led to the collapse of the 'liberal' government and to the strengthening of the political influence of the militarists. The policy of reflation adopted in 1932 coincided with a rearmament programme and with Japanese penetration into Manchuria and North China. During the period of the *junsenji-keizai*, immediately before the outbreak of the Sino-Japanese war in 1937, state control was steadily extended over an increasing range of institutions and transactions. This was achieved in part through the agency of certain newly organised industrial groups, the *Shinko-Zaibatsu* (new money-groups) which were considered more docile agents of the militarists than the old *Zaibatsu*. In part it took the form of increased official supervision over the associations of private industrialists and traders. Finally, it was brought about through the enlargement. of the public sector itself by nationalisation.

As their political influence grew, the military cliques insisted that the *Shinko-Zaibatsu*, which were heavily involved in the metal and engineering industries and in Manchurian development, should be used to carry out their strategic designs. The associations of manufacturers, which in the early 1930s had been fostered by the government with the object of handling industrial problems that arose out of the depression, were employed later in the decade as instruments of official control over production, prices and raw material supplies. The export associations were given a similar role in foreign trade. Certain basic industries were nationalised. In 1934 the government's Yawata Steel Works was joined with six private steel companies to form a concern wholly controlled and partly owned by the state—the Nippon Seitetsu, or Japan Steel Works. The electric power industry was nationalised in 1938, and in the same period a series of laws was enacted for the purpose of imposing more rigorous official control over the basic industries. After the outbreak of the Sino-Japanese War in 1937 the process was accelerated. In the strategic industries, or industries of outstanding national importance, a number of so-called 'national policy companies' were formed so as to ensure that development took the direction desired by the government. Companies such as these were established in the transport, mining, power, fertiliser, metal and aircraft industries as well as in many enterprises overseas. In Manchuria the Manchuria Industrial Development Company, which fell into this category, was of outstanding importance in the development of that country's resources. All these concerns obtained their capital in part from the state and in part from the *Zaibatsu*, new and old, and their resources were augmented by debenture issues under government guarantees.[9]

GOVERNMENT INVESTMENT

The economic importance of the government during the period of modernisation can be measured fairly accurately by its share in total national investment. According to Professor Rosovsky's estimates[10], from 1889 to 1938 gross national investment averaged 14·7 per cent of the national net product. The proportion varied widely over the period, being low in the early years and rising sharply during the 1930s when Japan was preparing for war. The share of the government's investment in the total also fluctuated, but for the whole period the tentative conclusion reached is that public investment was slightly more than private investment, 7·7 per cent compared with 7 per cent. There is some danger of exaggerating the government's share. Yet, if all the necessary qualifications are taken into account, the conclusion that government investment predominated during this period is not disturbed. Nor is this conclusion inconsistent with what has been said about the government's comparatively modest role in the actual ownership and operation of manufacturing and trading enterprise after the early years of Meiji. The government undertook the task of creating a modern infrastructure for Japan and its colonies. It found the resources for certain large-scale basic industries, such as steel; it was deeply engaged in various constructional works; and it spent lavishly on armaments and on founding the economic basis for military power. Most of the enterprises in which it was engaged were capital-intensive, whereas the bulk of private manufacturing industry, trade and agriculture remained labour-intensive, and made demands on capital resources that were small in proportion to output and employment.

THE PUBLIC SECTOR AFTER THE SECOND WORLD WAR

Between Japan's surrender to the Allies in August 1945 and the implementations of the Peace Treaty in the spring of 1952, the economy was in effect under American control. In the early years of the Occupation the policy of SCAP[12] was directed chiefly towards democratising Japan's institutions and destroying once and for all her warmaking capacity. In the economic sphere, this policy implied the strengthening of all forces favourable to a liberal market economy and the elimination of forms of organisation that had been associated with the war machine. So the *Zaibatsu* were dissolved into numerous constituent parts, for they were judged to have provided the economic basis of Japan's military power. Next, the industries that had been brought under state ownership and control during the 1930s, or in the course of the war itself, were denationalised. These included the iron and steel industry which now, for the first time since its original modern plants were set up, passed wholly into private hands. The generating and transmission equipment of the nationalised electricity industry was transferred to nine regional supply companies which were privately owned. Further, the special (or semi-official) banks which, as we have seen, had been used as instruments of national policy both in Japan itself and overseas, were completely reorganised. This was in accordance with the deliberate policy of the Ocupation Authorities who were intent upon loosening the grip of the state over economic processes and were determined to apply this policy without reservation to what they regarded as the financial instruments of Japan's imperialism.

In accordance with this policy, the special colonial banks and the Yokohama Specie Bank were closed, and the three debenture-raising investment banks (the Hypothec Bank, the Industrial Bank and the Hokkaido Development Bank) lost their privileges and their close connections with the government. The first and the third became ordinary deposit banks and the second ultimately resumed business as a private bank concerned with long-term loans to industry. Thus, by the end of the American Occupation the size of the public sector had greatly diminished and the trend towards the concentration of economic power had been reversed, at any rate in theory. In fact, the diffusion of economic power was less complete than it appeared. For the destruction of the *Zaibatsu* as centres of economic initiative at a time when capital resources were very scarce threw heavier responsibilities than ever on the government. For several years after the war the only important source of long-term finance for reconstruction was the Reconstruction Finance Corporation, an official concern which obtained its resources from the Bank of Japan, and many classes of transactions, including all foreign transactions, were subject to strict official control.

After Japan had regained her full sovereignty she modified

many of the reforms that had been imposed on her. The pursuit of this 'reverse course', as it was called, did not mean a return in all respects to the forms of economic organisation and control that had prevailed before the war, but there was a movement in that direction. It is true that no attempt was made to renationalise the iron and steel industry and that, although a publicly owned electric power company was established to build some new stations, the bulk of the generating and transmission capacity remained in private hands. Furthermore, no attempt was made to extend official ownership to other industries. But many instruments of official control which bore a close resemblance to those of the past were devised. We shall consider these in turn below.

It has been shown that the Japanese government had traditionally relied heavily on its financial institutions for controlling and directing the private sector of the economy. In the postwar period the importance of this instrument was enhanced. The continued shortage of liquid capital at a time when demand was urgent and when private financial institutions lacked resources, increased demands on the Central Bank. During the 1950s and early 1960s the commercial banks relied on the Bank of Japan for credit to enable them to finance industrial development, and this dependence strengthened the capacity of the monetary authorities to control not only the pace of development but also its direction. The controls over credit operated by the Central Bank were qualitative as well as quantitative.

At the same time the old special banks were replaced by several new banks with very similar functions. For example, the Bank of Tokyo rose out of the ashes of the Yokohama Specie Bank, admittedly without many of the latter's privileges. The place of the special banks concerned with long-term loans was taken by several institutions wholly owned by the government. These included the Japan Development Bank which supplied long-term loans to the basic industries, the Small Business Finance Corporation which conducted similar business with small and medium-sized firms, the Agricultural, Forestry and Fishery Finance Corporation which financed the industries mentioned in its title, and the Export-Import Bank which was concerned with providing long-term loans in connection with export transactions. These banks have continued to flourish. Other government banks are the People's Finance Corporation, the function of which is to meet the demand of small firms for temporary loans, the Small Businesses Credit Corporation which gives guarantees in respect of funds borrowed by small firms from private banks, the Housing Loan Corporation, and the Hokkaido and Tohoku Development Corporation, and several others. There are also a number of semi-official banks, such as the central banks for the cooperative credit societies, in which the government has substantial interests.[13]

The official banks have obtained the bulk of their resources from the Trust Fund Bureau (formerly Treasury Deposits Bureau) which handles the personal savings deposited in the Post Office, and their function has been to channel these savings into industries or classes of transactions considered by the government to deserve priority in the national interest. The pattern of lending has naturally changed from time to time according to the sector of the economy which the government has wished to promote. For instance, in December 1959, 52 per cent of the Japan Development Bank's outstanding loans were made to the electric power industry, 33 per cent to shipping and only 7 per cent to manufacturing industry, whereas in December 1966 the proportions were 33 per cent for both electric power and shipping and 16 per cent for manufacturing industries among which the chemical industry received the largest share.[14] The government's command over these investment resources has been an important source of its authority in influencing the policies of private firms.

Since the end of the Occupation the state's directing power has been exerted in other ways that are similar to those of earlier times. The *Zaibatsu* have been reconstructed and, although they do not dominate industry and finance to the same extent as formerly, they remain susceptible to official influence. They have been joined by new groups which operate in some of the most rapidly growing parts of the economy. The relations of government to private industry, however, are of some subtlety, and further discussion of them will be deferred until we come to examine postwar economic planning.

The postwar governments of Japan have been preoccupied, like earlier governments, with the problem of the balance of payments. Recovery in the early and middle 1950s, and expansion later on, were from time to time checked by the appearance of deficits in the international accounts. In dealing with this problem the government has possessed a weapon denied to its predecessors in the early Meiji era, namely effective controls over foreign trade and the foreign exchanges. These controls have been used systematically during much of the postwar period to stimulate exports and to promote import-saving, and it is only since 1960 that they have been partly dismantled under pressure from Japan's trading partners. Strict control over foreign investment in Japan was maintained for many years. It is evident that the shrinkage in the size of the public sector immediately after the war has proved to be quite consistent with the preservation of the state's influence over the economy.

Up to 1958 policy was concentrated on the encouragement of manufacturing industry and power production. Investment in these industries yielded quick returns and enlarged the country's exporting capabilities. This policy achieved its aims, but at the expense of the infrastructure, many parts of which were neglected. So, after 1958, it was decided to change the emphasis of policy and to direct much increased investment into the construction of roads and into social welfare. The change of policy involved the creation of new public bodies to carry it out. Already in 1948 the largest public concern in Japan, the National Railways, had been transferred from a government department to a public corporation, and this type of organisation was preferred when the government undertook other economic responsibilities. Such corporations were set up to deal with the construction of the major roads, the new trunk railway line from Tokyo to Osaka, and dwelling houses for letting, and also with various other projects, such as the provision of research into atomic energy. These corporations established by the central government supplemented local public corporations for dealing with ports, sewerage and water supplies.

THE SIZE OF THE PUBLIC SECTOR

It has been shown above (see p. 97) that the ratio of public expenditure to the GNP during the postwar period in Japan has been very low by Western European standards. On the other hand, a large share of the Japanese government's expenditure in recent years has taken the form of investment, ranging between 40 and 50 per cent of its total expenditure since 1950. The result is that the government has been responsible for a high proportion of the gross domestic capital formation which has itself been very large in proportion to the size of the national income. In the late 1950s its proportion was 26 per cent and in 1963–64, 29 per cent. If we make comparisons with prewar government expenditure as a whole, the most striking change is to be found in the rise in the relative importance of investment expenditure and the fall in that of consumption expenditure.[15] The latter is now small (when expressed as a ratio of gross national expenditure) in comparison with the expenditure of other advanced countries, as well as with that of Japan in prewar days. The chief explanation for this is to be found in the very small expenditure on defence (only about one per cent of the national income), as well as in the steep absolute increase in fixed government investment.

The state's contribution to capital formation has not been limited to direct investment by the central and local governments themselves or by the public corporations, for the official financial agencies already referred to have provided massive loans for the private sector. A glance at the direction taken by the government's investments and loans together will illustrate the nature of the state's economic policy. As a Japanese economist wrote recently, up to 1957–58 public loans and investments were 'heavily geared towards the promotion of private investment, especially plant and equipment investment by large corporations'.[16] Similarly, the generous depreciation allowances provided for by the company taxation system also stimulated private investment in equipment, while the official credit policy was aimed at 'fostering particular industries and enterprises by encouraging investments therein; this was accomplished by channelling to them, under the priority system, large volumes of investible funds, much of which was financed by the Bank of Japan's credits'.[17] Thus the government through its own investments and loans, its taxation system and the credit policy of the banks it controlled, exerted a profound influence on the development of the whole economy. If one glances at the other side of the account, one is impressed by the high level of public saving. During the later 1950s about 21 per cent of the nation's savings came from budget surpluses. From these the government found about two-thirds of the funds issued to finance its own investments. All this emphasises the fact that if the public sector, as narrowly defined, is comparatively small, this has little relevance to a judgement of the part played by the state in the postwar economy. On the other hand, it would be erroneous to suppose that the state has dictated policy to private industry. The Japanese method of decision-making is to proceed by consensus, and agreed policies normally emerge from discussions among interested parties. When one is comparing state intervention in Japan with that in other countries, moreover, one cannot fail to be impressed by the fact that, in her case, government investment since the war has been designed primarily to support private enterprise not to supersede it.

ECONOMIC PLANNING

The genesis of postwar economic planning can be found in the establishment of the Economic Stabilisation Board in 1946 by the government on the instructions of SCAP. The chief functions of the Board were to work out plans for the reconstruction of the war-torn economy and to indicate the priorities which would guide government departments and financial authorities in finding funds for industry. In particular, the Board collected information about the requirements of the economy in order to provide a basis for claims for United States aid and loans from the World Bank. One of its main reports was on the Economic Rehabilitation Plan of 1949–53. The Stabilisation Board came into existence at a time when, in default of any renewed private initiative, the government was obliged to assume almost universal functions. After 1950–51 the recovery of the economy proceeded rapidly and private enterprise reasserted itself. Yet Japan's economic problems could not be solved by following a *laissez-faire* prescription. The recurrent balance of payments troubles, the continued dependence on heavy special procurement expenditure by the United States, and the necessity for large investments in the basic industries, forced the government to concern itself with international trade, capital formation and technical development. A symptom of this preoccupation was the re-establishment in 1955 of the Stabilisation Board (or rather, the Economic Counsel Board which it had become in 1953) as the Economic Planning Board with new functions.[18] So began the first formal essay in economic planning.

The Board drew up a five-year plan which predicted an annual rate of growth in the gross national product of 5 per cent, and pointed to the conclusion that by 1958 Japan would have achieved a viable economy independent of any special procurement dollar revenue. It is difficult to believe that the plan had much influence on events. Its predictions were soon falsified since in the first two years GNP grew not by 5 per cent but by 10 per cent. This underestimation of Japan's capabilities was characteristic of all subsequent plans. For instance, in the case of the next plan, the new long-range plan for 1958–62, which forecast an annual rate of growth of 6·5 per cent, the target of production for the terminal year was hit by 1960. This plan itself was more elaborate than its predecessor. It provided targets for investment, savings and employment, production and foreign trade, and it laid down detailed plans for public investment in different parts of the infrastructure. It may have had some influence on the latter, for its existence may have encouraged the government to proceed with its own investment projects during the balance of payments crisis of 1957–58 rather than to abandon them in face of the clamour for retrenchment. But the activities of private entrepreneurs seem to have been unaffected by the plan. Certainly, the steep advance that occurred during these years in investment in the science-based industries had not been anticipated.

The next plan, both in its coverage and its aims, was more ambitious. This was the well-known income doubling plan for the decade 1961–70 (fiscal years) which was worked out by the Economic Planning Agency (formerly, Board) in conjunction wth a complex of committees and subcommittees of industrialists, bankers, civil servants and economists. The plan made provision for an annual average rate of growth of 7·2 per cent (9 per cent for the first three years and 6·4 per cent subsequently) and for an even faster rate of growth of exports (9 per cent throughout the decade). The most interesting feature of the plan was the change of emphasis given to investment. During the 1950s Japan had concentrated on investment in the manufacturing and power industries. Now it was proposed to devote a higher proportion of resources to the infrastructure—communications, housing and other forms of investment by the central and local authorities.

It was reasonable to suppose that, since the plan put so much stress on the kind of investment over which the government itself could exert direct control, the contrast between what was predicted and what was achieved would be less sharp than in the earlier plans. In fact, the opposite was true. The announcement of the plan led to a violent upward movement in private investment and production, and in 1960 and 1961 the rate of economic growth (in real terms) was far greater than that planned (15·5 per cent compared with 9 per cent). For the six years 1960–66 the average was just under 10 per cent. The planners raised their sights again in 1965 when they issued a medium term plan to cover the years 1964–68. For that period they put the annual average rate of growth at 8·1 per cent, and in the latest plan, for 1967–71, the prediction is the same. What is most significant about the latest plan is the increased importance given to social investment. The balance has turned further against private investment in manufacturing equipment and towards public investment in social overhead capital. Before 1960 so-called 'enterprise' investment was three times social investment. In the plan for 1961–70 the ratio was reduced to 2:1 and in fact in 1965 it actually fell to 1·8:1. According to the latest plan, by 1971 it will have been reduced to 1·65:1. In absolute terms social overhead investment in 1967–71 is to be twice that of 1961–65 (at 1965 prices). The largest increase is expected in housing, sanitation and the provision for social welfare, although as in the last few years there is also to be heavy investment in transport and communications.[19]

Such in outline were the central economic plans of the postwar period. But how effective were they in influencing the development of the economy? This is a vital question from the standpoint of the present paper, since central planning represents an important field for the exercise of the government's directive powers. As already shown, the influence of the first two plans was modest, even when judged by the undemanding standards of 'indicative' planning. The income doubling plan undoubtedly had a considerable effect on the economy, but the results were by no means those intended by the planners. The great upsurge of investment that followed the plan's announcement is attributed by Japanese officials to misunderstandings by the industrialists. These had observed that the Japanese government, in its previous essays in planning, had grossly underestimated the capacity of the economy for growth. Consequently, they thought themselves justified in concluding that the targets were simply minima, in some sense guaranteed by the government, and they acted accordingly. If this interpretation is correct, then one may hold that the plan was influential chiefly in giving fresh encouragement to industrialists already inclined towards optimism. Far from leading to steadier growth, which was one of the aims of the planners, it exerted a destabilising influence, for the boom was followed by a steep, though brief, recession.

Some Japanese industrialists deny that they are influenced by the plans or by the government's efforts to implement them. It is difficult to believe, however, that the market forces, to which they steadfastly geared their policies, have not been affected by government actions, or that on occasion entrepreneurs in the growing industries have not been compelled to bring their own plans into conformity with those of the government by the pressure of official measures of control. These have already been described—the regulation of foreign trade and exchange, the discriminatory lending policies of the official banks and the constant exercise of persuasion by officials and Ministers. As a recent commentator has stated:[20]

> 'The Ministries engage in an extraordinary amount of consultation, advice, persuasion and threat. The industrial bureaux of the Ministry of International Trade and Industry proliferate sectoral targets and plans; they confer, they tinker, they exhort . . . Business makes few major decisions without consulting the appropriate governmental authority; the same is true in reverse. The Ministries list three hundred consulting committees for this purpose!'

An outsider cannot, of course, be sure where power really resides in administrative relationships of this kind. Some great private industrialists try to resist or to disregard official pressure, and it is certain that the major impulse to expansion in the postwar period can be traced to private entrepreneurs rather than to the government. Nevertheless, the work of the latter in guiding, assisting and cajoling private industry has been at least a powerful contributory cause of Japan's economic success and it has certainly affected the direction of development.

Recent events do not suggest that the Japanese bureaucracy wears a seamless robe when it presents itself to the business community. The influence it exerts is far from homogeneous, for it is composed of factions in keen rivalry with one another. In most cases the contentions arise out of differences in policy and do not simply reflect quarrels among persons. They are found both in the great departments of state themselves and also in the bodies to which administrative functions have been delegated. They may at times frustrate action, but in general inter-departmental crises are resolved by constructive compromise before serious hurt to the state is sustained. The tensions between one part of the government and another, and between government and business, may themselves help to keep the policy-makers alert and decisive.

It would be wrong to suppose, however, that there have been no administrative failures, still less that the government or the bureaucracy always gets its own way. For instance, there have been bitter conflicts, still unresolved, among government departments and businessmen about proposed amendments to the Fair Trade Laws. This legislation was first introduced at the instance of the Occupation Authority. It was based on American precedents and was hostile to cartels and restrictive practices as well as to great aggregations of economic power. The laws were amended after Japan regained her sovereignty in order to exempt certain types of cartels from legal assault, for example, those formed to deal with temporary recessions and exports, but repeated demands by industry, supported by the Ministry of International Trade and Industry, for a virtual repeal of the anti-monopoly legislation were successfully resisted in the Diet. Since 1960, however, the liberalisation of foreign trade has threatened to expose certain industries to foreign competition in the home market and the government has encouraged those firms for whom large-scale operation is a condition of efficiency to consolidate their businesses. The motor industry provides the best example. It may be expected that government-inspired rationalisation schemes will be introduced into other industries, and there may be difficulty in reconciling some of these with the provisions of the Fair Trade Laws. In this respect, the Japanese government is now encountering problems very similar to those found in Europe.

REGIONAL PLANNING

Political disagreements and the opposition of industrialists have also impeded the execution of regional development plans. Ever since the war the growing concentration of industry and population in three great regions (Tokyo–Yokohama, Nagoya, and Kyoto–Osaka–Kobe)[21] has given rise to social problems besides depriving many outlying regions, especially those in the north of the main island, of enterprise and of workers in the more active age groups. The government has felt obliged to address itself to these issues. As early as 1950 legislation was passed to provide for regional planning; this was concerned with the planning of land use both at the regional and at the local level. Particular attention was given to Hokkaido and Tohoku. Development companies established to promote economic growth in those regions have tried to introduce new industries, and by the early 1960s the Tohoku Development Company operated factories producing cement, carbide, hardboard and various other goods; it also acted as a channel for directing government loans at low rates of interest to private companies within the area. Development Promotion Acts have also been passed to deal with other underdeveloped regions, such as Shikoku and parts of Kyushu.

The income doubling plan of 1961–70 approached regional planning more systematically. One of its objects was to reduce regional differences in income per head, and its regional programme was devised with that end in view. It sought to relieve the extreme congestion in the Tokyo conurbation and to divert industry to areas still underdeveloped. It proposed to build up, at some 13 points of growth in these underdeveloped areas, industrial cores from which further expansion would naturally proceed. There was to be public investment in the infrastructure at those points, and financial inducements, such as tax concessions, special depreciation allowances and low interest loans through the Japan Development Bank, were to be offered to industrialists who settled there. The schemes were ambitious, but in practice the achievements have been very modest, partly because industrialists for the most part have been sceptical about the whole regional plan, and partly because of the reluctance of the government to provide adequate finance in the face of disagreement among the politicians over the choice of sites for development. So it may be said that the regional policies of the planners have so far been thwarted by opposition from other interests. It is true that the so-called 'underdeveloped' regions are no longer impoverished and depressed, but their improvement has come about, not through planning, but through the generalised impact of the country's economic progress. The experience illustrates the limitations of the government's economic power and is inconsistent with the assertion that Japan possesses a completely centrally planned or state-moulded economy. In fact, in modern times as in the past, the bureaucracy is simply one important policy-making body among the several powerful groups which together, now in alliance and now in rivalry, determine the economic development of Japan.

CONCLUSION

The relations among these groups are complex and an outsider's interpretation of them can only be tentative. Nevertheless, it seems to the present writer that, as suggested at the beginning of this chapter, an identifiable thread of continuity has been present in the government's economic policy throughout the modern era. The means employed for guiding the economy have varied, but one is left with the impression of a determination on the part of the authorities to bring the activities of private entrepreneurs into conformity with the public purpose, although that purpose itself has altered from time to time. During the last quarter of a century, despite many contrasts with the previous period, both in the state's objectives and the means which it has employed, there can be little doubt that its influence on development has been profound. The small size of the public sector itself is likely to mislead the foreign observer in this respect. At the same time, it is also evident that Japan is a country where private entrepreneurship still shows exceptional vitality. The careers of certain individual industrialists of remarkable business capacity (for example, those of K. Matsushita and S. Honda) recall the great American and British industrial pioneers of the last century. It may be that one of the government's chief contributions towards economic progress during the last twenty-five years has been that of providing a congenial environment for such forceful innovators. Its overriding policy of ensuring that the energies of the nation were concentrated on a single purpose, economic recovery and expansion, has been amply rewarded. In the past Japan, like other countries, was moved by a variety of aspirations, not all of them consistent with one another. After the Second World War all these, with one exception, were relinquished, and the consequence of this wholehearted pursuit of a single ambition has astonished the world, and even the Japanese themselves.

A NOTE ON COOPERATIVE SOCIETIES

The cooperative movement in Japan can trace its origins far back in history, and many early forms of cooperation survived into the modern era and indeed still exist. The communal solidarity of the hamlet where the unit of organisation was the household rather than the individual, was an outstanding feature of Japan's rural life for many centuries.[22] Among the villagers a wide variety of societies existed concerned with religious and ceremonial affairs, the provision of common amenities and friendly society functions as well as agricultural and commercial matters. Cooperation among households was essential for the management of the common pasture and forest land from which the hamlets obtained fuel, fertilisers and food, and the irrigation problems faced by the paddy-farmers could be solved only by cooperative arrangements. Much the same was true of the fishermen who used boats and gear in common. In some parts of the country cooperative granaries and silk marketing societies existed long before the Meiji era. Even in the towns cooperatively owned equipment was used by groups of craftsmen for certain processes, such as the kilns required by the small potters. Throughout the country various kinds of mutual aid societies flourished, notably the *Mujin*, a mutual credit association, and a more elaborately organised species of loan society, the *Hotokusha*. The latter has been compared with the Raiffeisen cooperative credit societies.[23]

All these cooperative ventures arose spontaneously from the needs of the people, and their survival into modern times can be similarly explained. But the Meiji governments which sought to guide in greater or less degree the whole range of economic activities were determined to bring the country's institutions into conformity with accepted Western models. So in 1900 a Cooperative Law came into force, and from this the modern cooperative movement takes its origin. The Law was modelled chiefly on German precedents. Provision was made, and regulations laid down, for various types of societies both for producers and consumers. The producers' societies included those concerned with credit, marketing, the purchase of materials and the use of machinery, and these formed the most flourishing branches of the movement. Although the Law also dealt with consumers' cooperatives, this form never took firm root in Japan, while the Law itself was silent about self-governing cooperative workshops.

The reasons for these disparities are not far to seek. The type of cooperative movement that flourishes in any country is closely related to the nature of the economy. When the government began to encourage the modern cooperative movement, Japan was still largely a country of peasant farmers, fishermen and small-scale industrial producers. Organisations to support the financial and commercial strength and the technical capacity of these small producers were clearly the form of cooperation most required. In 1900 and for many years afterwards there was no substantial class of factory wage-earners. The chief large-scale manufacturing industry, then in an early stage of development, was cotton-spinning, and the labour force employed in the mills consisted predominantly of young girls who were recruited from country families and who returned to their homes after a few years of industrial work. The environment that produced the Rochdale Pioneers had no parallel, and consequently there was little encouragement for consumers' cooperation. Moreover, Japan had been well supplied with shops for centuries. In the early eighteenth century the Dutch traveller, Kaempfer, had been impressed with the number of shops and the variety of goods sold in them. By no means all the establishments were small; some very large retail enterprises had flourished in the Japanese cities long before the Meiji era. The lack of cooperative workshops and the failure of the legislation to cover them may be explained by similar reasons. In the absence of a large urban proletariat, there was no point in seeking to encourage forms of organisation which nineteenth-century idealists in Europe imagined would rescue the wage-earner from his servitude.

The rural cooperative societies developed rapidly in the early years of the century under the influence of the new legislation. By 1914 there were over 11,000 cooperative societies in the villages. They included over 9000 cooperative credit associations, many of which also undertook marketing and purchasing functions for their members.[24] The credit associations helped to foster savings habits and there was a rapid increase in the amount of money deposited with them in the early years of the century. The societies were particularly active in handling supplies of fertilisers for their members. In 1917 an amended law was passed and a few years later, under the provisions of this law, a Central Bank for Agricultural Cooperative Associations was formed. This coordinated the credit activities of all the local societies and strengthened their competition with local moneylenders and merchants. In a similar way, the other types of cooperative society were coordinated by national federations; the purchasing societies, for example, were affiliated to a central wholesale association.

After the onset of the world depression in 1929 the importance of the societies increased, and by 1935 about 65 per cent of all agricultural households had joined them. The societies purchased seeds, fertilisers and other materials and sold these to their members. They handled the bulk of the business for some classes of chemical fertilisers at this time, and played an important part in stimulating their use and so in increasing agricultural productivity. Some societies even set up their own fertiliser factories and made compounds for their members. Cooperative warehouses were established for storing rice and other cereals, and the marketing societies handled a large proportion of the cocoons. The growth in the business of the societies during the 1930s occurred at the expense of local merchants who complained that this competition was subsidised by the government, as indeed it was. It seems that the societies were chiefly beneficial to the rural landlords and substantial peasant proprietors, and that these persons were dominant in the administration of them. The small peasant proprietors and the tenant farmers, though not excluded from the benefits, found the societies of comparatively little assistance.

As Japan moved towards war in the later 1930s, the cooperative societies, like other producers' associations, were transformed into agents of government policy. Eventually they were merged with the agricultural associations (which had been formed to encourage technical improvements) and became the instruments of official control over agriculture and the rural population. After the war the agricultural cooperative societies were reborn and the Agricultural Cooperation Act of 1947 was passed to define and regulate their activities.[25] But their new career was clouded by memories of their wartime functions. These were not readily forgotten because the societies continued to act as agents of the government's staple food control system. On the other hand, the postwar land reform, which abolished the landlords and turned the tenant farmers into peasant proprietors, provided opportunities for the democratisation of the cooperatives, previously under the thumb of the landlords. By the early 1960s there were 31,000 associations in the villages of which about 12,000 combined the functions of providing credit, purchasing and selling. During the postwar period the local associations have been federated at the prefectural and national levels, and they have been served, as before the war, by a central bank. It is estimated that in recent years the money deposited with the associations has represented about 60 per cent of the total savings of farm households and that the associations have been responsible for about 40 per cent of all farm loans. The purchasing sections of the movement have supplied about two-fifths of the total purchase of materials by farmers, and the sales sections have been responsible for about half the total farm sales.[26]

It is evident that the postwar agricultural cooperative movement has an important place in Japan's rural economy.[27] But it has shown certain weaknesses. Its business has been concentrated largely on the staple crops and on fertilisers, and it has done little to interest itself in the more rapidly developing sections of Japan's diversifying agriculture, for example, livestock, dairy farming and fruit-farming. A leading authority on Japanese agriculture has pointed out that in the staple products (grains and soya beans) the distributive channels have long been well established and that, in places where a cooperative exists, it has usually handled the whole of the rice supply as the government's delegated agent. Further, for wheat, barley and soya beans the cooperatives have an advantage in that they can offer the farmers a higher price for the goods which they sell to the government than the merchant who sells in a free market. But farmers have been reluctant to entrust to the cooperatives the perishable crops which require speedy handling and careful packing, and they have found the commercial concerns more efficient in the marketing of their industrial crops. The cooperatives have the advantage, in some of their transactions, of being backed by the savings banks or credit societies; the farmers can buy their fertilisers from the cooperatives on credit which is later extinguished by deductions from the proceeds of their rice deliveries. But private merchants usually give better service than the cooperatives, especially in the provision of tractors and other hired machinery. Indeed, the societies have taken only a modest part in the mechanisation and reorganisation of agriculture that began in the later 1950s. It is true that an amendment of the law in 1962 permitted the societies to acquire farmland for the purpose of engaging in cooperative ventures in large-scale agriculture and this policy has enjoyed some success. But the real strength of the movement since the war has depended on its functions in the official rice control system. If this were abandoned, it is probable that many of the cooperatives would go with it.

In the industrial sector examples of cooperative enterprise are to be found among the small producers who still form a large but declining class in Japanese society. In their efforts to adapt themselves to changes in technical and marketing conditions some small producers have cooperated in setting up new industrial centres each of which is composed of firms in a particular trade and is provided with certain common facilities. The government has helped these ventures by giving grants, tax concessions and loans at low rates of interest. The small business sector is, like agriculture, an important area for the operation of various types of mutual loan and cooperative credit association. There are central organs to coordinate the local societies, notably the National Federation of Credit Cooperatives and the Central Bank for Commercial and Industrial Cooperatives. These are private institutions, although they receive government support.

The mutual loan societies, which grew out of the older bodies already referred to, combine the functions of savings banks and of instalment loan institutions for small manufacturing and trading businesses. Under a *Mujin* contract, the customer agrees to make regular deposits for a stated period with a society, and he gains the right of borrowing a certain sum during the currency of the contract. The conditions under which these societies trade are controlled by law. They make both long-term and short-term loans and, with the country's economic expansion, their business has much increased, like that of all financial institutions. Besides the mutual loan associations, there are urban credit cooperatives organised by local groups of small businessmen. They accept deposits from their members and make loans to them; their methods of trading are subject to some degree of official supervision. The Central Bank for Commercial and Industrial Cooperatives, which was established by law in 1936 to coordinate the business of the local credit societies, has been capitalised partly by member-societies and partly by the government. This Bank is supervised by both the Ministry of Finance and the Ministry of International Trade and Industry which appoint its officers.

What emerges from this survey of cooperation is the ubiquity of the state's interventionist activity. Yet, in this as in most other sectors of Japan's economy, government influence falls well short of control. Moreover, there is often a long step between the assertion of an intention, even when it is given legislative and institutional embodiment, and its actual achievement in the gritty world of economic reality.

7 The Causes of Japan's Economic Progress[1]

The several periods of rapid economic growth which Japan has experienced during her modern history have always taken the world by surprise. Even the Japanese themselves have, on occasion, been astonished at their recurrent good fortune. This is certainly true of the postwar period. Ten years ago, even eight years ago, Japanese businessmen, officials and economists surveyed their industrial and commercial prospects with apprehension. They spoke of their country as a high-cost, 'marginal' supplier of goods. The economy, they said, was exceptionally vulnerable to any recession in international trade and rested upon precarious sources of income. The outside world took the same pessimistic view. Yet the succeeding period witnessed one of the most remarkable economic advances in history, and everywhere observers are casting about for plausible explanations. Is the development firmly based and can one expect it to continue at the same rate? What importance should be attached to fortuitous causes? To what extent can an identity with previous periods of rapid growth be detected, or have quite new factors been mainly responsible?

An attempt will be made to answer these and related questions in the course of this article. But, first, let us recall the main facts of growth, although these are now so well known as to require little emphasis. Between 1955 and the end of 1961 the index of mining and manufacturing production rose from 100 to 197; on a very broad estimate, industrial production last year was probably at least four times that of the middle 1930s. The general growth has been associated with a considerable broadening of the basis of production. The former extreme specialisation on a narrow range of textiles has gone. As in other advanced industrial countries, development has been associated chiefly with the expansion of the metal, engineering and

126

chemical industries. Finished steel production in 1961 was about two-and-a-half times that of 1955 and over four times the prewar output. Japan has become the fourth largest steel producer in the world. She is also the world's largest shipbuilder, one of the leading producers of electrical and electronic apparatus, and a considerable manufacturer of motor vehicles. Her chemical industry has expanded and its scope has greatly increased, especially through the development of a petrochemical industry which provides oil-derivatives for a variety of new products, such as plastics and synthetic fibres. The rise in agricultural production has been equally remarkable. This production since prewar times has grown much faster than the increase in population (which amounted to about 28 per cent between 1940 and 1960), and it has become more highly diversified. The former specialisation on cereals (especially rice) has diminished, and dairying, fruit and vegetable growing and livestock farming have been widely extended. The gross national product has risen faster than that of any other country, except Western Germany; the average annual rate of increase between 1953 and 1959 is estimated at 7 per cent, and 10 per cent between 1955 and 1960.

The postwar development of the Japanese economy cannot be described as 'stable growth'. Since Japan regained her autonomy in 1952, the advance has been checked on three occasions because of the appearance of serious disequilibria in the balance of payments. These crises occurred in 1954, 1958 and 1961. In the first two instances restrictive measures applied by the government were quickly effective, and the upward trend in production was soon resumed. It is likely that the same result will attend the application of the monetary restrictions introduced in 1961, although on this occasion the difficulties may be less readily overcome. Between each period of boom and recession prices fluctuated widely. For instance, wholesale prices rose by about 12 per cent between the middle of 1955 and the end of 1956, but by the early months of 1958 they had fallen back to the 1955 level. There has been no secular rise in prices. The Bank of Japan's wholesale price index for 1960 was just about the same as for 1953. Its consumer price index also showed no significant upward movement until 1960; since then there has been a sharp rise. So in Japan inflation has not been a concomitant of rapid growth. This also must be explained.

Before acclaiming these economic successes as a 'miracle', we must safeguard our sense of proportion by a glance at Japan's previous experience. This will show that very rapid economic development is no new phenomenon in Japan. From the outset of her modern career she has pursued a vigorously expansionist policy. It would be misleading to speak of 'planned growth' in the modern sense, but it is evident that her political ambitions and her institutional arrangements were such as to induce an exceptionally high rate of development. Throughout her modern history, up to 1937, there was a remarkable convergence of diverse factors conducive to rapid growth, such as heavy state or state-induced investment in new industries of national or strategic importance, a wide extension of opportunities in export markets for products which Japan was well fitted to supply (especially raw silk and cotton textiles), a concentration of power in a few great business houses (a concentration that gave the economy expert leadership and promoted a high rate of capital accumulation and investment), a steep rise in agricultural productivity which, together with the growth in the population as a whole, enabled an ample supply of labour to be made available for the secondary and tertiary industries, a social structure and social traditions favourable to a high rate of personal saving, a financial system well designed to mobilise and direct liquid resources into industrial investment, and finally an educational system capable of producing competent business executives, civil servants, technicians and skilled workers.

The rapid pace of the advance was largely responsible for a succession of crises in the balance of payments, but by a combination of luck and readiness to apply remedies ruthlessly, Japan found her way out of them without more than temporary hesitations in her growth. This was so even in the world depression of 1930–31. Thus, the very rapid expansion of the last decade is by no means novel to her experience. Between 1925 and 1939, for instance, a period that included not only the world depression, but also two serious financial crises, the annual rate of increase of the gross national product averaged 4·6 per cent. The ratio of gross capital formation to national income during most of the interwar years is estimated to have been well over 20 per cent. So, if we recall what has happened in the past, the development of the economy since 1950 appears less surprising. Nevertheless, the rate of growth in the last ten years (that is to say, since the time when prewar levels of production had been restored) has been much higher than in any decade in the past. One must consider, therefore, whether this achievement is primarily attributable to the operation of the same factors as were responsible for previous rates of growth, or whether some new cause can be detected.

A new cause was certainly present during the first half of the postwar period (1945–52). There can be little doubt that at that time Japan owed her recovery in large measure to factors outside her own control, particularly to American policy. It is true that in the first years of the Occupation, SCAP (Supreme Commander of the Allied Powers) was intent upon democratising Japan and permanently destroying her capacity to make war rather than upon economic recovery. Hence the land reforms, the breakup of the great concerns (the *Zaibatsu*), and the labour legislation which called into existence a militant trade union movement. But with the outbreak of the Cold War, Japan's strategic importance to the United States was enhanced, and enthusiasm for reform gave place to a determination to render the economy viable. By 1950 steps had been taken to check inflation and to set going industrial recovery. Yet, although the great institutional reforms were now pushed from the centre of the stage, at least one of them, namely the land reform, played a significant part in subsequent progress. For this reform, which in effect converted agricultural tenants into peasant proprietors, not merely removed a source of social unrest that had contributed to the militarist and anti-parliamentary movements of the 1930s, but it also, at first, promoted agricultural efficiency by strengthening the farmers' incentives. The other reforms, which at the outset impeded recovery, were modified even before the Peace Treaty came into effect (in the spring of 1952), and they were later abandoned or accommodated to Japan's requirements. During these early years American 'aid' was lavishly given, and without it Japan would scarcely have been able to avoid starvation or to supply materials to her industries. On balance, then, American policy during the Occupation period was of great benefit in rescuing the economy from chaos and in preparing the way for the future development.

It was to be expected that Japan would face grave difficulties after the end of the Occupation, when American 'aid', dried up. Her sources of foreign income were then exiguous, for her export trade remained very small and her mercantile marine had not yet been rebuilt. From these difficulties Japan was rescued by the outbreak of the Korean War. Substantial orders for industrial goods came in from abroad; American expenditure within Japan vastly increased; and high foreign earnings enabled her in the next few years to re-equip her industries and to create substantial foreign exchange reserves. Even when the war was over, Japan continued to earn large sums in dollars on account of United States' 'special procurement' expenditure, chiefly in connection with American forces stationed in Japan. In the early and middle 1950s when Japan's costs were relatively high and her export trade still small, these payments were invaluable. Between 1952 and 1956 they amounted to 3380 million dollars, equivalent to more than a quarter of the value of her commodity imports at that time. 'Special procurement' continued as a useful source of foreign income for much longer than had been expected. Even in the late 1950s it was equivalent to 14 per cent of the imports. All this Japan owed to good fortune—to her key position in American strategy at a time of tension in the Far East. It may be argued that, apart from the measurable financial benefits, the momentum gained at the time of the Korean War and the continued stimulus of American demands, set the pace for future growth. Certainly, in the absence of these factors, Japan's subsequent history would have been very different.

The American participation in Japan's development was, then, a leading new factor in growth. Let us now consider the importance for postwar growth of certain factors that operated powerfully in the past. Foreign trade, a powerful stimulus to development throughout Japan's modern history, has probably played a less important part since the Second World War than ever before. Its recovery lagged far behind the rise in production. After 1955 the pace increased and in the next six years exports doubled in value. But in 1960 they accounted for only 3·6 per cent of world exports, compared with 5·4 per cent in 1938, and their volume is now probably not more than 25 per cent greater than in the middle 1930s. The growth in imports was also very moderate when compared with the massive expansion of production.

The disproportionately small growth in foreign trade can easily be understood. When Japan set about rebuilding her economy after the war, she found that her most important markets and sources of supply had been permanently lost. In the middle 1930s, China, Korea and Formosa took about two-fifths of the exports and supplied over a third of the imports. They provided the chief markets both for manufactured textiles and for capital goods, and the growth of Japanese industry and the expansion in its scope in the prewar decade were geared to this trade. In 1959 these countries together accounted for only 4 per cent of the exports and 3 per cent of the imports, and their shares were tending to fall. Meanwhile, raw silk, the chief export to the United States, the other leading market, had been replaced in the American hosiery trade by synthetic fibres. (Silk was the commodity from which the agricultural population had derived much of its money income.) So Japan had to rebuild her foreign trade from its foundations. This necessity has certainly stimulated her to branch into new lines of production and to seek markets outside the areas to which her trade was previously specialised. Her export trade has become more widely distributed and diversified than formerly, and in 1961 metals, engineering goods and chemicals accounted for 44 per cent of it. An increasing proportion of her exports now consists of high quality goods in the manufacture of which her relatively cheap, skilled labour affords her considerable advantages. In general, she now supplies labour-intensive products to the advanced nations and capital-intensive products to the rest of the world.

Yet, unless procurement expenditure is counted as an export, one cannot regard the export trade during the last decade as having achieved its former importance as a factor in growth, except in particular periods (1950–51 and perhaps 1960) and for particular industries, such as shipbuilding and camera manufacture. What is especially remarkable about the postwar trade is that Japan was able to organise a rapid industrial expansion without raising her imports substantially, for it was once a commonplace that her economy was exceptionally dependent upon foreign trade. The explanation is to be found partly in the structural changes in industry already referred to and partly in her success in finding adequate substitutes for

imported materials. In prewar days when manufactured textiles, especially cotton goods, formed a high proportion of industrial production and exports, the import-content of
Japanese manufactures was high. Textiles have now, in part,
given place to goods that depend less heavily on imported materials, and in textile production itself pulp and other materials
from home sources of supply have been substituted for
imported raw cotton and pulp. A similar process of substitution
has affected other manufacturing industries, but the most striking import-economy has occurred in food. Despite the rise in
population of over 28 per cent since the 1930s, the proportion of
foodstuffs in the import trade has fallen steeply. This change
has been made possible by the increased productivity of agriculture. Japan is now almost self-sufficient in rice. Until recently this process of substitution, and indeed the composition
of the foreign trade as a whole, have been much influenced by
an elaborate system of controls designed to restrict imports and
stimulate exports at the expense of domestic consumers. The
reluctance of the Japanese to abandon this system indicates
that they still regard their foreign trading position with anxiety.

In the past the government played a prominent part in development chiefly for the purpose of realising its political and strategic aims. Industries considered necessary for national power
were founded by the government, or its agents, the *Zaibatsu*,
and were sometimes subsidised and protected. During the
1930s official control, through 'national policy' companies,
was extended over a considerable part of the economy. Investment in the heavy industries of Manchuria and China as well
as in those of Japan itself contributed to the steep rise in industrial production. The 'special', or semi-official, banks
were active in financing these developments, and the government's loan-financed expenditure on armaments gave another
impetus to the boom from 1932 onwards. A well-known
Japanese economist, indeed, came to the conclusion that
Japan's development had been promoted and sustained primarily by wars and preparation for war.

   In all these respects the change has been profound. Military and strategic investment on the part of the Japanese
government (as distinct from that provided by the Americans) has played an insignificant part in the postwar growth.

The budgetary deficits of the 1930s and earlier times by which some of this investment was financed have no counterpart in the Japan of the 1950s and 1960s. Recently only one-tenth of the government's annual expenditure has been for defence, compared with over two-fifths in the middle 1930s. Then, since the dissolution of the old 'national policy' companies by the Occupation Authority and the denationalisation of steel and electricity generation, the extent to which industrial ownership is concentrated in the state has declined. The ratio of direct government expenditure to the national income is now comparatively small; it was about 19 per cent in 1958, excluding transfer payments.

Yet it would be wrong to conclude that the part of the government in economic development has become unimportant. Through a number of new state banks, notably the Japan Development Bank, the government has encouraged investment in certain key branches of industry, such as steel and electricity generation, and the Central Bank's loan policy has exerted a major influence on the development of the economy as a whole. Further, with the rehabilitation of the *Zaibatsu*, the government has again found to its hand instruments through which its policies can be contrived and executed. Since 1955 these policies have been expressed as 'plans' worked out by government officials, ministers and representatives of great industry. In these plans estimates have been made of production and of resource-allocation both for the economy as a whole and for its various constituents. The estimates are supposed to act as a guide to those responsible for determining the production and investment policies in both the public and the private sectors. Plans and planning are now fashionable, but it is debatable whether they have contributed a great deal to Japan's progress. Indeed, some critics consider that, by encouraging excessive investment, the plans helped to produce the crisis of 1961. But it would be quite consistent to hold that planning has fostered growth, even if one concedes that it has at times accentuated the instability of the economy.

Most students are agreed that the *Zaibatsu* contributed 'strength, efficiency and sureness of purpose' to Japan in the course of her development, and that their dissolution by the Occupation Authority destroyed the main centres of economic initiative in Japan. Since 1952 the leading *Zaibatsu* (Mitsui, Mitsubishi and Sumitomo) have re-established themselves. They have, however, changed in form. They are less closely knit; they are no longer controlled by central holding companies owned by members of the *Zaibatsu* families. But the formal change is of little significance. For many years past real authority rested with salaried officers, and each of the groups is now focused on the bank which has always played a key role in its operations. It has been noted that the various *Zaibatsu* are now inclined to associate with one another in establishing new, joint enterprises, but this may be regarded simply as a revival of their prewar practice of combining to capitalise and manage 'national policy' companies set up by the government. Undoubtedly some very large enterprises have appeared outside these privileged circles; a few of them emerged from the empires of the lesser *Zaibatsu* which have not been reconstructed. Yet, despite these changes, it remains true that control in the modern sector of the economy is still highly concentrated, that the close links between industry, trade and finance (which gave the *Zaibatsu* their distinctive character) have been reforged, and that the formulation and execution of economic policy depend on the close association of the government and large business concerns. Without doubt, the efficiency of economic administration at the centre, in recent years as in past times, has been a major factor in Japan's growth.

Among the most prominent features of the prewar banking system were, first, the integration of commercial banking and industrial enterprise, and secondly, the presence of 'special' or semi-official banks which were used as instruments of government policy both in Japan itself and in her overseas territories. The efforts of the Occupation Authority to destroy this system had no enduring effect. In place of the old 'special' banks, the government instituted a number of state-owned banks with functions in the spheres of home investment and foreign trade, and the revival of the *Zaibatsu*, as we have seen, renewed the links between particular industrial concerns and particular banks. As before the war, personal savings have gone for the most part into postal savings accounts, where they have helped to finance government-fostered ventures, or into fixed deposit accounts in the commercial banks which have thus been supplied with funds for investment in related industrial undertakings. In these respects, the identity between the prewar and the postwar situation, at any rate since the middle 1950s, has been very close. In other respects, however, there have been fundamental changes which have affected the mechanism of growth. Before the war the money market was undeveloped and the Bank of Japan could exercise little control over the credit policies of the commercial banks which were then very numerous. During the 1930s one of the Bank's chief functions was to absorb the increasing quantities of government bonds issued to finance the huge budgetary deficits of the time and to pass on as high a proportion of these issues as it could to the commercial banks. It was in this way that reflation was engineered after the world depression.

After the war the situation was transformed. At first both the banks and industry were short of liquid capital. Personal savings were exiguous and industrial self-financing, once a leading factor in growth, could satisfy only a small part of the needs. At the outset a special government financial agency advanced the loans for reconstruction. Later this function was taken over partly by the new official investment banks (such as the Japan Development Bank) and partly by the Bank of Japan which provided the commercial banks with the funds required. Even after the revival of industry, firms remained far more dependent than previously on bank loans. Despite the rise in personal savings which went to swell the resources of the commercial banks, the latter were unable to provide the credit necessary to sustain a high rate of growth without borrowing heavily from the Central Bank. What is known as the 'overloan' position had its origin in this process.

So (to compare postwar with prewar conditions), in the assets of the Bank of Japan loans to the commercial banks have replaced government securities (which are, indeed, scarce because of the postwar fiscal policy). Whereas the Bank of Japan formerly had only slender links with the commercial banks, it is now heavily committed. This new relationship has greatly strengthened the control of the central monetary authorities over the credit supply. By restricting its loans to the commercial banks, the Bank of Japan can quickly enforce a contraction throughout the economy, and it can readily persuade the banks to follow credit policies of its choosing. Its power has been ruthlessly displayed on several occasions when Japan's external imbalance has required her to scale down her costs and prices and to curtail investment. On these occasions equilibrium has been quickly restored. The execution of this policy has become all the easier because of the consolidation of the banking system. Today, a dozen large city banks and their branches conduct the bulk of the business; in prewar days there were some hundreds of independent banks.

It is reasonable to conclude, then, that the postwar changes in Japan's banking system have not merely assisted in mobilizing the country's resources for industrial investment but that they have introduced a fairly effective system of credit control. The result is that the authorities have been able to take risks in regard to the pace of development since they could count on being able to check any overexpansion without delay. This in itself can certainly be regarded as an important factor in fostering rapid secular growth. Obviously, however, the effectiveness of this monetary policy has depended upon the capital structure of Japanese industrial firms. Moreover, such a policy could not win its success quickly unless costs and prices were extremely sensitive to deflationary pressure. This sensitivity is not, of course, new. It is a function of the structure of the economy as a whole and of certain relations and practices pecular to it, notably the wage system. Here we approach the heart of the problem of Japanese expansion.

A dichotomy between the large-scale sector and the small-scale sector of the economy has been evident since the early years of the present century, and until very recently it was tending to become sharper. In the former sector the equipment is modern and productivity high. In the latter conditions vary widely, but in general productivity is relatively low. In the very small establishments wages are, on an average, only about half those in the large factories. These contrasts are to be found not merely in textiles and the consumption goods trades but also in many branches of engineering and distribution. In the small-scale sector highly competitive conditions prevail both in the product market and in the labour market, and prices and wages respond readily to any change in economic fortune. During the postwar period, as during the 1930s, costs and prices in this sector fell steeply whenever deflationary pressure was exerted; hence the resilience for which the Japanese economy has been distinguished. As long as the overpopulated countryside could provide a stream of recruits for industry, these conditions were likely to persist.

Even the large-scale sector was (and is) susceptible, though to a smaller extent, to the same forces. The large employers and their employees have been well aware of the pressures exerted by the abundant labour supply, while the system of industrial relations has assisted in preserving the same resilience. In every factory a sharp distinction is drawn between the established workers, towards whom the employer recognises onerous obligations, and the temporary workers who enjoy little security, are seldom members of trade unions and can be laid off at once in case of a recession. The wage system itself is peculiar. There is seldom a standard rate for a job. The typical worker's monthly earnings are made up of a wide variety of payments that have only a slender relationship to his job, and in addition his annual earnings are linked to the firm's prosperity by the payment of biannual bonuses, which may be very small in bad years and equivalent to from two to six months' wages if the firm's profits are high. This wage system has survived the growth of a powerful trade union movement since the American Occupation. Thus wages and costs even in large establishments are flexible. Moreover, the 'lifetime employment system' and the practice of relating wages to age and seniority have the effect of discriminating in favour of expanding firms and industries since (in comparison with the less progressive) a higher proportion of their workers are young.

These conditions in the labour market lie at the root of Japanese progress. At the same time there has been an abundance of labour to meet the rapidly rising demand from the factories, without provoking a steep increase in wages. And it has not been raw labour. Most Japanese villages have for many years occupied themselves with industrial by-employments, and small and medium workshops are scattered far and wide. In these circumstances it is not surprising that while industrial productivity rose by 55 per cent between 1955 and 1960, real wages rose by only 25 per cent. Here is one of the main reasons for the massive industrial investment during recent years—gross investment has lately amounted to over 30 per cent of the gross national expenditure—without which

Japan's rapid progress would have been impossible. Furthermore, the fact that wages are flexible means that costs can be easily adjusted downwards if disequilibrium should appear. It is noteworthy that each of the brief recessions which Japan experienced during the 1950s, by removing inefficiencies and reducing costs in other ways, prepared the economy for a further leap forward.

In considering both the provision of new capital and the avoidance of inflation, one must also have regard to the high propensity to save among townsfolk and peasants alike. This propensity, rooted in traditions of austerity and frugality, was a source of strength in the past. In the postwar period the postal savings accounts and the fixed deposits in the commercial banks have grown vastly with the rise in Japanese personal incomes.[2] According to the United Nations Economic Survey for 1960, the ratio of personal savings to total domestic production has been far higher in Japan than in any other country.

The reports of the recent Census of Population give additional support to the arguments set out above. It is well known that after the Second World War the Japanese birthrate fell steeply and that it is now no higher than that of most Western European countries. The consequence is that the largest increases in population during the last decade have occurred in the active age groups. Between 1955 and 1960 the gainfully occupied population grew by 11·3 per cent (or 4·4 millions) compared with 4·6 per cent in the total population. At the same time, employment in agriculture and forestry, which in the late 1940s was larger than for many decades, has been rapidly falling. In 1955–61 the decline amounted to 2·6 million. This is an indication of the vast reserves of labour on which Japan has been able to draw; in that period employment in secondary industry increased by 2·9 million and in tertiary industry by 3·1 million.[3]

It is reasonable to conclude that during the last decade Japan has been favoured by a convergence of factors congenial to industrial growth. Her traditional sources of strength for the most part lent their aid—for example purposeful leadership and efficient organisation, a corps of well-trained managers and technicians, an ample supply of high-quality labour, a high rate of investment and of saving, both institutional and personal, and a very flexible economic system. Her chief weaknesses in this period were to be found in her lagging foreign trade and her technical backwardness. The first of these has been mitigated partly by resourcefulness in economising imports and partly through the flow of American 'special procurement' expenditure. Her technical deficiencies she has overcome by importing foreign 'knowhow' through the medium of her great business houses whose prestige has made possible the necessary arrangements with overseas firms. At the same time her admirable system of technical education has provided conditions for the successful assimilation of the 'knowhow'.

The question now arises: will these favourable conditions persist? Will Japan in fact succeed in doubling her national income by 1970, as her latest plan proposes? Will she be able to maintain the high rate of investment upon which this advance will in part depend without inflation and trouble with her balance of payments? And if that trouble does appear, will she be able to deal with it as promptly as during the last decade?

Japan has played the game of 'Confound the Prophet' too often to encourage one to make confident predictions. It is tempting to suggest, however, that some of the favourable influences may operate less powerfully in the future. For instance, the labour reserves hitherto available from agriculture are now drying up, and the first symptoms of tightness in the labour market have shown themselves in the narrowing of the wage-disparities between large and small firms. If the flow of recruits to industry seriously diminished, this might be accompanied by a decline in the proportion of temporary to established workers and by an increase in trade union bargaining power. The flexibility of wages and costs might then diminish and thus the rate of development at which it would be safe to aim without the risk of inflation.

There is also the question of the *nature* of future investment. During the last decade a high proportion of the new capital was directed into manufacturing industry and power generation. Investment in certain forms of social overhead capital (such as housing, roads) was modest, and Japan is backward in these respects. The plan for 1961–70 looks forward to heavy investment of that type. In the long run such investment is, of course, as necessary to economic development as to social wellbeing, but it is not likely to yield its returns so quickly as the kind of investment on which the Japanese concentrated during the 1950s. Finally, to turn to foreign trade, 'special procurement' expenditure has diminished, and although Japan proposes to economise still further in imports, it is doubtful whether this will be compatible with growing production, rising standards of life and the more liberal trading arrangements to which the government is committed. The necessity for effecting a large increase in the export trade may, therefore, become more pressing than in the last decade, and such an increase may not be easy to achieve so long as Japanese goods are discriminated against in foreign markets.

Yet an optimistic outlook is justified, for there is much to be put on the other side. There are still large labour reserves in the small-scale manufactures and trades that are available for transference to high-productivity occupations, and it will probably be a long time before the dichotomy between the two sectors of the economy in respect of wages and efficiency disappears. On the side of capital, it can be said that accumulation becomes easier as incomes rise, and that Japan is now attracting funds from overseas both for long-term investment in industry and also for bridging her current account difficulties. By reason of her social stability and her commercial enterprise, she should offer considerable attractions to foreign investors. Her technique is no longer backward, as it was in 1950, and her range of high-quality products has greatly widened. It would not be rash to predict that by 1970 there will be very few markets in which Japanese industry has no share and very few highly finished manufactured goods of which it is not a leading producer.

POSTSCRIPT

It does not become an economist to call attention to the rare occasions when his predictions are fulfilled. But, at the expense of modesty, it may be useful to compare the forecasts in the last paragraph with actual achievements. An indication of the extent of Japan's economic progress between 1961 and 1971 is given in the figures set out in Table 10 at the end of Chapter 9, but something more should be said. Industrial production was certainly not hampered, as some had feared in the early 1960s, by any shortage of manpower. Adequate supplies of labour were found to maintain, and even to increase, the rate of industrial expansion, although the main factor in the continued success was the rise in productivity. This rise was chiefly dependent upon heavy investment in new technology. Contrary to the expectations of the early 1960s, the increase in the *proportion* of total investment directed into the infrastructure and the public sector did not take place, and an even larger share of the new capital than before was embodied in new equipment for manufacturing industry. For the economy as a whole the annual average investment during the decade amounted to nearly 34 per cent of GNP.

The major industries in which Japan by 1961 had already become a leading producer (notably steel, ships and electronic goods) continued to grow rapidly and, in addition, by 1970–71 she had achieved eminence as a manufacturer of a wide range of other metal and engineering goods, including motor cars. During the decade industrial production rose threefold, and in 1971 GNP (in real terms) was well over two-and-a-half times that of 1961. As for the prediction about Japan's commercial progress, during the 1960s her exports increased at twice the rate of international trade as a whole, and their volume in 1971 was about five times that of ten years earlier. A much higher proportion of them consisted of the products of the high-technology, capital-intensive industries; textiles and other traditional exports declined in relative importance. Japan's accomplishments in production and trade raised her credit in foreign money and capital markets, and by the late 1960s she had become attractive to foreign investors, within the limits allowed by her government. Her balance of payments no longer gave her monetary authorities cause for anxiety; indeed, after 1968 her large and growing surplus on current account, and especially her very favourable trade balance, began to provoke criticism from among her trading partners. Although as time went on they exerted increasing diplomatic pressure on her to dismantle her import restrictions, liberalisation failed to redress the imbalance in her international accounts. Foreign countries continued to discriminate against Japanese goods, but this discrimination was not sufficiently serious, as the author had thought likely, to arrest the country's advance in world markets.

8 The Problems of Economic Growth [1]

In its planning forecasts the official body now called the Economic Planning Agency has consistently underestimated Japan's rate of economic growth. (The disparities between forecasts and achievements have been set out in Chapter 6 above.) Conscious of their past errors, the forecasters have cautiously raised their sights, and in the plan for 1967–71 they have estimated the annual average rate of growth (in real terms) at 8·1 per cent. If this rate is achieved, by 1971 Japan will have the national gross product which she would have reached if there had been no Second World War and if the prewar average rate of growth of 4·5 per cent had been maintained. Some economists seem to attach significance to this statistical accident, and think that the rate of growth will fall back sharply after 1971. But it is difficult to justify their implied assumption that there exists some 'natural' rate of growth which Japan is destined to achieve in the absence of catastrophes. An attempt to estimate what would have happened to the economy if there had been no Second World War is about as useful as speculation about the fate of Europe if Napoleon had won the Battle of Waterloo!

There are many Japanese who hold that, in its latest prediction, the Economic Planning Agency has again been too cautious. They can see no reason why Japan during the next five years should not maintain the 10 per cent annual rate of growth which she enjoyed between 1955 and 1965, and they are not convinced by the arguments of the planners to the contrary. They point out that the shortage of labour, a subject of active discussion since the early 1960s, has so far had less serious consequences than was once expected. It has certainly not prevented a very high rate of growth. These objectors to the Economic Planning Agency's forecasts also dismiss the possibility that Japan's future international competitive position will be damaged by a cost inflation.

The difference between a 10 per cent and an 8 per cent rate of growth (which is what is in dispute) hardly seems worth worrying about to British observers for whose own economy a 4 per cent rate of growth is at present an unattainable ideal. But it rests on an important divergence of view between those who believe that the Japanese economy has now entered upon a new phase of its development, and those who hold that the economy will continue to function much as before and who deny that structural changes are likely to slow down growth.

An appraisal of these opposite viewpoints requires us to examine the outstanding movements in the Japanese economy during the last few years and in the forces that have driven it forward. During the 1950s, indeed up to and including the great boom of 1960–61, the forward surge in production was associated mainly with heavy investment in manufacturing industry (including power production) and with the introduction of advanced technology made possible by the investment. Since the boom of 1960–61, which led to overinvestment and surplus capacity in many industries, an important contribution to growth has been made by exports and more lately by increased government expenditure. For instance, the recovery from the recession of 1964–65 was brought about largely by a steep rise in exports (26·6 per cent between 1964 and 1965 and 15·7 per cent between 1965 and 1966) and by heavy investment in public works and utilities financed partly by the government. However, private industrial investment, which has been growing comparatively slowly in recent years, is now taking another leap forward.

In the plan for the next quinquennium 1967–71 the balance has turned against private investment in manufacturing equipment and towards public investment in social overhead capital. The new plan is significantly called the economic and social plan and not simply the economic plan like all its predecessors.

In providing for the increased public investment last year the government for the first time for nearly two decades incurred a budgetary deficit, and it is preparing for another budgetary deficit in the current fiscal year. But whereas the deficit for 1966 was thought of primarily as a means of compensating for the fall in private investment and so of hauling Japan out of the recession, this year it is the direct result of decisions to increase public expenditure on overhead capital and amenities which the policy-makers now consider essential. Thus the targets have changed. In the 1950s Japan concentrated her efforts on re-establishing and developing her manufacturing industries and she neglected many parts of her infrastructure. The plan for 1961–70 pointed to the need for correcting the balance. Now this need is being urged more decisively and has been accepted by the government.

In absolute terms, social overhead investment in the next five years is expected to be more than double that of 1961–65 (at 1965 prices). Transport (roads, railways, harbours) and telephonic communications will claim a large share of this investment, as in the early 1960s, but the greatest increase will take place in housing, sanitation and provision for social welfare, areas where Japan is still backward compared with other industrial nations. The new programme accords with Japan's general postwar policy of addressing herself to particular sectors of the economy in turn, a policy which has certainly led to success so far, even if it has meant that the Japanese citizen has had to wait for certain amenities that are commonplace in the West while enjoying Western standards of provision for a wide range of consumer durable goods.[2]

The proposals officially accepted are the 'indicative plans' of a government which, though capable of influencing the direction of investment and growth, cannot determine it, for Japan still has a market economy. In fact the proposed new emphasis in Japanese investment is attuned to the needs of the private industrial sector. Higher investment in the infrastructure is no longer to be regarded simply as an alternative to further industrial investment but rather as a condition of future industrial growth. For instance, improvements in transport and communications will lead to economies in working capital because they will enable firms to reduce the heavy stocks which they normally carry. Better housing and the relief of urban congestion are probably necessary simply to maintain efficiency as well as for promoting social welfare.

In the new plan one can observe not only a shift in objectives, but also a shift in the views of the leaders about the main problems that lie ahead. In the past the major anxieties turned on the balance of payments. In the early and middle 1950s, when the export trade was weak and when the maintenance of a balance in the current account depended heavily on the 'special procurement' expenditure of the United States, such anxieties were very acute. Even during the next decade this problem remained at the heart of Japanese policy. It was found that every leap forward in production had to be cut short because it led to deficits in the balance of payments. Japan's reserves in relation to her short-term liabilities were such that drastic restrictive measures had then to be taken by the monetary authorities to restore equilibrium. This action was indeed the chief cause of the recession of 1964–65.

Japan's progress has thus been characterised by 'stop and go', although, unlike Britain, in the 'go' periods she has advanced very fast while the 'stop' periods have been short. It seems probable that up to the present time a policy that allowed or even fostered these oscillations in activity was more conducive to a rapid secular advance than a policy aimed at securing a steady rate of growth. But the consequential recurrent threat to the balance of payments was a frequent source of anxiety to the monetary authorities.

It would be an exaggeration to say that these anxieties have now completely disappeared or that Japan will never again encounter those wide fluctuations in activity so familiar throughout her economic development. Indeed, in the summer of 1967 the deterioration in the balance of payments that accompanied industrial recovery obliged the monetary authorities to introduce mildly restrictive measures. But the balance of payments has certainly ceased to be the chief long-term preoccupation of the economic planners and policy-makers. For this there are good reasons. As already shown, growth in recent years has been to some extent export-led, and the rise in exports is by no means mainly attributable to fortuitous factors, such as the Vietnam war.[3] Japan's exports for some years have been expanding at a rate more than twice as fast as world trade, and the stability in her export costs and prices, compared with those of other countries, suggests that her relative strength is still increasing. So, even if the growth of world trade should slow down, Japan is unlikely to be the chief sufferer.

It is true that her large deficit on invisible account is increasing and that a change in the composition of the import trade—the shift from raw materials to foodstuffs, fuel and manufactured goods—has lessened the responsiveness of imports to restrictive measures imposed by the monetary authorities to correct deficits in the balance of payments. Moreover, the loosening of quantitative controls over imports under the liberalisation policy, if carried further, may also blunt the government's still powerful instrument of trade regulation. On the other side, however, one can point to Japan's increasing financial strength, as shown by the magnitude of her gold and dollar reserves, by her transference from the position of a capital-importing to that of a (net) capital-exporting country, and by her improved credit in foreign money markets which now enables her to borrow readily to correct any temporary disequilibrium. In other words, the long-term basis of her international position is strong, and for dealing with temporary disequilibria she is now well-equipped. Although structural changes in the economy mean that costs and prices are becoming less responsive to restrictive monetary policies than formerly, the development of the money market may enable the Central Bank to exert more continuous control over the creation of credit than in the past. For instance, with the increase in the supply of government bonds[4] the possibilities of open market operations by the Bank of Japan have been enlarged. Fiscal policy will probably play a more important part than hitherto in the control of demand, and in fact the government is now trying to moderate the current growth in its expenditure in order to reinforce the deflationary measures recently taken by the monetary authorities. It is quite likely that the country is moving towards a condition in which the policy of 'boom and bust', hitherto consistent with a high secular rate of economic growth, will give place to one that aims at a steadier, if slower, rate. It would, however, be premature to conclude that this condition has been reached.

Much turns on the structural changes to which reference has already been made. Those who believe that Japan has entered on a new phase in her development are influenced chiefly by the disappearance of the labour surplus which previously characterised the economy. The chief symptoms of the change are the narrowing of the wage gap that formerly existed between large and small firms and the rise in the price of services and of labour-intensive goods.[5] The new conditions in the labour market have increased the bargaining power of trade unions, and there are indications that wage increases are pressing hard on increases in industrial productivity, a fact that has helped to disturb the long-continued stability of the wholesale price index.[6] The chief causes of the change in the labour market are the large increase in the demand for labour that has accompanied industrial growth and the reduction in the former reserves of labour in rural areas. The movements in the size of the population of working age are a contributory cause. In the late 1950s the rate of increase declined because the low birthrate during the war was then exerting its effect. This was followed by an increase in the annual increment to the working population, an increase which reached its maximum in 1965. A decline has now set in, and it is expected that by 1970 the annual increase in the population of working age will have fallen to under half that of the middle 1950s. The labour-participation ratio is likely to decline because young people will stay longer at school.[7]

The extent of the changes must not, however, be exaggerated. The foreign observer can be easily misled by the fears of Japanese economists who, when they speak of a labour shortage, have in mind comparisons with the conditions that have previously prevailed in Japan and not comparisons with other industrial countries. Judged by European standards, Japan's labour reserves are still large and the annual increment to the working population, 1,200,000 in 1966 falling to 600,000 in 1970, is considerable. Moreover, as we shall argue below, labour is being extravagantly used in the service industries; and in small-scale manufacturing and even in agriculture there are still ample opportunities of economising labour. Thus, while in the years ahead the supply of labour available for transference from low-productivity to high-productivity occupations will be less lavish than in the past, it should be sufficient to sustain what Western countries would regard as a very high rate of growth. The chief contrast with the past lies in the fact that in future the provision of greatly increased supplies of labour for modern industry may be conditional upon far-reaching modifications in institutions and social conventions. This is a point which will be discussed subsequently in this paper.

Considerations such as these lie behind the change of emphasis in Japan's economic planning. In the new plan three related policies are given priority, (1) price stabilisation, (2) the promotion of industrial efficiency, and (3) social development. These we will now consider in turn. Until recently, wholesale prices have been very stable, but consumer prices since 1960 have increased steeply, by about 6 per cent a year. When this rise first became evident, many economists were inclined to argue that it gave no reason for disquiet. The rise was attributable largely to increases in the price of services, rent and food, and it was plausible to argue that these increases were symptoms of Japan's approach to economic maturity. Formerly services and all labour-intensive goods had been very cheap because of the existence of a surplus of labour which could not find well-paid alternative employments. The disappearance of this surplus was simply the result of industrial progress and was certainly not to be deplored. Those who held this view comforted themselves by pointing out that Japan's competitive power was not being affected by the rise in consumer prices as this had not communicated itself to export prices.

Today this complacent view is less widely held. It has been realised that different kinds of prices are related to one another, and the recent upward movement of wholesale prices has underlined this fact. Further, the contention that services were becoming more expensive because the tertiary trades were being starved of labour seems at first sight to be inconsistent with the fact that those trades have recently been absorbing a growing share of the recruits to the labour market. One can, of course, argue that as the Japanese become richer their demand for services will increase disproportionately and that this must raise their prices. But the problem cannot be dismissed so lightly. The Japanese habits of consumption were formed when services were cheap, and it has not been found easy to modify these habits to meet the new circumstances. In other words, services are now being used extravagantly. Until habits of consumption have become adapted to the new level of service-prices, consumers will complain of increasing hardships.

No doubt this is a passing phase, for social customs, however deeply rooted, yield ultimately to economic necessity. Already some of the retail food trades, which are very labour-intensive, are being transformed by innovations in packaging. For example, *tofu* (bean-curd), traditionally made by small vendors at night for sale early the next morning, is now being produced by large manufacturers who pack the *tofu* so that it remains fresh for a considerable time and sell it through the supermarkets. A similar change is affecting the production and supply of *udon* (a kind of macaroni). On the other hand, men's hairdressers, who have been accustomed to provide every customer with an elaborate service, strongly resist efforts at simplification and, despite their customers' complaints, merely raise their charges. The result is that Japan has twice as many hairdressers as the United States in proportion to the size of the population. Again, the newer forms of retail distribution, such as supermarkets and chain stores, seem to have advanced much more slowly than was expected a few years ago. This is attributable to the preservation of traditional shopping habits, the existence of a large number of elderly people among the small shopkeepers who continue to run their businesses even if their incomes fall, and restrictive official policies.

The problem of the service trades, though serious enough for the ordinary householder, will be solved as time goes on mainly by changes in consumption habits and the introduction of modern forms of organisation. That problem will be shortlived. But some part of the rise in the cost of living can be attributed to increases in the price of the basic foodstuffs. Since this is for the most part the direct result of government decisions, it seems that a complete solution to the problem of consumer prices must depend on a fundamental change of policy in regard to agriculture and food imports. Such a change, however, raises political and social questions of a most delicate kind, and some of these deserve detailed examination.

During the last decade agriculture in many of its aspects has been transformed. It has lost about 4·5 millions from its labour force and the proportion of agricultural workers to the total occupied manpower has fallen from nearly 40 per cent to 23 per cent. Despite the diminution in the number of workers, agriculture has succeeded in raising output very substantially by resort to mechanisation and other labour-saving devices. By now, however, it is approaching a crisis. Far from providing a ready source of recruits to other sectors of the economy it is short of labour itself. There is little likelihood that this shortage will be overcome, and productivity further increased, without a drastic reorganisation of the whole industry. So far, however, little has been attempted in that direction. Despite the steep fall in the numbers engaged on the land, the number of separate holdings, or agricultural households, has declined very slowly. Japan still remains for the most part a country of tiny peasant farms laid out in scattered strips, where the economies of large-scale farming cannot possibly be realised. It is generally agreed by economists that if agriculture is to raise its efficiency further and to cease its still extravagant use of labour and capital, holdings must be concentrated into large units. The argument is sometimes heard that the early postwar land reform law, which was designed to strengthen the class of peasant proprietor, raised a barrier in the way of consolidation by limiting the right of the peasant to sell his land. However, the rules regarding sales are now liberally administered, and the chief obstacle to the introduction of larger-scale agriculture seems to be the reluctance of the farmers to sell an asset which, they observe, is constantly rising in price. The possession of land is highly regarded for the security that it confers on the owner in a country which has not yet advanced very far towards being a welfare state. This security is valued not only by the elderly men and women who now make up a high proportion of the full-time labour force, but also by their children who have found full-time or part-time work outside agriculture but who look on the parental holding as a refuge from the uncertainties of urban life.

The maintenance of the existing agricultural structure, in the face of rising costs and the competition of other industries for land and labour, has been possible only because of agricultural protection, subsidies and price-support. The main crop is still rice, and the price annually fixed by the government for this commodity determines to a large extent the size of the farmers' incomes. Every year the price is hotly debated between the government and the representatives of the farmers. The trend has been steadily upward. After the most recent discussions the government has agreed again to a substantial increase in prices, although, of course, this increase still leaves the farmers dissatisfied. The price of Japanese rice is now more than twice the world price. (By 1978 it was five times the world price).

The question is: how far is the government prepared to go in buttressing the existing agricultural structure? It is clear that the cost of doing so will continue to rise steeply, for the farmer expects to share in the country's mounting prosperity and labour will not stay on the land unless it can earn an income which reflects the productivity of the economy as a whole. Despite the increase in agricultural output which the financial support has made possible, Japan's dependence on food imports has been intensified during the present decade, and such imports now account for 17 to 18 per cent of total imports compared with 12 per cent in 1960. This trend is likely to continue, for home agriculture cannot hope to meet the rapidly growing demand. This applies not only to grain but also to meat, dairy products and vegetables which are being consumed in increasing quantities by the urban population. During the postwar period there has been a considerable extension of livestock farming which has been based in part on the import of feeding stuffs. But there are now signs that this expansion is nearing its limit mainly because of the lack of grazing land.

It is arguable that the future growth of industry and trade will depend to some degree on the government's being ready actively to foster fundamental changes in agriculture. The economy of resources obviously requires that a smaller, large-scale commercial agriculture should be substituted for small-scale peasant agriculture—at any rate for the staple products—and also that Japan should accept a much greater dependence than hitherto on food imports. Such a policy would require the government to spend heavily on the consolidation of farms instead of on supporting the existing organisation. By this means the government would help to counter the rise in consumer prices and also to mitigate the labour shortage.

This policy, however, raises some very awkward social and political problems. The strength of the farmers' vote is something that no political party can ignore, and the introduction of what appears to many as the rational economic solution would provoke a strong reaction among the millions of small peasants which might well affect the fortunes of the dominant political party. Even more serious matters are at stake. Rural Japan still remains the rock on which the social order rests.

For a considerable section of the Japanese people, even those engaged in industrial pursuits, the family farm is a haven of security to which they can return if bad times should come. The agricultural life is still regarded as the repository of old values and virtues in a time of social disintegration. It offers some barrier against the wave of urban squalor that threatens to engulf much of this beautiful land.

The present agricultural structure will certainly be transformed when the present generation of elderly farmers has passed away, and in twenty years' time the farming population is likely to fall to 8 or 9 per cent of the working population. Would it not be prudent, some ask, to allow the slow transformation of the size and shape of Japan's agriculture to proceed, even at the cost of increasing subsidies and of some retardation of industrial development, rather than to expose the rural community to the pressures of a free market? On the other hand, the urban population is loud in its complaint of the rise in consumer prices to which the constant increase in the price of food contributes. If the farmers are to be heavily protected, will it be possible to moderate the annual rise of consumer prices from the present 6 per cent to 3·2 per cent over the next five years, as the planners hope? The Japanese leaders have seldom lacked tact and adroitness in handling complex social situations, and it may be that in this case they will succeed in avoiding a violent confrontation of the opposing interests. But a successful compromise which allays social and political discontent and at the same time serves Japan's ambitions for further economic growth will not be easy to reach.

The agricultural problem is the most extreme instance of the problem of the small-scale sector of the economy as a whole. In industry the 'dual economy', the coexistence of a large-scale, high-productivity sector and a small-scale, low-productivity sector, has been frequently described both by foreign and by Japanese observers. But the small-scale industrial sector differs from agriculture in that it is largely exposed to market forces. In recent years, under their impact, it has been modifying its role in the economy. Some small firms have found themselves well-fitted for providing the speciality goods which the more affluent country requires. Others, by mechanisation and specialisation, have raised their productivity and have survived, sometimes as subcontractors to the great firms, sometimes by means of co-operative arrangement with other small firms. Those unable to make these adjustments have gone out of business under the pressure of rising costs. It would be an exaggeration to say that the 'dual economy' is now in its final stages. But the dichotomy becomes less evident year by year, and the government through various financial institutions actively assists firms in this sector of the economy to re-equip themselves so that they can meet the new conditions. In this way some of the social stresses caused by market pressures are alleviated.

Since Japanese progress towards a higher gross national product must depend mainly, in the years to come, on increases in productivity rather than on increases in labour supply, the improvement in the efficiency of the small-scale sector or, as an alternative, the transference of its resources to the large-scale sector, will be of the highest importance. Moreover, success in stabilising prices can only be achieved if those sectors of industry in which productivity is now relatively low are modernised.

Let us now turn to the planners' proposals for large-scale industry. For this sector the main issue during the next five years is not so much that of extending the range of output or the import of fresh techniques, but rather rationalisation. Japan's industry now covers the whole field of modern production. She ranks third among industrial countries and her output of manufactures is exceeded only by that of the United States and Russia. She is easily first in shipbuilding, second in chemicals and motor-cars, and third in metals and machinery. She considers that she ranks as the equal, or even the superior, of European countries in technology, and she is now bracing herself for rivalry with the United States. She seeks to do this partly by increasing investment in scientific research and development, and in education, and partly by a reorganisation of her industry. The recent steps towards the liberalisation of foreign trade, which may expose certain of the industries to foreign competition in the home market, has strengthened the need for reorganisation for the twin purposes of reducing costs and of increasing the market power of producers *vis-à-vis* their foreign rivals. Hitherto Japan's modern industry, though oligopolistic in structure, has been the scene of fierce rivalry among the dominant groups for shares in the market for every new product that has been introduced. This competition has led not only to periodical overinvestment in certain industries but also to a lack of specialisation among plants and a failure to secure the full economies of scale. Now, with American industry as the chief prospective rival, the Japanese authorities are trying to persuade their own manufacturers to concentrate production on plants of optimum size. Consolidation in the motor industry and in some others has already occurred, but elsewhere (as in the steel industry) the major firms are offering a stubborn resistance to the efforts of the government. In the end, their opposition is likely to be overcome, for the government possesses powerful weapons of persuasion because of its control over the credit resources of the official investment banks. In pressing forward this policy, it encounters a familiar dilemma. How can industries achieve the maximum economies of scale and establish forms of organisation which enable them to confront their foreign rivals, without destroying the vigorously competitive conditions which have hitherto contributed much towards Japan's industrial advance? The Fair Trade Commission, an inheritance from the period of the American Occupation, is being confronted with some awkward problems.

It might have been thought that since Japan now regards the United States as its most formidable economic rival, she would have welcomed American participation in her industries. American technique is, of course, received unreservedly when it is made available by royalty agreements or by means of joint ventures which leave the Japanese in unqualified control of the operations. But both government and industry are strongly opposed to the intrusion of American management or financial control, and it is this that explains their reluctance to liberalise foreign investment in Japan. In the general view, American control would be too high a price to pay for more rapid technological progress, for it would be offensive to the spirit of Japanese nationalism and might disrupt the country's unique system of social and industrial relationships. Official apologists for Japan's attitude assert that, since the capital structure of Japanese companies is very highly geared, takeovers by foreign firms could be easily accomplished in the absence of official regulation. Despite pressure from her trading partners, Japan will not easily yield on this point.

The third problem to which the planners have addressed themselves is that of urban congestion and rising urban land values. Since the Second World War an exceptionally high proportion of industrial development has taken place in the narrow belt that runs from the Tokyo plain in the east to Osaka–Kobe in the west. Indeed, in some of the Prefectures remote from this centre the population has actually declined. In all the great urban areas land prices have risen very steeply, by ten times in Tokyo in the last decade. Rents have soared and housing standards have lagged far behind industrial progress. For the ordinary metropolitan wage and salary earner the journey to work has become more fatiguing than in most other countries.

Under the new plan it is proposed that 7·3 million houses shall be built during the quinquennium; of these, 3 million are to be financed or built by the government and the rest by private enterprise with help from the government in the provision of sites. Up to the present, however, it cannot be said that any real attempt has been made to grapple with the problem of land prices. A policy of fixing prices by law has been rejected as futile. Instead, the policy-makers favour the programming of land use, the redevelopment of cities, improvements in transport and the dispersal of populations from the most congested centres. This policy would require the government to provide very large sums for acquiring land needed for new housing developments. So far no great progress has been made except perhaps in regard to improvements in urban road and rail transport.

These problems are closely related to the government's location of industry policy. This has been aimed at reversing the trend of industry and population towards Tokyo and other great cities by establishing points of growth in the less developed areas.[8] Little has been done in practice. Industrialists have been sceptical about the whole scheme, and the execution of the policy has been handicapped by the unwillingness of the government to provide adequate finance and by quarrels among the politicians over the choice of localities for development. Yet the need to solve these problems of urban congestion, housing and land prices is even more urgent in Japan than elsewhere because of the exceptionally rapid industrial growth of the last two decades.

It is reasonable to conclude that the most difficult problems that will face Japan in the next decade lie outside the sector of manufacturing industry and trade. It is in that sector that she has won her main successes since the war, and the forces responsible for her industrial progress do not yet appear to have spent their strength. She is still pressing forward with ingenious technical innovations. She is still saving and investing an exceptionally high proportion of her national income. Although she is now being called on to play a more positive role than hitherto in international affairs, she will not easily be persuaded to divert substantial resources to military and strategic purposes. Her industrial leadership remains as alert and resourceful as ever. The 'purge' of those in control of affairs at the end of the war brought youth to the helm at a critical moment, and it may well be that her progress in the 1950s owes much to that fact. As yet there is no sign that the energies and ambitions of her industrialists are flagging, and until her income per head approaches that of the United States (a distant goal to which the Japanese confidently look forward) she sees no reason for the slackening of effort. Those in control of the great companies are indeed concerning themselves more actively than in the past, not only with the training of their staff in modern techniques but also with the question of morale. Thus, some firms seek to relieve the tensions created by prolonged application to business affairs by sending their young executives to Zen monasteries for a period of spiritual refreshment. It is true that the condition of the labour market is less favourable to rapid growth than it was in the 1950s, but here the difficulties can easily be exaggerated.

Whether the surge forward will long continue is likely to depend on the timely solution of the social problems associated with industrial progress. It would be calamitous if the social cohesion and discipline on which the leaders have so far been able to rely were destroyed by the confusions of modern urban life. That the government is aware of these emergent issues is shown by its plans for increased social investment. These, however, follow a fairly conventional path. The strain is likely to come when further economic growth calls for fundamental institutional and structural changes. This problem in connection with agriculture and food supply has already been discussed at some length. Manufacturing industry may also be faced with novel issues not only in its administration and organisation but also in its labour relations. The present practice of settling wages and working conditions by negotiations between each company and a union composed solely of that company's employees proved to be admirably fitted to the conditions of the postwar period. At the same time, the 'lifetime engagement' system and the seniority wage system helped to strengthen the workers' loyalty to the firm. Demarcation troubles have been avoided and unrestricted labour mobility within the firm has been made possible.

In recent years, however, many employers have been seeking to introduce modern systems of wage-payment in the interests of efficiency, while the extreme shortage of young workers, which has raised their relative bargaining power, has threatened the seniority wage system. Structural changes in industry and the arrival of automation may progressively increase the need for labour mobility *between* industries and create difficulties for the 'lifetime engagement' system. Meanwhile, the leaders of the workers' organisations are pressing for wage-bargaining on a nationwide or industry-wide scale.

These processes are in their initial stages and so far they have proceeded smoothly. But as they and other changes in social and economic relations are carried further, they may well give rise to strains within society and new problems for government. This outcome is probably inevitable for other reasons also. The wholehearted pursuit of industrial growth, which served the nation well in the 1950s, can no longer be expected to satisfy the complex purposes and ambitions of Japan as she approaches economic maturity.

9 Social Institutions and Economic Purpose[1]

Japan's economic achievements during the last twenty-five years (1948–73) cannot be fully understood if attention is concentrated on the events of that period. It is for this reason that I have thought it necessary, in a paper concerned primarily with Japan's recent material progress, to extend my scrutiny to the historical background. This paper is directed to an analysis of the *economic* factors and such a limitation is convenient because of the difficulty of covering the subject 'in the round' within a reasonable compass. But I am aware that an explanation that looks to economic factors alone is likely to be incomplete. I must, therefore, state at the outset that, important as these factors obviously have been—they include the supply of national resources, human and material, their organisation and direction, the distribution of responsibilities and authority, capital accumulation and allocation, the management of demand and the functioning of markets—they cannot be dissociated from the country's social institutions and political purposes.

Soon after my first visit to Japan, some fifty years ago, I noted Alfred Marshall's brief but penetrating analysis of Japan's achievements and promise:

> . . . the singular power of self-abnegation, which the Japanese combine with high enterprise, may enable them to attain great ends by shorter and simpler routes than those which are pursued where many superfluous comforts and luxuries have long been regarded as conventionally necessary. Their quick rise to power supports the suggestion, made by the history of past times, that some touch of idealism, religious, patriotic or artistic, can generally be detected at the root of any great outburst of practical energy.[2]

Marshall was fully aware of the extent to which outstanding economic accomplishments rest upon 'non-economic' factors.[3]

Having said that, I should like to put forward another general proposition. It is that great economic achievements can scarcely ever be explained by one or a few causes. They are usually the result of the convergence, sometimes fortuitous, of numerous favourable influences. With hindsight one can often identify them. But it is seldom that one can predict the result for, even if one is aware of their presence, it is impossible to say whether, or when, the convergence will take place. In this respect, the experience of a nation resembles that of a firm. Resources and energies are frequently invested for years in a line of business with only mediocre results. Then, in a way that surprises even those in command of the firm's affairs, a number of favourable factors converge to lift the firm to some outstanding success. A certain capability has been created; a turn of fortune brings the opportunity for its profitable exploitation. There is much in Japan's history that justifies this analogy. Good fortune as well as good management has made a conspicuous contribution to progress at several critical points in the country's economic experience. I shall give examples below.

Nations, like individuals, achieve those things upon which they are ready to concentrate their energies. They fail when they are uncertain in their aims, when they diffuse their energies and when they allow themselves to be distracted from what is ostensibly their main purpose. In my view, a fundamental cause of Japan's economic success since the Second World War is the concentration of her energies on a single purpose, economic recovery and expansion, which was calculated to enable her to draw level with the most advanced nations of the world in commercial and technical achievement. This was a choice forced upon her by defeat. Imperialist ambitions could not have been resumed, even if the people had had any stomach for them. She was in no shape to model her policy on those of the emerging welfare states. Economic growth was the only rational choice. Elsewhere, I have tried to point the contrast between Japan's singleness of purpose and the ambiguities of British policy which paid merely lip-service to economic efficiency.[4]

This contrast may be illustrated by the different attitudes of

Japan and Britain towards investment and technical innovation. The difference is revealed not only in Japan's higher ratio of gross investment to GNP, but in the use made of her resources. Britain wasted much capital in bolstering up decaying industries or in investment in 'prestige technology'. As has been observed by a critic of her policy, she showed a tendency 'to back technological horses before they were really fit to run'.[5] Japan, more sensibly, allowed others to spend lavishly on research and development, and then bought the 'knowhow' when it had been proved useful. In her circumstances, this was rational economic conduct. One question which has not received much attention from economists is how far Britain's poor economic performance can be ascribed to the diversion of huge resources, including some of the most valuable scientific expertise, to defence. Among the causes of Japan's success I place high the fact that she was precluded from spending more than a very small proportion (about 1 per cent) of her national income on the armed forces and munitions. In the UK, in the period 1961–71, defence expenditure averaged $6\frac{1}{2}$ per cent of GNP.

Concentration on economic growth was, of course, a postwar phenomenon. From the beginning of the Meiji era[6] down to 1945 economic development was widely regarded as a handmaid to political power. Throughout the greater part of her modern history defence expenditure absorbed a large share of the total budget. Furthermore, the development of the Japanese Empire and of 'spheres of influence' in East Asia required heavy investment of a strategic kind. This was to a large extent at the expense of investment in the domestic economy. Even if we consider that much of the expenditure was unavoidable, because of threats to Japan's security or to her markets and sources of supply (such was the contention of many Japanese before the war), the fact remains that it represented a diversion of resources from economic growth. What has been achieved since the war is some measure of what can be done if there are no competing purposes.

From these general considerations let me examine some of the factors that had a direct influence on Japan's development from the beginning of the modern period. The importance of a country's 'initial position' at the time when it first enters upon a course of growth is commonly recognised, and historians have stressed the significance for Japan of the pre-Restoration changes in her economy.[7] In several respects Japan had been following a path which made her ready for the new era and receptive of influences from outside. I need refer only briefly to some of these changes. First, there were the agricultural developments of the previous Tokugawa era which led to a rise in productivity. In preindustrial societies, in which agriculture must be relied on to provide the investment resources needed for a widening of the scope of production, such a rise is a condition for generalised economic growth. The surplus of income which these improvements made available was thus essential to the subsequent 'takeoff'. I do not propose to engage in the controversy about whether agricultural production increased steeply during the early decades of Meiji, or whether there was merely a continuance of an upward trend that had begun earlier. What is almost equally important is the distributional aspect of agricultural incomes in the years that followed the post-Restoration settlement, a settlement that involved the abolition of feudal dues paid by the holder of land and their replacement by a land tax paid to the state. The fact that much of the increase in the net revenue from agriculture accrued to the landlords meant that the surplus formerly used for the maintenance of the *samurai* became available for investment both in land improvements and in new industrial activities. This was certainly a factor in growth. It demonstrates the difficulty of treating economic influences in isolation from social and political changes.

Another example of Japan's preparation for the new era is provided by the spread of industrial by-employments among the peasants, for this not only furnished them with new sources of income but also accustomed them to working for wages and to production for a market. At the same time, commercial and entrepreneurial aptitudes were fostered among an increasing population of local merchants, the pivot of the 'putting out' system according to which the new forms of production were organised. At another level the great merchant families, with their sophisticated financial techniques and nationwide operations, provided a foundation for large-scale enterprise in banking, commerce and industry. I should also mention the fairly extensive education system, which prepared men's minds for new communications.

On the productive side, therefore, Japan was quite well prepared for her new career, although this was not apparent to contemporary observers. In most sectors of the economy she was open to admit influences from outside and this receptivity, brought about by the economic changes of past years, was actively fostered by the central authorities, intent upon modernising their country's institutions in the interest of national survival. It must be rare in history for a political revolution to bring into power an *élite* which was fundamentally conservative in its social and political attitudes and yet eager for economic and technical change. What is probably even more unusual was the coincidence of enthusiasm for innovation in production and conservatism in consumption. Professor Firth, writing of the peasants of South-East Asia, has called attention to the fact that, while they were conservative in techniques of production, they had shown themselves enterprising in consumption, anxious to sample novel products from overseas. 'The result' he concludes, 'is that at many points, without realising it, the peasant has become geared to the Western economic system.'[8] Similarly, Sir George Sansom argued that for Asian peoples as a whole 'objects of trade, which are silent but convincing, have had more influence upon their lives than Western ideas'.[9] Japan presents an obvious contrast. The people were eager to adopt, or to adapt, Western methods of production, but their consumption remained peculiar to themselves. We must not make too much of this. The Japanese have always been interested in new things. But until recent times their habits of consumption, their houses, furnishings, food and articles of everyday use bore the imprint of tradition hardened by the former isolation of their society.

The economic consequences of this peculiarity struck me when I first lived in Japan fifty years ago. At that time we in Britain were already troubled by heavy unemployment brought about by depression in our staple industries, most of which were of the 'unsheltered' kind. It seemed to me that Japan's peculiar standard of living had created a condition in which a substantial part of the productive system was safeguarded against the competition of imports and that the existence of this large 'sheltered' sector was especially significant in periods of general depression. Nowadays we emphasise a different aspect of this insulation of part of the domestic economy. As

Professor Rosovsky has pointed out, Japan's resistance to the influence of foreign consumption patterns, or to what are called 'the demonstration effects' of foreign contacts, meant that, in times of rapid expansion, increases in consumer demand were satisfied to a large extent from domestic sources.[10] The consequence was that the demand for imports in such periods rose more slowly than would have been the case if Japan's consumption had been cosmopolitan in character. This was of benefit to her balance of payments. In effect, it meant that expansion could be pushed forward more rapidly than would otherwise have been possible, without producing external payments deficits which would have brought the expansion to an early end. I suppose that the strong preference of the Japanese for home-grown rice, and the fact that most of the consumption of this cereal was satisfied by domestic (or colonial) producers, provide the most obvious instance of this general characteristic. Of course, the advantage for growth was won at the expense of the immediate standard of consumption, a sacrifice of present benefits for future advantages or, as List put it, of 'values in exchange' for 'productive powers'.

Rosovsky also points out that it was not only consumption goods that were affected. The rise in incomes was not attended by marked increases in the demand for higher standards of housing or more elaborate furnishings. And, since the building industry belonged to the labour-intensive sector, the provision of housing for the rapidly growing population resulted in a comparatively modest demand on Japan's exiguous capital resources.[11] One must not overstress the importance of a traditional consumption pattern as a factor in growth, but it ought not to be ignored. The inelasticity of imports in the face of changes in income has persisted down to our time, although the factors responsible are more diverse than in the past. Since the war the most potent of them has consisted of stringent import controls, which made the expansionist policy easier to maintain without danger to the balance of payments. These controls have, however, become less rigorous in recent years, when the balance of payments has ceased to give rise to anxiety.

When one looks back on Japan's advance during the Meiji and Taisho eras,[12] one is tempted to conclude that her progress was guided by a consistent plan. This is how it appeared to Bertrand Russell when he came to record his impressions in the light of his brief residence in the Far East. 'Modern Japan,' he wrote, 'is almost exactly what it was intended to be by the men who made the revolution of 1867.'[13] But the notion of Japan as a planned economy cannot be justified. It is true that certain broad objectives of national policy were pursued, analogous to those that can be detected in the history of most other countries. In the last quarter of the nineteenth century the ending of the 'unequal treaties' was an ambition that lay behind many acts of policy. But, even at the time when the government was most clearly taking the lead in building up the new economy, the motives that inspired particular acts were diverse and were often directed, not by any long-term aim, but by the need to solve immediate and urgent problems. I need not give examples, for the story is well known. Nevertheless, a survey of events and policies leaves an impression of exceptional farsightedness and sound judgement on the part of the leaders.

Of none is this truer than of Count (later Prince) Matsukata, the architect of the financial system which served Japan well up to the Second World War. He realised the vital importance of a satisfactory financial structure to the encouragement of adequate investment in the new economy and for fostering foreign trade. Hence his establishment of the various investment banks, the Yokohama Specie Bank (founded in 1880), and the Treasury Deposits Bureau (set up originally in 1877) through which the savings of the people were channelled into investment via the debentures of the official banks. The technical accomplishment of Matsukata in finance was matched by his good sense as shown in the conduct of economic affairs in general. He came into office at a time when, in the then esteemed West, private competitive enterprise was regarded as the norm and state intervention was viewed with deep suspicion. Matsukata, as a reading of his reports shows, was willing to accept those fashions in ideas and practices as statements of general principles of economic management, and was impressed by the success of their application in the West.[14] But he remained sceptical of the wisdom of applying them, without modification, to the Japan of his day. This reluctance to mould policy according to a set of general principles derived from different types of social experience, this empiricism in the face of persuasive examples from the most advanced nations of the world, is itself evidence of the high quality of the leadership. On the other hand, the spirit of emulation has played an active part in making the Japanese what they are. They themselves realise that their determination to show that they are at least as good as any other people has been a sharp spur to effort. They have a joke to the effect that when their GNP per head has drawn level with that of the United States their progress will come to a halt; with no one ahead of them, there will be no inducement to go further!

I now consider a policy which Japan has consistently practised throughout the modern era and which, in my view, has made a weighty contribution to her rapid economic growth. I am encouraged in my belief in the importance of this policy by the support given to my views by the eminent scholar, Professor Shinohara.[15] Broadly speaking, my contention is that Japan has not been much concerned about 'allocative efficiency' in running the economy, that is to say, with the maximisation of welfare in the short period. This is not to deny that her allocative efficiency has been high; but she has achieved it as a byproduct of her efforts to promote rapid growth. As I have said, this has been an almost exclusive ambition since the war. To attain this objective she has pursued a resolutely expansionist policy, characterised by the maintenance of a high level of demand induced by heavy investment. Since the war something like a virtuous circle has existed; strong demand has brought rising production and incomes, which have helped to finance high investment, which in turn has led to still higher production and incomes.

Until recently, adherence to such a policy inevitably produced strains on the balance of payments. J. Inouye, the famous Minister of Finance, was acutely conscious of this danger and called attention to the persistent import surplus from which Japan suffered in the early years of this century.[16] At that time, the condition was the result of heavy expenditure on armaments and on large colonial investment. But troubles of this kind were not allowed to get out of hand, for the authorities seldom hesitated to apply ruthless checks on demand and investment when the deficits became menacing. These alternations of periods of rapid growth and short but sharp recessions have been identified by a number of economists,[17] and I need not discuss them here. The point I want to make, however, is that Japan's growth throughout her modern history has not taken the form of a steady advance, or 'stable growth' as it is called. It has been attended by violent fluctuations, and in this respect it does not differ greatly from Britain's experience in the nineteenth century. Nowadays, recessions have generally been regarded as impediments to growth and in most countries it has been a leading aim of policy to avoid them. In Japan, on the other hand, they have had a therapeutic effect, inasmuch as they have usually brought about a quick restoration of equilibrium by eliminating high-cost producers and establishing a sound basis for the next advance.

The problem has been examined by Professor Bronfenbrenner in a recent article.[18] He does not consider proved the proposition that Japan's 'growth path' has been one of 'disequilibrium', but he is inclined to support it. As he rightly implies, those who believe that growth has been mainly 'market oriented' will not like this conclusion, for such a 'growth path' requires frequent intervention by the central authorities. In Japan's case, in recent times, this intervention has been effected not only by the close, if subtle, relationship between industry and the officials of the Ministry of International Trade and Industry, but also by the monetary authorities. The dependence of industry for financing capital extensions on the commercial banks and their reliance, in turn, on the Bank of Japan for resources to provide this accommodation have given the central monetary authorities a most powerful influence over the investment policy of firms and, indirectly, over their costs and prices. To a considerable extent, these authorities have been able to stimulate or to limit industrial expansion in accordance with the needs of the economy as a whole, and at the same time to exert strong pressure on the cost-price structure. They have generally been able to achieve a quick effect.

The contention that rapid and substantial growth can be achieved in a modern economy only if the authorities actively pursue the policy of maintaining a high level of effective demand is widely accepted. This policy is believed necessary not only for the purpose of achieving full employment, but also because, unless the pressure of demand is strong, it is impossible to reap the full rewards of increasing returns, such as those accruing from a rise in the scale of production and the adoption of labour-saving techniques. Yet, this analysis of the process of growth is incomplete as an explanation of Japan's success. One reason why her recessions have exercised a therapeutic effect is to be found in the flexibility of her costs. This, in turn, can be explained by the highly competitive character of the economy, especially the large, small-scale part of it, and also, in recent times, by the system of wage payment (for instance, the payment of variable biannual bonuses) which means that annual earnings are geared to the changing fortunes of firms. The mobility of resources is another factor of importance in this connection. Until recently, mobility was a function of the vastly excessive agricultural labour supply. In the past, it owed something to the organisation of the labour market (for instance, the method of recruitment of female labour for the textile mills) and the practice of establishing new productive units in close proximity to the local labour supply in what for many years was the largest industry (raw silk). In modern times, mobility has been promoted by the system of industrial relations, which facilitates the transfer of workers from job to job within a firm and so avoids demarcation disputes and resistance to innovation, such as have hampered progress in Britain.

The assertion that the Japanese economy has been highly competitive does not accord with the view of Japan as a country where the state exerts great influence over the economy and where economic power is concentrated. In fact, keen competition is not confined to the small firms. The old *Zaibatsu* are what we now call 'conglomerates' rather than monopolists and compete with one another vigorously in many lines of business. Since the war the rivalry among the great concerns has become fiercer through the appearance of new groups which include some of the most dynamic undertakings in the country. Among the old *Zaibatsu* themselves, the 'purges' of the former leaders immediately after the war had a salutary effect, since they put enterprising young men in the seats of authority. (It is tempting to speculate on the improvement in Britain's economic performance during the last thirty years that might have resulted from 'purges' of men in command of affairs similar to those that occurred in Japan, France and Germany.)

The keenness of competition in Japanese industry is shown by the ineffectiveness of cartels and price-fixing bodies. The different fortunes of the British and Japanese steel industries, for example, are not wholly unconnected with the contrasts between their price policies. Flexible pricing has favoured rapid structural changes in response to altered markets, for a readiness to discard old industries and to turn to new ventures is necessary to keep up a high pace of economic growth. The government, except in its policy for agriculture, has been faithful to this principle. It has not gone out of its way to bolster up decaying industries, nor has it wasted resources on prestige products. It has sensibly bought its advanced aircraft after others have poured out their treasure in developing them.

Most students of Japan's economy agree that it has been well managed, but we must not forget the part played by luck at critical stages in her history. Even disasters to other people have turned out to be of advantage to Japan. The outbreak of the First World War probably saved her from a crisis in her balance of payments. The Korean war set her on the road to industrial recovery after the disasters of the Second World War. The value of the American 'special procurement' expenditure during the years before Japan's exports had revived can hardly be overestimated, for without it she could not have financed the imports necessary for reconstruction.[19] Sometimes, policies adopted with one purpose in mind brought unexpected benefits. For example, the deflationary policy of the late 1920s, introduced in order to make possible the return to the gold standard in 1930, was, on the face of it, as ill-advised as Britain's return to gold in 1925. But the ultimate results were in many respects salutary. The accompanying recession, painful as it was at the time, had a remarkable effect in stimulating technical and economic efficiency during the next few years and so in preparing Japan for the great structural changes of the 1930s. Unfortunately, the benefits were lost, in part at any rate, by the diversion of resources to armaments.

Luck was with Japan from the outset of her modern career. Consider the circumstances in which her great silk export trade began: the demand for silkworm eggs to replace the disease-ridden stock of the European silk industries. The demand for eggs opened the way to the export of raw silk itself. Right up to 1929 Japan depended heavily on the foreign exchange earned from this trade. If foreign market conditions had been less favourable, her progress would have been jeopardised, for she had no other major export for many decades. On the other hand, Japan succeeded because she seized the opportunities offered to her. It was largely her skill in organisation which enabled her to oust China from her position as the world's chief supplier of silk. Here was a small-scale, labour-intensive industry, conducted in numerous peasant households and small filatures, and highly decentralised. Yet, the authorities realised the necessity for imposing control over quality at a few key points in the interests of filament uniformity, and the great financial and merchant houses came in to assure the smooth flow of products from the local filatures to the export markets.

It is plausible to argue that Japan's social system has proved to be an efficient instrument for economic growth, at any rate in recent times. Not everyone accepts this proposition. The author of an excellent study of the *Zaibatsu*, while appreciative of Japan's achievements, cannot free herself, like many Westerners, from the assumption that American institutions and socio-economic ideals are the norm to which all mankind should pay obeisance.[20] It is evident from her criticisms that she deplores that postwar Japan has not emerged as the kind of individualistic democracy that conforms to the ideal of an American society laid up in Heaven. Of course, these are value judgements which it is not very fruitful to debate. Yet, from the point of view of economic growth, there are reasons for supposing that Japan's traditional social arrangements, modified as they have been by contact with the West, especially during the American occupation, are well attuned to the requirements of a rapidly developing modern economy. At any rate, it does not seem to me that we can challenge the Japanese way of doing things until we have become more completely satisfied than we are at present with our own institutions and economic arrangements. There is no telling what the future has in store and it is foolish to expect present trends to continue indefinitely. But, so far, Japan seems to have succeeded reasonably well in the difficult task of reconciling great technical and economic changes with social stability.

I conclude by suggesting that the expansionist economy, which I have already discussed, is not simply the product of the successful application of the technical devices of economic management. It has derived its nourishment from the nation's social and political institutions and the attitudes they foster. This point is well exemplified by the words of one of the most forceful of Japan's postwar industrial innovators. When S.

Honda was beginning to build up his company, he was criticised for what appeared to be his recklessness in pushing ahead

TABLE 10 *(Statistical)*

	1961–71 *Average annual rate of increase* %
Gross national product	+10·1
Manufacturing	
Output per man-hour	+10·3
Hourly earnings	+13·8
Earnings per unit of output	+3·1
Exports: volume	+9·2
Imports: volume	+2·9
Capital investment: % of GNP	33·7 (average 1961–71)

Production	1961	1971
Steel (million tons)	27·8	87·2
Cement (million tons)	24·2	58·4
Synthetic yarn (thousand tons)	119·3	512·5
Cotton yarn	560·9	525·5
Electricity (million kWh)	132,036	385,608
Motor cars (thousands)	250	3,715
TVs (thousands)	4,584	12,192
Ships launched (thousand gross tons)	1,799	11,993

Employment (1971)	m	%
agriculture	*8·1*	*15·9*
industry	*18.4*	*36·0*
services	*24·6*	*48·1*
	51·1	*100·0*

with expansion. To this charge he replied: 'Even if my business becomes bankrupt because I expand my plant too fast, the plant itself will remain to be of use for the development of Japanese industry. So I will take the risk.'

10 Education, Science and Economic Development [1]

The subject of this chapter is the change that took place in Japanese education and in the Japanese attitude to science, technology and professional or vocational training in the period just before the Restoration of 1868 and during the early years of the Meiji era (1868–1912). The relation of this change to the economic development of the country during the last quarter of the nineteenth century and the first decades of the present century will be considered in the course of the discussion.

I must begin by stressing that Japan in 1868 was better prepared for her new career, by reason of her attitude to education and her provision for it (as well as in other ways) than was once supposed in the West. Among the ruling classes there was a reverence for learning that had deep roots. In the eighth century an Imperial University was in existence, with departments of ethics, history, jurisprudence and mathematics, and scholars pursued their studies even during the long and turbulent feudal period that ended with the establishment of the Tokugawa Shogunate at the beginning of the seventeenth century. The Tokugawas themselves tried to foster learning, and by the middle of the nineteenth century, when their day was almost over, formal education of some kind was widespread. It is as difficult to estimate the numbers who attended schools and colleges as it is to judge their quality. But Professor Dore and others seem to agree that by the middle of the nineteenth century some 40 or 50 per cent of the boys and from 10 to 15 per cent of the girls were receiving some kind of formal education. [2]

The education differed profoundly according to orders and ranks in society. The *Shogun* had set up schools in Yedo (Tokyo) for training officials for the fiefs directly administered by him. The feudal lords (*daimyo*) had founded schools for the education of the sons of their retainers (*samurai*). There was a special boarding school in Yedo for the scholarly study of Chinese classics and philosophy. Finally, for the masses there were village schools (*terakoya*—literally 'temple schools') originally established by the Buddhist monks and later by well-to-do peasants and merchants.[3] The subjects studied by those of *samurai* rank were mainly the Chinese classics, Confucian ethics, calligraphy, military arts and etiquette. The purpose of this training was not vocational or utilitarian, but rather character-building. The aim was that of fitting pupils to practise the Confucian moral code as interpreted by a martial society. The education received by the masses was simply in reading, writing and arithmetic, including the use of the abacus. Towards the end of the Tokugawa period, when feudal society was disintegrating, the divisions became blurred. The sons of rich peasants and merchants were getting above themselves and were beginning to study subjects properly reserved for their betters. Some of the *terakoya* became so well thought of as to attract the sons of *samurai*. Moreover, the minds of men were coming under an influence that owed nothing to Chinese learning or to Japan's own educational traditions—this was *Rangaku*—Dutch learning.

Although the *Shogun* had forbidden intercourse with foreigners, except, to a limited extent, with the Dutch in their settlement at Deshima,[4] derogations were allowed to Satsuma, the clan in the south-west part of Kyushu, and individual *samurai* from other parts of Japan had found their way to Deshima in the later eighteenth century. There they studied the Dutch language and found out what they could about Western conditions and Western knowledge. Unlike the Chinese, who were complacent about their moral and intellectual superiority, the Japanese had always been outward-looking and welcomed new knowledge and ideas (before these were proscribed for political reasons). Sir George Sansom refers to them as 'a friendly people, given to hospitality, disposed to good manners and extremely curious to learn new things'.[5] Here he echoes the words of St Francis Xavier and the Portuguese missionaries of the sixteenth century. The branch of Western knowledge for which the Japanese first displayed an interest was medical science. Doctors enjoyed a high status in old Japan and the medical properties of plants had been studied in a botanical garden cultivated for that purpose since the seventeenth century. One of the first Dutch books to be translated into Japanese was the *Tafel Anatomia* in 1777. As the translation revealed disparities between Western and Chinese descriptions of human anatomy, the Japanese, no despisers of experiment, dealt with the problem by dissecting the bodies of executed criminals and found the Western description correct. The curious went on to study other sciences, learning Dutch in order to do so. Textbooks on physics and chemistry were published in the 1830s and 1840s. Western military science interested the clan governments, and schools where the Dutch language was taught were established privately.

Even the *Shogun* was worried by what he heard of the technical accomplishments of Western nations, as well as by the attempts by foreigners to breach Japan's seclusion. So, in 1811, he himself provided for the translation of Dutch books, and in the 1850s, as the lessons of the Opium War began to have a persuasive influence on his policy, he actually set up in Yedo a bureau for the study of barbarian books. By the time of Perry's arrival (1853–54), a considerable number of *samurai* were addressing themselves to Western studies and, after they realised that English rather than Dutch was the most important medium of international communication, they turned to that language. The bombardment of Kagoshima by British warships (1862) and the helplessness of the Japanese authorities before that assault may have helped to persuade them to change the direction of their linguistic interests. Some of them tried to introduce Western techniques simply by the study of textbooks; for instance, it was by such methods that the 'six wise men of Saga' succeeded at length in building a reverberatory furnace. Other local governments, with more sagacity, imported Western machines and engaged Western technicians to operate them and to train Japanese in their use.

Up to the Restoration (1868) most of the initiative in these changes came from individuals, or clan governments, rather than the central government which remained a reluctant host to the new learning. The pioneers had to fight hard to overcome long-entrenched conventions and institutions before their views prevailed. They had convinced themselves, not of the moral worth of Europeans ('a dirty, mannerless and clumsy race, with little self-control'), but simply of Europe's technical superiority. They had no doubt that education must be given a practical, materialistic bent, and that Japan must adopt the Western scientific method in her approach to the problems of the new era, even though it was repellent to men trained in the ways of Confucius. Carmen Blacker has made clear to us the gulf that had to be crossed before men trained in the Chinese classics could be brought to accept the scientific attitude to nature. Few Chinese were able to take that step until very recent times. To look on nature as something to be studied, as if it were a dead thing, was impious as well as a waste of time.[6] What the superior man had to strive for was to reach a harmony with nature, a harmony that was beyond the grasp of sordid experiment.[7] The Japanese for their part were similarly constrained. Yet many members of the intellectual *élite* seemed ready to spurn the old learning and to give an enthusiastic welcome to the new. This contrast with the Chinese reception may perhaps be attributed to the foreign origin of Japan's culture. This had been imported from China and grafted on to her native traditions, which, indeed, had at times been invoked by men in revolt against the weight of Chinese precedent. There was, of course, conflict between the old and the new, but in the end the two were welded, one ministering to the moral fibre of the nation and the other to its practical capacity. Some have regretted the survival of the influence of the past; others have hailed the combination as a prescription for success.

A more difficult obstacle in my opinion was that of overcoming the prejudices of the *samurai* against participating in commercial and industrial activities. Fukuzawa Yukichi, the renowned educational pioneer, has left on record the resentment of his father, a *samurai*, whose inclination was towards scholarly pursuits, because he was forced by his poverty to argue with merchants about rates of interest and prices and to engage in business transactions in his lord's service. It is difficult to believe that the *samurai* would have changed so quickly their attitude to education and business affairs in the absence of two conditions, first, the crumbling of the status of their order as the system established by the Tokugawa moved towards collapse, and, second, the threat to Japan's security presented by the incursions of the technically superior Westerners. The exigencies of national need left the patriotic Japanese with no choice but to respond to the appeals of leaders who saw clearly the path that Japan must tread.

The outstanding educational pioneer was Fukuzawa Yukichi. Early in life, and with his father's experience to warn him,
he became convinced that Japan must abandon her traditional
education and must turn her attention to the useful arts and sciences. The watchword was utility. Only by acquiring new techniques and skill could Japan hope to match the West in
practical accomplishment, compel the abrogation of the 'unequal treaties', and confront the barbarians on their own terms.
Fukuzawa himself, with help from his clan, set up schools for
the study, at first of Dutch, and then of English and other lan-
guages. The chief purpose was to obtain access to Western
knowledge, especially in science and technology. He was an effective propagandist. One of his books *Gakumon no Susume* ('Inducements to Study') sold three-and-a-quarter million copies
in the 1870s, and some ten million copies of his published works
were sold before the end of the century. His publications included books on chemistry, physics, economics, politics and,
notably, a description of conditions in Western countries entitled *Seiyo Jijo*. The school he founded at Tokyo in 1858 developed into the most famous of the private universities, Keio.
Fukuzawa also tried to simplify the Japanese language so as to
make it a more suitable instrument of communication for the
new life. Among the terms her introduced was *Jitsukyoka*, 'a
man who undertakes a real job of work', as a preferred alternative to *Chonin*, a merchant who merely ministered to the
needs of the feudal lords.

In his teaching he stressed the importance of independence,
and urged his pupils to strike out for themselves instead of
depending on government office. They should not defer to
officials and stand in awe of them. He took England as a
model. The books that influenced him and his disciples included Mill's *Representative Government* and *Principles of Political
Economy*, Smile's *Self-help*, Spencer's *Social Statics* and Buckle's
History. Fukuzawa's opinion of the old learning was summed
up in a typical passage:

The only purpose of education is to show that Man was
created by Heaven to gain the knowledge required for the
satisfaction of his needs for food, shelter and clothing, and
for living harmoniously with his fellows. To be able to read
difficult old books or to compose poetry is all very nice and

pleasant but it is not really worth the praise given to great scholars of Chinese and Japanese in the past. How many Chinese scholars have been good at managing their domestic affairs? How many clever men have been good at poetry? No wonder that a wise parent, a shopkeeper or a farmer, is alarmed when his son displays a taste for study . . . What is really wanted is learning that is close to the needs of a man's daily life . . . A man who can recite the Chronicles but does not know the price of food, a man who has penetrated deeply into the classics and history but cannot carry out a simple business transaction—such people are nothing but rice-consuming dictionaries, of no use to their country but only a hindrance to its economy.[8]

Yet, despite this fervour for utilitarian education, Fukuzawa held fast to the virtues of Old Japan. He would, indeed, have failed to persuade his students to follow him (for at the beginning they were nearly all *samurai*) if he had not appealed to qualities they understood, duty, loyalty, self-abnegation. He, and they, approached the goal of material prosperity through the practice of traditional virtues. He urged his students to seek their careers in business, and Keio University became the source of recruits for the great houses, the *Zaibatsu*. One of the most eminent of these, Mitsubishi, was said to be founded on Iwasaki's money and Fukuzawa's men. But there was resistance to his ideas. What he had to struggle against is shown by the experience of another pioneer, Shibusawa. When *he* tried to recruit graduates of the Imperial University for the Tokyo Gas Company, he was rebuffed—such occupations were for common men, not for the sons of *samurai*. As a footnote to Fukuzawa's career and influence, one must record that he did not escape the common fate of successful revolutionaries. At Keio, the university he founded, his memory is revered like that of a god. In universities and colleges in general teachers are referred to by the honorific term '*sensei*'. At Keio this appellation is reserved for Fukuzawa alone!

The pioneering work of individuals preceded the establishment of a national system of education in 1872.[9] Based on Western models, it was obedient to the principles which Fukuzawa and other reformers had advocated, although it retained the Confucian insistence on moral training. The preamble to the Act which called the new system into being asserted that learning was the key to success in life, and that henceforth there should be no village with an ignorant household and no household with an ignorant member. It was the first duty of a family to subordinate all things to the education of its children. Besides aiming at equipping the people for the new era, the national system served other purposes. For one thing, it provided jobs for the now functionless *samurai* who, if they had remained unemployed, might have been a disruptive political force. Fortunately, teaching was a highly respected profession in Japan, and *samurai* could take it up without loss of dignity. The nationwide character of the system also helped to overcome the particularism of the feudal era and the distinctions of status inherent in it. This unifying influence may be contrasted with the divisive tendency of the French educational reforms introduced about the same time. When the Third Republic instituted a system of education *gratuite, laïque et obligatoire*, it split the nation into two, for it was regarded by a large section of the population as a means of destroying the people's religion. In Japan there was no established church or powerful religious institution capable of opposing or influencing the state's educational policy. The contrast with Britain was equally striking. The Education Act of 1870 was not intended to provide for common, universal primary education. The schools which it called into existence were not 'all class' schools like the national primary schools of Japan or the common schools of the United States. The pupils for whom they were designed were the children of the working class, and they alone. The significance of this limitation did not elude the understanding of such perspicacious critics of British society as Matthew Arnold.[10]

The national system was intended to be comprehensive. The first aim was to establish universal and compulsory elementary education on a nationwide scale. This goal was not reached for many years, but by the first decade of the present century, when fees had been abolished, it was estimated that 98 per cent of boys and girls of school age were covered. At the beginning, the period of education was only four years; it was extended in 1908 to six years and later became eight years. In addition to the state's primary schools, middle schools were set up which normally took pupils from twelve to seventeen years of age. Above them there were normal schools, high schools (with a two or three years' course), and at the summit five imperial universities. Besides the institutions for general education or training for what *we* call the 'professions', technical and vocational education was provided by an array of schools and colleges at various levels. As early as 1871 the Department of Public Works set up a technical school for training engineers and staffed it with Europeans; in 1886 this became the College of Engineering in the Tokyo Imperial University. In 1874 the Ministry of Finance founded a school for training bank officials, and in the twenty years of its existence it turned out 600 graduates. Japan remained until the First World War predominantly an agricultural country, and from an early date the government exerted itself to improve agricultural techniques. Between 1874 and 1877 several agricultural and forestry schools were established; some of these later on became colleges of agriculture in the various imperial universities. There was a particularly striking development in commercial education, which entitles Japan to be regarded as one of the pioneers in this field. In 1875 Viscount Mori, then Minister of Education, in cooperation with Shibusawa Eiichi, who played a distinguished part in Japan's industrial and commercial modernisation, founded a business school. This was, at the outset, a private institution, but was later taken over by the government. In 1920 it became the University of Commerce (*Shodai*) and it is now well known as Hitotsubashi University, a leading centre for economics and business studies. In the early years of the new century several new higher commercial colleges (*Koto Shogyo Gakko*) were established on the model of the German *Handelshochschulen*. In the 1920s there were eleven of them, each with 500 to 600 students. About the same time as the first business schools were founded, several higher technical colleges (*Koto Kogyo Gakko*) came into being, modelled on the German *Technischehochschulen*; there was always a strong demand for *their* graduates. Provision was also made for technical training at a lower level, for instance, in technical schools of middle grade and technical continuation schools. By 1920 there were 12,000 of the latter type, with 800,000 students. They provided ten hours teaching a week for a course of two years.[11]

The new system took several decades to complete. As shown above, elementary education did not become universal until the 1900s. Further, it has been pointed out by historians that, while the new institutions for higher education (and especially for higher scientific and technical education) were impressive, the number of their graduates for many years remained small.[12] Compared with what was being done at the same time in Germany, France and Switzerland the achievement in advanced technical training was modest, as judged by the number of highly qualified experts produced during the last quarter of the nineteenth century. Yet such provision as was made fulfilled Japan's needs at the different stages in her development. In the 1870s and 1880s, and indeed much later, small-scale agriculture was her main business, and her industrial development until the late 1890s was conspicuous only in textiles and raw silk. The first large-scale, steam-driven cotton-spinning mill did not begin production until 1882.[13] There was no modern steel works until 1901. The building of oceangoing steamers remained inconsiderable until after the Sino-Japanese War (1894–95). Apart from munitions factories, the engineering industry made little progress until the period just before the First World War. Of the total occupied population, some 70 per cent were engaged in farming and fishing until the end of the century, and in 1900 the number of 'factory' workers was only 420,000, mainly textile operatives.[14] Japan's task in the early and middle years of Meiji was that of creating the infrastructure of a modern state, increasing agricultural productivity, improving the efficiency of the traditional industries by technical innovation, and building up an export trade so that she could import the capital instruments required for her new career.

The assimilation of Western knowledge necessary for achieving these aims did not call at once for large numbers of learned scientists and technologists. Japan needed a small *élite* well qualified in technology and administration, fairly large numbers of skilled technicians trained in the new methods of production, and also a body of men versed in Western trading methods and financial operations. As the range of her industries extended, the skeleton of her educational system could be, and was, clothed, and the number of experts under training increased. By 1934 there were about 3500 engineering students in the imperial universities (by then, eight), about 7500 in the *Koto Kogyo Gakko* (*Technischehochschulen*), and some thousands of such students in the private universities.[15] At that time there were also some 18,000 students of economics and business studies in the universities and the *Koto Shogyo Gakko* (*Handelshochschulen*), apart from an even larger number in private institutions of various grades.

The schools and colleges were not the only source of state-sponsored training for industry and commerce. In the first years of Meiji the government set up a number of factories equipped with Western machines and staffed with Western technicians and managers. In these factories many Japanese who were later to initiate and staff the undertakings of later years were trained. The future officers and crews of Japan's mercantile marine learnt their business in the same way from Europeans who made up a high proportion of the captains and mates until the end of the century. The farmers were assisted to improve productivity by instructors who were sent throughout the countryside to disseminate new techniques. A few of the industrial firms introduced systems of 'training within the factory'; Hitachi was a pioneer in this field. The old apprenticeship system lasted for many years, but it gradually yielded to the new methods of training.

The cost of the national educational system and of the other means employed by Japan in early Meiji for assimilating Western knowledge is not easy to discover. But some rather general statements can be made. In the 1870s payments to foreign teachers and technical experts absorbed most of the expenditure of the Department of Industry; these payments amounted to 5 to 6 per cent of the total expenditure of the central government. In addition, numerous foreigners were employed by private firms to train their personnel and to instal and operate equipment. All the foreigners earned salaries that were extremely high by Japanese standards.[16] In early and middle Meiji most of the public expenditure for primary, middle school and technical middle school education was borne by the local authorities; in the 1880s one-third of the prefectural expenditure went for these purposes.[17] But the public purse was not the only source of income for the national educational system. The pupils had to pay fees, and until primary education became free early in the present century, these were a heavy burden on the poor. In particular, the peasants who, in the first decades after the Restoration, were called upon through their taxes to finance much of Japan's modernisation, including her heavy expenditure on defence, found the fees exceptionally oppressive. In the absence of the institution of the 'extended family', it is difficult to see how the money could have been found. Some Japanese historians, looking back on those hard times, wonder if the burden was not too heavy, whether the building of the modern state was not achieved at too great a social cost. No one, least of all a foreigner, can give a confident answer. All that one can say is that the new educational system ensured for Japan a competent, well-trained labour supply at all levels, and that it produced leaders professionally equipped for what they had to do.

It is often asserted that Japan's development was state-led, but this is only a half-truth. In education, as in other branches of national life, much can be attributed to the initiative of private individuals. Down to the present time, the state system has supplied only part of the educational needs. Fukuzawa was not the only pioneer, though he was the greatest of them. Numerous schools and colleges at all grades, except for the primary grade, were established and run independently. Private businessmen in the early days took a prominent part in the development, and not all those who founded schools had themselves been well educated. One must also record the important contribution, especially to women's education, that was made by foreigners, notably by foreign missionaries. For the private sector, or for most of it, the fees charged, especially in the private universities, were, and are, high; but the demand of the Japanese for education has been insatiable, and competition for places in the most reputable institutions has been fierce. The government and the Imperial House have made donations to the private schools and universities; but even today less than a quarter of their expenditure is covered by official grants.

Japanese education was thus not a seamless robe. It has depended, and still depends, heavily on government direction and finance, but the private sector pioneered the changes from the old to the new order and has been complementary to the state system, especially in higher education. In neither sector, however, was educational policy fashioned by men committed to a belief in the sufficiency of a liberal education; it seemed essential to them that adequate provision should also be made for professional and vocational training, directed towards producing experts. It would be quite wrong to deduce, however, that Japan's higher educational system was wholly concerned with turning out technical and administrative specialists. Japan set out to assimilate every branch of Western knowledge, literature, art and pure science. She brought a long line of English poets to Tokyo for the Lafcadio Hearn Chair of English Literature. At the beginning of the period of Westernisation, the Japanese were ardent students of the British empirical and utilitarian philosophers, and when they later took up German idealist philosophy, they came to it through the writings of T. H. Green. Nor did they abandon the aestheticism which is, perhaps, the most enduring and admirable thread in the pattern of their culture.

In these respects there were differences only of emphasis between the state and the private institutions. Practically, however, their functions were separate, at any rate in the higher reaches. The independent universities and colleges, apart from those founded by foreign religious bodies, aimed primarily at meeting the demand of private industry for trained personnel; they also turned out journalists and politicians. Keio and Waseda (founded in 1881 by Count Okuma) sent their best graduates to the *Zaibatsu* and big business; Meiji University trained lawyers for private practice. The imperial universities, on the other hand (especially Tokyo Imperial University, *Todai*) supplied the civil servants and administrators, as well as scholars. One may conclude that, broadly speaking, the national educational system, in addition to providing Japan with an efficient bureaucracy, was successful both in assuring a wide diffusion of knowledge and also, since almost everyone went to the state primary schools, in giving a common background to all. The private sector had the distinction of training leaders in business and politics, and of pioneering changes in many branches of national life. But, of course, there was (and is) no clearcut division between functions. Indeed, certain developments in the public service have narrowed the gap. Japanese civil servants are accustomed to retire at an early age (the late forties) unless they are destined for the highest office. Those who retire commonly find administrative jobs in private industry or the public corporations—a process known in the civil service as *Amakudari* ('Descent from Heaven'). Cynics have even suggested that there is a causal link between this practice and the proliferation of public corporations during the postwar years!

From the beginning of the Meiji era—indeed, from late Tokugawa times—until very recently, Japan was content with her
role as an assiduous pupil of Western science and technology,
happy that Europeans and Americans should spend their substance in original research and in devising the major industrial
innovations. She did not take it amiss that others should enjoy
the honour of scientific and technological leadership, provided
that she could obtain access to the results of their originality.
She resisted any temptation to the kind of cultural chauvinism
that has seduced postwar Britain into wasting her resources on
projects that confer prestige but are economically disastrous.
The temptation for her to do so can never have been very strong.
In the early days of modernisation her technical inferiority to
the West was so obvious as to discourage rivalry in research and
development. Nor had she the capital with which to finance
such activities. Immediately after the Second World War she
was again conscious of the wide gap between herself and the
West in technology, and at the same time she was desperately
short of capital for reconstruction. So a concentration on acquiring and assimilating Western 'knowhow' was the only sensible course for her to follow, especially as one of the chief
stimuli to competition in the technological race (military ambition) could no longer exert an influence on her policy.[18] Defeat
and the subsequent peace treaties left no way open to her except
that of cooperation with her victors in the reconstruction of her
economy. It can be understood, therefore, that Japan's educational system was devised from the beginning to facilitate the
acquisition and wide dissemination of the 'knowhow' that
foreigners could provide, and consequently to produce men
who could make use of, and sometimes improve upon, what
others had originated. In the fulfilment of this purpose the
system has been very successful. Now that Japan has caught up
with the West in most branches of technology, the role of fol-
lower has ceased to be adequate to her industrial needs. Research and development have increased their share of total
industrial costs, and the flow of new technical knowledge between the West and Japan is no longer a one-way traffic.

Many critics have claimed that Japan has placed too much
emphasis on formal educational qualifications as a path to a
career, and there is some justification for such a charge. Shibusawa, a pioneer in both business and education in early Meiji,

was, *inter alia*, President of the Dai-Ichi Bank, one of the first modern banks. He refused to grant a loan to an applicant named Suzuki on the ground that Suzuki was not well educated. The rejected applicant later became the leader of the new sugar-refining industry! Yet, although Japan, in this instance as in others, often showed herself inclined to rate too highly the qualities of conformity and convention, the educational system achieved what it intended. It kept Japan supplied with men trained for the jobs they were called upon to do. The Japanese worlds of business and administration have no respect for the inspired amateur, the man with a general education but without specific expertise. Japanese officials, bankers and businessmen are astonished, on meeting their counterparts in London, to find that these have often received no formal professional or vocational training. I myself became conscious of the contrast years ago. In the 1920s, and later in the 1930s, I spent some time in research into Japan's industrial organisation, and I was impressed by the fact that almost every company official or businessman whom I encountered had received an education, in a university or a higher technical or commercial college, that was relevant to the work he was engaged upon. Between these two periods in Japan I spent several years in research into industrial organisation in the West Midlands. I met many business executives in the course of that work, but it was exceptional to find one who had had an advanced education that could be described as vocational or professional. The number of those with any kind of university education was very small. Since then there have been many changes, and the contrast would not now be so clearly marked. But, in this respect, Britain lagged behind Japan by two generations.

The charge of excessive reliance on the academy as a preparation for careers in practical affairs remains, but it can be said at least that the reliance is not unqualified. In the first place, the larger companies have for a long time organised systematically 'training within the firm'. In the second place, it is clear that, at certain times in Japan's modern history, men of energy and business genius have found it possible to force their way to the front, despite their lack of formal education or close links with the Establishment. At the time of the Restoration, when the old order was overthrown, there were many instances of outstanding success achieved by men of that type, some of lowly origin. Again, immediately after the Second World War, when the restraints of the past were loosened, institutions trans-

TABLE 11

Number of students in Japanese schools, colleges and universities

Average for period	Total	Primary schools	Middle schools	Higher education	Percentage of total population in educational institutions
			(in thousands)		
1878–82	2589	2559	23	8	7·0
1893–97	3815	3752	47	16	9·1
1908–12	7413	6854	512	48	14·9
1923–27	11,561	9544	1886	131	19·3
1938–42	17,208	12,749	4226	233	24·0

formed by external influences and the former leaders dismissed from the seats of power, new men were given scope for exerting their talents as innovators. It is significant that, while some observers of the country's postwar economic successes see the Japanese in terms of a disciplined people obedient to the direction of a central authority, others stress the importance of the new freedom and the enlarged opportunities for individual enterprise which it conferred. One may offer as examples the careers of S. Honda and K. Matsushita, self-made men who have each made a massive contribution to the country's industrial development since 1950. Although the Japanese are conformists who like to work as members of cliques, they have a soft spot in their hearts for non-conformists and, in the opinion polls that record the most admired business leaders, it is the self-made men who come out on top.[19]

11 Japan's Post-war Economic Prospects: The British View[1]

I should declare initially that I have no special knowledge that would justify my commenting on the attitude of the British public at large towards Japan in the years just after the war. I recall that, when I was in Japan in the early 1950s, a Japanese journalist asked me if he was right in thinking that the chief grudges of the British against the Japanese had their source in, first, the treatment of British prisoners in South East Asia, and, second, the inroads that Japan had made into the British textile markets overseas. I told him that he was probably correct, and he then went on, with characteristic realism, to ask me to tell him, first, the number of such prisoners now returned to Britain, and, second, the postwar importance of the cotton industry to the British economy.

I am not concerned today with popular opinions about Japan at that time. What I shall try to do is to describe the views held of Japan's economic prospects, and the attitude to her economic future, that I found among politicians, civil servants and some businessmen with Far Eastern interests, immediately after the war. I must explain why I am speaking of these matters with perhaps more assurance than may be justified. In the summer of 1945 a Far Eastern Advisory Commission was set up at Washington on which eleven Allied Powers were represented.[2] The Commission was concerned with policy towards Japan during the Occupation and with the directives to be sent via the American government to General MacArthur, a proconsul, it may be recalled, who was not noted for willingness to lend an ear to outside advice. A section, known as the Economic and Industrial Planning Staff (EIPS), was brought into being at the Foreign Office to produce briefs for Sir George Sansom, our representative on the Commission, and I was put in charge of this section.[3] I also presided over an interdepartmental committee which considered the first drafts of the briefs. These were then passed to an official committee under the chairmanship of a secretary to the Cabinet and thence to a Cabinet Committee presided over by the Foreign Secretary. When agreed, the briefs went off to Sir George Sansom. As I attended all these committees and also met other interested persons, I obtained a fairly clear idea of both ministerial and official attitudes to the problems.

The views expressed by ministers and civil servants certainly did not proceed from any deep knowledge of the subject. It is perhaps symptomatic of Britain's supply of expertise at that time that, while our representative on the Commission was pre-eminent in his understanding of the Japanese and much respected by his colleagues there, knowledge of the subject at lower levels in the administration was scarce. I am speaking, of course, about Japan's *economic* affairs. The Foreign Office had little interest in them; one official, in the course of a discussion of some technical economic problem, complained of the sordid subjects that we were being forced to occupy ourselves with. Even on the Cabinet Committee some strange attitudes were revealed. One of the members was a Parliamentary Secretary whose firm before the war had had extensive dealings with the great Japanese trading companies. When he began to enlighten his colleagues about the nature of the *Zaibatsu*, the Chairman cut him short by saying: 'My God, N. . . . , what company you keep'! Ignorance, however, has never been a reason for the lack of strong convictions, and these were present in abundance. Some of the convictions, even when held by the same person, were inconsistent with one another. Thus, while most of the members of my committee were very pessimistic about Japan's economic prospects, this pessimism did not prevent some of them from pressing for various restrictions on her industries with an eye, not only on the war potential of such industries, but also on their future competitive capability in international markets. In general, I found ministers more sensible and far-sighted on these questions than the civil servants, but the comparison may not mean more than that the best of the officials on these committees were preoccupied with German affairs, and left Japan to their less experienced auxiliaries. The ministerial discussions, on the other hand, were dominated by Bevin and Cripps.[4]

EIPS began by distinguishing what were regarded as the outstanding economic problems, Japan's own problems and those arising out of the future economic relations between Japan and the outside world. Before we could venture to formulate policy proposals, however, we thought it essential to make some kind of forecast of the state of the Japanese economy after the initial difficulties of reconstruction had been overcome. Our plan, I remember, was supposed to describe the likely economic conditions in Japan in what we rather comically called 'the first normal, postwar year, or 1951'! We thought that, if things went well, Japan might by that time have achieved 'viability', but only if she accepted a standard of living significantly lower than that of the middle 1930s. The predicted levels of production and consumption were set out in detail. By 'viable' we meant her being able to obtain the imports she required to sustain the postulated standard of living, without dependence on foreign aid. The chief constraint was likely to be the difficulty of finding sufficient exports. (A few years later (1948) an official American forecast put the 'viability date' forward to the middle 1950s, but the level of consumption postulated in that forecast was higher than in our estimate.) Of course, in 1945, the Cold War, the Korean War, and all that these meant for American involvement in Japan, were unforeseen.

Most of the officials and businessmen with whom I had dealings thought that I was being very optimistic about Japan's economic future. A high-level Board of Trade official, who had had experience in the Far East, put it to me in this way. Japan's prewar economic position was precarious in spite of her territorial possessions and commercial privileges in East Asia. Two-fifths of her trade was with that region. Now that she had lost it all her economic position was wellnigh hopeless, since her industrial recovery depended on access to imports of raw materials from which she was deprived by her territorial losses and the collapse of her export trade. It is odd that this critic, like others, seemed implicitly to have accepted the Japanese defence of aggression in Asia. As a Mitsui executive had argued in 1936 when we talked of events in Manchuria: 'We had to do what we did in order to live'. It was not a proposition to which I had ever subscribed, and in 1945 I judged that the recovery of Japan was more likely to be impeded by the state of her morale than by the loss of territories. But this was not the prevailing view. I found that British businessmen who had learnt to fear Japan as a competitor in prewar days rated her chances of recovery low and even as late as the middle 1950s thought little of her prospects. I recall that, at the IPR Conference at Kyoto in 1954, Japanese businessmen seemed to share this pessimism.[5] One of them, a participant in the Conference, stated the problem in this way: 'Before the war our main exports were cotton manufactures and raw silk. Silk has been killed by manmade fibres. The prospects for recovery in cotton are bleak because of the development of new capacity in our former markets. Our other exports are insignificant. What can we do?' He invited suggestions. The only exports that the foreign members of the Conference could think of were labour-intensive speciality goods, artistic wares, fishing tackle, binoculars, cameras and so on—suggestions which the Japanese received with easily restrained enthusiasm. No one predicted the triumphs that would come later in steel, shipbuilding, electronics, manmade fibres and motor vehicles. Even when Japan's exports of capital goods began to increase, the explanation commonly offered was that she was a marginal supplier and was benefiting temporarily by the world investment boom. The same pessimistic views long prevailed in circles where Japanese affairs were discussed by businessmen, officials and academic persons (for example, at Chatham House).

Other papers from EIPS dealt with the chief items of economic policy discussed on the Far Eastern Commission —reparations, the constraints to be placed on Japanese industries that might constitute a future war potential, the organisation of the economy (particularly the treatment of the *Zaibatsu*), land reform, population trends, industrial relations and trade unions, financial problems, including the treatment of Japanese foreign debts, prewar British assets in Japan, exchange rates and so on. The British attitude to these problems (and to the American proposals in regard to them) was strongly influenced by the prevailing pessimistic views about Japan's long-term economic prospects. EIPS and the various committees, on the whole, looked with favour on the proposition that, except where security was closely affected, the fewer the impediments placed on recovery the better. For instance, it was urged that agricultural production should be restored as soon as possible. This required the rapid restoration of the chemical fertiliser industry, and, despite the fact that nitrogen plants could be easily converted to explosives manufacture, it was argued that the restoration should be encouraged. The American proposals for land reform were examined mainly from the same point of view—how they would affect production.[6] Of course, the relations in prewar days between rural impoverishment. and aggressive militarism were not ignored, but the Labour ministers showed much less interest in social reform in Japan for its own sake than might have been expected.

The initial American proposals about reparations and the level of industrial capacity to be left to Japan—the Pauley proposals—seemed excessively harsh to the British, not because they felt much sympathy with the Japanese in their plight, but because they were judged to be impracticable.[7] According to these first proposals, a high proportion of the plants that remained in the heavy industries were to be removed as reparations, and the country was to be left with a very modest amount of equipment in iron and steel, shipbuilding, chemicals and machine tools. Even the textile industry was to be restricted by ceilings on its capacity. No ships larger than 5000 gross tons were to be built. The American notion was that the Japanese had brought their trouble on themselves; let *them* get out of it! This policy did not, of course, long survive the realities of the Occupation.

The policies referred to had their supporters in Britain, but not among the most influential officials and ministers whom I met at that time. *They* took the line that, since Japan's economic prospects were very bleak, she might sink into chaos and despair if she were squeezed too hard. Such a condition would be fatal to peace and stability in the Far East. It was right for Japan to pay compensation to those she had injured, but such payments would have to await her own economic reconstruction. This, I think was the tenor of our policy. I like to think that, in these first months after the victory, the British authorities strayed more frequently within the boundaries of rationality and commonsense than did the Americans, at any rate to judge by the early American proposals. But, if this was so, it was not because of any moral superiority. Good policies only emerge when there is a happy, and usually accidental, coincidence of self-interest and wisdom. The Foreign Secretary knew only too well that Britain's hands were full because of the German problem. He was determined not to get involved in any commitment in Japan that he could avoid. He certainly could not contemplate any large provision of aid, and he thought that the sooner the Allies were free of any possible burden the better. His standpoint naturally weakened our influence in all the negotiations. It may be that, if Britain had been forced to shoulder more of the responsibilities at that time, her attitude would have been less detached and rational. Britain's very lack of interest in Japan (it amounted almost to indifference) may also have played a part.

I must not, however, give the impression that everyone took the same line. There were undertones of dissent from departments that represented sectional interests. For instance, the Board of Trade, being concerned with future markets for British manufactures, made representations in favour of measures to prevent the re-emergence of competition with British textiles in overseas markets. Similar representations were made about shipping. One of the most *outré* suggestions came from a senior Treasury official who seriously proposed that the Japanese mercantile marine should be limited to the use of sailing ships, partly on the grounds of their beneficial moral effects on those who would man them! I made fun of this proposal by suggesting that the moral effects would be even greater if we sent out a team to teach the Japanese to sing sea shanties, but he deplored my frivolity and insisted on putting his scheme to Cripps, who, of course, sank it without trace. Cripps also turned down his officials' proposals for restricting Japan's textile capacity. But the notion survived that some kind of regulation of her competition with Britain in overseas textile markets was desirable. I remember that a former British Minister of State suggested at a meeting of Osaka cotton-spinners and manufacturers in the early 1950s that they and their British counterparts should get together and agree to restrict competition by quotas on exports, a proposal by no means welcomed at Osaka. And, as we know, this was not the end of the matter.

There were other examples of the inclination of certain officials to think that, while Japan could not be allowed to sink into economic chaos, it would be a good thing for British industry if her economic recovery were less than complete. Thus some of them praised the American proposals for new labour laws on the grounds that the more powerful the trade unions, the better it might be for Japan's competitors in the years ahead. It was not foreseen, certainly not by me, that Japan would adapt the reforms imposed on her so as to create a type of trade union and a system of industrial relations that were perfectly in accord with the efficient administration of an industrial state in an age of high technology.

The American proposal to dissolve the *Zaibatsu* led to discussions that illuminated the several different strands in British policy. The dissolution, it will be recalled, had its origin in the proposition that the *Zaibatsu* had armed Japan for war and that, unless economic power were more widely diffused, it would be impossible to establish the liberal, democratic, free-enterprise society that the Americans favoured. I had myself unwittingly provided a small amount of fuel to stoke up this reforming zeal. In 1936, when the West (or at any rate, Western economists) knew little about the *Zaibatsu*, I had contributed an article about them to the *Economic Journal*.[8] In 1945 SCAP circulated copies of this article among its economic staff, and ex-Viscount Kanō Hisaakira afterwards chided me for having been responsible for initiating the policy.[9] This, of course, was complete nonsense. But the charge was embarrassing because, though I regarded monopolies and cartels as being among the chief enemies of a system of free enterprise, I was lukewarm about the dissolution policy. For one thing, the *Zaibatsu* were what we now call 'conglomerates' rather than monopolists. But the main reason was my doubt whether it was prudent to embark on a large experiment in industrial organisation at a moment of crisis in Japan's affairs, especially when it meant the destruction of the main centres of economic initiative. I was also convinced that the policy would not survive the end of the Occupation. After that, Japan would go her own way, and since capital was likely to be very scarce for many years, large organisations capable of mobilising investment funds and directing them into productive uses would be indispensable.

The reaction of ministers was what might have been expected. Most of them applauded the American proposal to break up these great concentrations of economic power, especially as the policy was coupled with a capital levy on the wealth of the *Zaibatsu* families. But they had no sympathy at all with the

American zeal to create a competitive, market economy. On the contrary, the *Zaibatsu* undertakings, they thought, should be nationalised. It is ironical that that particular consequence of the dissolution—a transference from the frying pan of concentrated private power to the fire of state ownership—was what some of the Americans who reported on the scheme most feared! However, Bevin soon silenced his colleagues. On large questions of foreign policy he was a romantic imperialist, but in dealing with immediate, pressing issues, he was realistic and the reverse of doctrinaire. He accepted the argument that to embark on elaborate experiments in industrial organisation and to destroy established centres of economic authority might jeopardise recovery and store up dangerous problems for the Allies in future. He brushed aside the contention that the *Zaibatsu*[10] were to be condemned because they had been so closely associated with Japan's war effort. Great industrial concerns inevitably had to play a prominent part in any war economy. 'Think what happened here', he said; 'when the war came to an end, I fully expected to see the directors of ICI marching down Whitehall to hand back the British Empire to the government'. As to monopolists and cartels, he had always found them much easier to negotiate wages with than firms that were subject to the discipline of the market. So, for all these reasons, he would have preferred to let the *Zaibatsu* alone. Nevertheless, on this question of policy as on others, he insisted on the principle that, while we should do our best to persuade the Americans to come round to our point of view, in the end we had to acquiesce in what they wanted. Our hands were too full, as it was, with the problems, especially the financial problems, of the German occupation. It was a British interest to have Japan restored to economic 'viability', if not to rude health, but it was not for Britain to assume any substantial share in the financial responsibility of aiding her. The Americans, being closer to the problem, might sometimes confound the contingent with the essential. So be it; the British were in no shape to offer more than advice. Anyhow, such influence as we could exert, even with Sansom as our representative on the Far Eastern Commission, was far removed from the place where decisions were being taken, at SCAP headquarters in Tokyo.

To sum up, these are my recollections of British attitudes to Japan just after the end of the war. A deep pessimism about both her short-run and her long-run economic prospects permeated the circles in which British policy towards her was being shaped. The mere fact that her prospects were bleak did not in itself greatly disturb the British ministers and their advisers who deliberated on the problem. The Japanese, they thought, were after all the authors of their own troubles, and the British could easily tolerate a long delay before Japan reappeared as a competitor. At the same time, it was clearly not sensible to put obstacles in the way of such modest recovery as seemed possible, since a descent into hopeless impoverishment would be inconsistent with stability in the Far East. This consideration seems to have weighed more heavily with the British than with the Americans at that time. Among the British there was scant concern with the social and economic reforms that the Americans proposed, except from the standpoint of economic expediency having regard to our judgement about Japan's probably dismal economic future. Anyhow, there was little that the British government could do to divert the Americans from the course on which they were set, or seemed to be set, just after the war, even if it had wished to oppose them. With our anxieties about the financial burden of the British Zone in Germany, we were obliged to leave decisions about Japan's economic and social problems to others. Of course, there were individuals among us who thought that the postwar world would be deeply affected by Japan's success or failure in rebuilding her industry and trade, and who, therefore, advocated a more positive policy. But they made only a feeble impact on political and official attitudes. These were compounded largely of indifference towards Japan's future (now that the menace of her military power had been removed) and a recognition that her fate must lie in other hands than the British.

Notes and References

CHAPTER 1

1 According to the *National Institute Economic Review* (July 1961), Japan's real product grew at an annual rate of 4·4 per cent between 1880 and 1913 and 3·8 per cent between 1913 and 1959. Comparable rates for the latter period were 3·1 per cent for the USA, 1·3 per cent for France and the UK and 2·4 per cent for Germany. From 1950 to 1967 Japan's real GNP rose by 9·5 per cent a year compared with 6·2 per cent in Germany, 5·6 per cent in Italy, 5 per cent in France, 3·9 per cent in the USA and 2·8 per cent in the UK. See A. Maddison, 'Japan's Explosive Growth Explained' in *The Economic Review*, Vol. 21, No. 2 (May 1970) (Tokyo: Hitotsubashi University), p. 116.

2 G. B. Sansom, *The Western World and Japan* (The Cresset Press, 1950), p. 449.

3 G.E. Hubbard, *Eastern Industrialization and Its Effect on the West*, 2nd edition (Oxford University Press, 1938), p. 160. In 1938 the real product per head in Japan was estimated to be only 24 per cent of that of the UK (*National Institute Economic Review*, July 1961).

4 See Freda Utley, *Japan's Feet of Clay* (Faber and Faber, 1936), passim.

5 G. C. Allen and A. G. Donnithorne, *Western Enterprise in Far Eastern Economic Development: China and Japan*; and *Western Enterprise in Indonesia and Malaya* (Allen and Unwin, 1954, 1957).

6 Boston Consulting Group, *Japan in 1980* (*Financial Times*, 1974), p. 22; and W. W. Lockwood (ed.), *The State and Economic Enterprise in Japan* (Princeton University Press, 1965), p. 503.

7 Mitsui and Co., *The 100 Year History of Mitsui and Co. Ltd., 1876–1976* (Tokyo, 1977), p. 11, for the statement: 'Children were adopted, and marriage partners were carefully selected, to ensure that outstanding men were available to fill positions of authority within the Mitsui structure'.

8 Mitsui and Co., op. cit., pp. 184–5.

9 For a brief description of *Ringi-sei*, see D. F. Henderson, *Foreign Enterprise in Japan* (University of North Carolina Press, 1973), pp. 114–116.

10 J. Hirschmeier and T. Yui, *The Development of Japanese Business, 1600–1973* (Allen and Unwin, 1975), p. 190.

11 OECD, *Income Distribution in OECD Countries* (OECD Economic Outlook Occasional Studies, 1976), passim., and A. Boltho, *Japan, An Economic Survey, 1953–1973* (Oxford University Press, 1975), Chapter 8.

12 'Measured in terms of number of rooms per person, diffusion of water supply and sewage, ratio of paved roads or area of city parks, Japan lags sadly behind countries with which it likes to compare itself . . . The percentage ratio of social security payments to national income was 6·2 per cent in 1966 and has hardly risen since then. Comparative ratios were 7·6 per cent in the United States, 13·8 per cent in Britain, 19·9 per cent in West Germany and 19·2 per cent in France and 15·0 per cent in Italy' (K. Ohkawa and H. Rosovsky, *Japanese Economic Growth* (Stanford University Press, 1973), pp. 242–3. See *Japan Times Weekly* (10 December 1977), for comments on the Japanese Government's *White Paper on Welfare* (1977).

13 For an analysis of the causes of Japan's export surpluses, see, G. C. Allen, *How Japan Competes* (Institute of Economic Affairs, Hobart Paper 81, 1978).

CHAPTER 2

1 This chapter has resulted from the conflation of two articles. The first was published in the *Economic Journal* in March 1925 under the title of 'The Recent Currency and Exchange Policy of Japan', and the second in *Economic History* (a supplement of the *Economic Journal*) in January 1933, under the title of 'The Last Decade in Japan'. The latter had previously been read before Section F of the British Association at York on 5 September 1932.

2 Y. Yagi, 'Relations between Japan and Korea as seen from the Standpoint of Rice Supply', in *Kyoto Economic Review* (December 1931).

3 S. Uyehara, *The Industry and Trade of Japan* (P. S. King, 1926), pp. 284–6.

4 H. G. Moulton, *Japan: An Economic and Financial Appraisal* (Washington: Brookings Institution, 1931), p. 588.

5 This and subsequent statements apply to the early 1930s; the bank ceased to exist after the Second World War.

6 J. Inouye, *Problems of the Japanese Exchange* (Macmillan, 1931), pp. 185–6.

7 Ibid., pp. 1–2.

8 Sources of statistical data, unless otherwise stated, are the *Financial and Economic Annual of Japan*, and the *Statistical Year Book of the Empire of Japan*. For the purpose of these comparisons, China includes Hong Kong and Kwantung.

9 The American financial crisis of 1907 led to a steep decline in the value of Japan's exports of raw silk (see S. Uyehara, op. cit., p. 102).

10 M. Matsukata, *Report on the Post-Bellum Financial Administration in Japan* (Tokyo: Japanese Government), p. 215.

11 Ibid., pp. 224–5.

12 Part of this foreign reserve belonged to the government and part to the Bank of Japan.

13 A detailed description of Japan's banking system and monetary system at that time is given in *United States National Monetary Commission, Reports*, (1910), vol. XVIII.

14 G. Odate, *Japan's Financial Relations with the United States* (Columbia University Press), p. 29.

15 J. Inouye, op. cit., p. 156.
16 Ibid., Chapters 2 and 3.
17 H. G. Moulton, op. cit., p. 274.
18 Ibid., p. 318.
19 A. Andréadès, *Les Finances de l'Empire Japonais et leur Evolution* (Paris: Felix Alcan, 1932), p. 90.
20 H. G. Moulton, op. cit., pp. 306ff, 495.
21 T. Jones, 'The Recent Banking Crisis and Industrial Conditions in Japan', in the *Economic Journal* (March 1928), and J. Inouye, op. cit., pp. 123ff.
22 J. E. Orchard, *Japan's Economic Position* (New York: McGraw-Hill, 1930), Chapters 16 to 18.
23 The exports considered here are those from Japan itself to countries outside the Japanese Empire. It should be noted that exports from Japan itself to the rest of her Empire increased in relative importance, from 12·5 per cent of the total export trade in 1920 to nearly 20 per cent in 1928. This growth took place under privileged conditions for Japanese exporters. Trade between Japan and her colonies was virtually free, while the colonial tariffs against foreign goods were on the same scale as those of the mother country.
24 H. G. Moulton, op. cit., pp. 517ff.
25 W. R. Crocker, *The Japanese Population Problem* (Allen and Unwin, 1931), p. 111n.

26.

Year	Bank of Japan's index number of general wholesale prices (1913 = 100)	Index number of silk prices (1913 = 100)
1923	199	236
1924	207	203
1925	202	214
1926	179	175
1927	170	148
1928	171	142
1929	166	141

27 B. Ellinger, 'Japanese Competition in the Cotton Trade', in the *Journal of the Royal Statistical Society*, Part 2 (1930); A. S. Pearse, *The Cotton Industry of Japan and China* (Manchester: Taylor, Garnett and Evans, 1929).
28 K. Iwasaki, 'The Economic Outlook in Japan', in *A Picture of World Economic Conditions at the Beginning of 1932* (United States: National Industrial Conference Board, 1932).
29 At the beginning of June 1932, when the government made an unsuccessful attempt to unload part of its stocks of silk, the price fell to 400 yen a bale.
30 In volume the decline was only 8 per cent.
31 The Satsuma and Choshu clans exerted a powerful influence over national policy in the early years of modernisation. Satsuma was dominant in the Navy and Choshu in the Army.
32 The Japanese banks are said to have held about 100 million yen in London

198 Japan's Economic Policy

in September 1931 (*Financial Times, Japanese Supplement* (29 February 1932), p. 15).

33 A. Andréadès, op. cit., p. 106.

34 T. Uyeda, *The Small Industries of Japan* (Oxford University Press, 1938), pp. 287ff.

CHAPTER 3

1 First published in the *Economic Journal* (June 1937) under the title of 'The Concentration of Economic Control in Japan'.

2 By analogy with *Hanbatsu* ('clan groups' or 'cliques') and *Gumbatsu* ('military cliques').

3 Okura was concerned chiefly with trading, mining, textiles and motor transport; Asano with cement, mining, steel and heavy engineering; Kuhara with heavy engineering, chemicals, mining and aquatic products; Ogawa-Tanaka with chemicals; Kawasaki with banking, insurance, rayon and shipbuildings; Shibusawa with banking, shipbuilding and engineering; Furukawa with copper-mining and refining and electrical plant; Mori with chemicals and electric power.

4 Mitsui Gomei Kaisha, *The House of Mitsui* (Tokyo, 1933), p. 6.

5 R. Iwai, *Mitsui Mitsubishi Monogatari* (*The Story of Mitsui and Mitsubishi*) (Tokyo, 1935), Part 1, Chapter 2.

6 Ibid., Part 2, Chapter 1: and Mitsubishi Goshi Kaisha, *An Outline of Mitsubishi Enterprises* (Tokyo, 1936), pp. 1–6.

7 Sumitomo Goshi Kaisha, *Sumitomo* (Osaka, 1936), passim and personal enquiries. The second largest shipping line in Japan (Osaka Shosen Kaisha) was under Sumitomo's control.

8 For instance, many of the properties of the Suzuki firm, which collapsed in the financial crisis of 1927, were acquired by Mitsui.

9 This applies particularly to Mitsui, Mitsubishi and Sumitomo. Yasuda's interests were mainly in banking, but it was able to control many industrial concerns through the medium of its financial institutions.

10 Asano appeared at this time to be falling under the dominance of Mitsui. Early in 1937 Asano's shipping company, Toyo Kisen Kaisha, joined with Mitsui Bussan (Mitsui Trading) in organising a new shipping company called the Toyo Kaiun Kaisha (Oriental Trading Company), and it was expected that this would ultimately be merged with Mitsui (*Oriental Economist*, Tokyo, January 1937), p. 63.

11 R. Iwai, op. cit., Part 1, Chapters 4 and p. 358 (chart).

12 M. Suzuki, *Nihon Zaibatsu Ron* (An Essay on the Japanese *Zaibatsu*) (Tokyo, 1935), Chapter 1 and passim.

13 'A Study of the Shipbuilding Boom', in *Economic Knowledge* (Tokyo, vol. II, series 16, 1 August 1936; also *Mitsubishi Monthly Circular* (April 1937), pp. 22–23.

14 At the time a single *Zaibatsu* could build ships in its own yards, operate them, bunker them from its own mines and oil storage tanks, insure them and their cargoes, warehouse the cargoes and discount the warrants at its own bank. Moreover, a high proportion of the cargoes consisted of goods

shipped by its own merchanting company and made in its own factories.

15 The trading company of Mitsubishi.

16 Mitsui has long supported the Tokyo University of Commerce (*Shodai*) and has recruited many of its administrative staff from that institution, which, after the Second World War, became Hitotsubashi University.

17 M. Suzuki, op. cit., Chapter 6.

18 R. Iwai, op. cit., p. 358; M. Suzuki, op. cit., pp. 41ff and Mitsui Gomei Kaisha, *The House of Mitsui*, passim.

19 M. Suzuki, op. cit., pp. 41–8.

20 Ibid., p. 57; and pamphlet issued by the Oji Company in January 1935.

21 M. Suzuki, op. cit., pp. 394–400.

22 H. Wada, 'How Big Capitalists Camouflage Themselves', in *Nippon Hyoron* (June 1936).

23 Mitsui Gomei Kaisha, *The House of Mitsui*, p. 21.

24 Ibid., p. 24.

25 M. Suzuki, op. cit., Chapter 1.

26 Ibid., Chapter 6.

27 Nippon Sanyo Kaisha (Nissan) was managed by Y. Aikawa who became prominent in business when he took over the Kuhara Mining Company in 1927.

28 M. Suzuki, op. cit., pp. 109ff, 129–37.

29 Several studies have been made of the dissolution of the *Zaibatsu* and their subsequent history, notably E. M. Hadley, *Antitrust in Japan* (Princeton University Press, 1970); see also the present author's *Japan's Economic Expansion* (Oxford University Press, 1965), Chapter 10.

CHAPTER 4

1 Paper read before the Manchester Statistical Society on 10 March 1937, under the title of 'Recent Changes in the Organisation of the Japanese Cotton Industry'.

2 The figures in this paper have been taken from the half-yearly reports of the Japan Cotton Spinners' Association, except where otherwise stated.

3 *Statistical Year Book of Ministry of Commerce and Industry* (Tokyo), various years.

4 See Table 8, p. 68.

5 T. Uyeda and T. Minoguchi, *The Cotton Industry* (Institute of Pacific Relations, International Research Series, 1936), p. 19.

6 Ibid., pp. 19 and 67–70.

7 Mitsubishi Economic Research Bureau, *Japanese Trade and Industry* (Macmillan, 1936), p. 242.

8 Estimate based on figures from Ministry of Commerce and Industry (Tokyo) and Japan Cotton Spinners' Association.

9 T. Uyeda and T. Minoguchi, op. cit., p. 19.

10 From memoranda supplied by Mitsubishi Economic Research Bureau.

11 According to leading men in the cotton trade, over a period of nearly thirty years, fifty-eight cotton merchants went out of business through bankruptcy. Failures were especially numerous between 1924 and 1928.

12 A competent authority informed the author that four-fifths of the savings were due to this cause.
13 From monthly reports of the Japan Cotton Spinners' Association.
14 Manufacturers' Associations.

CHAPTER 5

1 First published in *International Affairs* Vol. XXX, no. 3 (July 1954).
2 The number of factory workers was estimated to be 1,076,000 by Ou Pao-San and Wang Foh-Shen in their article 'Industrial Production and Employment in Pre-war China', in the *Economic Journal* (September 1946), pp. 426–34; a factory was defined as a workplace employing more than thirty persons.
3 G. C. Allen and A. G. Donnithorne, *Western Enterprise in Far Eastern Economic Development: China and Japan* (Allen and Unwin, 1954), p. 243.
4 Ibid., pp. 165–6. The same fate attended the efforts of Li Hung-chang, another enlightened official, to modernise the Chinese economy about the same time (see Hou Chi-ming, *Foreign Investment and Economic Development in China, 1840–1937* (Harvard University Press, 1965), p. 156; and A. Feuerwerker, *China's Early Industrialization* (Harvard University Press, 1958), passim.

CHAPTER 6

1 This chapter is the result of the conflation of two articles. The first was published in the *Annals of Public and Co-operative Economy* (Liège), vol. XXXIX, no. 2 (April–June 1968), under the title of 'The Public and Co-operative Sectors in Japan'. The second was published in the *Economic Review* of Hitotsubashi University (Tokyo), vol. 21, no. 2 (May 1970), under the title of 'The State and Private Enterprise'.
2 *The Currency of Japan* [A reprint of articles, letters and official reports published by the *Japan Gazette* (Tokyo, 1882)], pp. 76–80.
3 The number of foreigners employed by the national and prefectural governments rose from 369 in 1872 to a maximum of 527 in 1875. Of these about two-fifths were technical advisers, between a quarter and a third were teachers in schools and universities and the rest were military and naval experts, lawyers, managers, doctors and mechanics (see G. C. Allen and A. G. Donnithorne, op. cit., p. 270).
4 Y. Horie, 'Government Industries in the Early Years of the Meiji Era', in *Kyoto University Economic Review* (January 1939), pp. 67–87.
5 *The Currency of Japan*, p. 260.
6 This Bureau obtained its funds from the people's savings entrusted to the Post Office. Its resources were mainly invested in enterprises sponsored by the state both in Japan and in the colonies.
7 Bank of Japan, *Hundred Year Statistics of the Japanese Economy* (Tokyo, 1966), pp. 130–5.
8 W. W. Lockwood, *The Economic Development of Japan* (Princeton University

Press, 1954), p. 454.

9 For a detailed account of the government's economic policy at this time, see E. B. Schumpeter (ed.), *The Industrialisation of Japan and Manchukuo* (New York, The Macmillan Company, 1940), pp. 728–82, 817–53.

10 H. Rosovsky, 'Japanese Capital Formation: The Role of the Public Sector', in the *Journal of Economic History* (September 1959), pp. 350–73.

11 For a detailed description of the management of the economy during and just after the Second World War, see J. B. Cohen, *Japan's Economy in War and Reconstruction* (Minneapolis: University of Minnesota Press, 1949).

12 SCAP stands for Supreme Commander of the Allied Powers. It was used to designate both a person and also the Occupation Authority in general.

13 For a description of these institutions, see: Bank of Japan, *Money and Banking in Japan* (Tokyo, 1964); and Fuji Bank, *Banking in Modern Japan* (Tokyo, 1961).

14 Bank of Japan, *Economic Statistics of Japan, 1966* (Tokyo), p. 147.

15 R. Komiya (ed.), *Postwar Economic Growth in Japan* (University of California Press, 1966) pp. 17–25.

16 Ibid., pp. 21–3.

17 Ibid., p. 20.

18 In 1958 it was renamed the Economic Planning Agency.

19 In the event, because of the steep increase in private investment in industry, public investment actually fell as a proportion of the national expenditure in this period. (see Chapter 1 above).

20 W. W. Lockwood (ed.), *The State and Economic Enterprise in Japan* (Princeton University Press, 1965), p. 503.

21 In 1961 these regions turned out nearly three-quarters of the country's industrial production and housed nearly half the population.

22 R. P. Dore, *Land Reform in Japan* (Oxford University Press, 1959), p. 351.

23 K. Ogata, *The Co-operative Movement in Japan* (P. S. King, 1923), passim, for an authoritative survey of the movement up to the end of the First World War.

24 T. Ogura (ed.), *Agricultural Development in Modern Japan* (Tokyo: Japan FAO Association, 1963), p. 22.

25 Ibid., pp. 84–7, and passim.

26 R. P. Dore, op. cit., pp. 277–97.

27 In the fishing industry the cooperative societies are governed by a law of 1948. These societies provide credit, purchase and sell products on behalf of their members and make available facilities for refrigeration and cold storage.

CHAPTER 7

1 First published in the *Three Banks Review*, No. 55 (September 1962), under the title of 'The Causes of Japan's Economic Growth'.

2 In the postwar period the high rate of personal saving is also attributed to the assumption by families of responsibility for many welfare services which, in the West, are provided by the state. Further, there is the practice by which employees receive a high proportion of their annual income in

the form of bonuses at New Year and midsummer (bonuses dependent on the firm's prosperity). A family's consumption tends to be related to the monthly wage and the bonuses are mainly used either for the purchase of consumer durables or as additions to savings.
3 Numbers employed in the electricity and gas supply industries are included with employment in tertiary industry.

CHAPTER 8

1 First published in the *Three Banks Review* (December 1967), under the title of 'Japan's Economic Problems and Prospects'.
2 It was estimated that in 1966 the ratio of households in possession of such goods was as follows (as per cent of total households in each case): television sets, 94; sewing machines, 77; washing machines 76; electric fans, 66; refrigerators, 62; vacuum cleaners, 41; motor cycles, 30; motor cars, 12.
3 Exports directly or indirectly attributable to the Vietnam War have been put at about 8 per cent of Japan's total exports in 1966.
4 Issues required to finance the budgetary deficits of 1965 and 1966. Up to then the budgets in the postwar period were 'balanced'.
5 *Wages by size of firm* (as percentage of monthly wages paid by firms with 500 employees or over)

Employees per firm	1959	1965
5–29	44.3	63.2
30–99	56.1	71.0
100–499	69.6	80.9

6 In manufacturing industry average productivity increased by 49 per cent between 1960 and 1966, cash earnings by 63 per cent.
7 That is, the proportion of persons of working age who are actually in employment.
8 In 1963 the Kanto area (Tokyo–Yokohama region and its hinterland) was responsible for 47 per cent of total manufacturing production, compared with 44 per cent ten years earlier.

CHAPTER 9

1 This paper was originally presented to a Conference on Modern Japan held by the British Association for Japanese Studies at St Antony's College, Oxford, in April 1973. It was published in *Lloyds Bank Review*, No. 111 (January 1974), under the title of 'Why Japan's Economy has Prospered'.
2 A. Marshall, *Industry and Trade* (Macmillan, 1921), p. 161.
3 The Japanese themselves are also well aware of the importance of such factors. Professor H. Kitamura, in a contribution to a discussion on economic development at a Conference of the International Economic Association in Japan, affirmed that social attitudes were vital in that context. The revolution in social attitudes in Japan after 1870 was, he said, the most

important difference between China and Japan and was crucial to the explanation of the new period of Japanese growth. (see K. Berrill, *Economic Development with Special Reference to East Asia* (New York: St Martin's Press, 1964), p. 247.)

4 G. C. Allen, *Japan's Economic Expansion* (Oxford University Press, 1965), p. 261.

5 M. V. Posner, 'Industrial Policies and Growth', in A. Cairncross (ed.), *Britain's Economic Prospects Reconsidered* (Allen and Unwin, 1970), p. 160.

6 The Meiji era was 1868–1912.

7 The term 'Restoration' refers to the political change of 1868 which overthrew the Tokugawa *Shogun*, (military governor of the house of Tokugawa), and restored the Emperor as the *de facto* as well as the *de jure* ruler of the country. The Tokugawa house had ruled from 1603 to 1868.

8 R. Firth, 'The Peasantry of South-East Asia', in *International Affairs* (October 1950), p. 507.

9 G. B. Sansom, *The Western World and Japan* (The Cresset Press, 1950), pp. 152, 158.

10 H. Rosovsky, *Capital Formation in Japan* (New York: Free Press of Glencoe, 1961), pp. 86–7.

11 The rate of growth in the population after 1868 was high by the standard of the pre-Restoration period, but it was low—about 1 per cent a year—when compared with that of most Asian countries in recent times.

12 The Taisho era was 1912–26.

13 Bertrand Russell, *The Scientific Outlook* (Allen and Unwin, 1931), p. 212.

14 M. Matsukata, *Report on the Adoption of the Gold Standard in Japan* (Tokyo: Ministry of Finance, 1899), passim.

15 M. Shinohara, *Growth and Business Cycles in the Japanese Economy* (Tokyo: Kinokuniya, 1962), pp. 107–8.

16 J. Inouye, *Problems of the Japanese Exchange, 1914–1926* (Macmillan, 1931), p. 156.

17 Including Professor Shinohara mentioned above. The well-known 'Matsukata Deflation' in the 1880s is a classic example.

18 M. Bronfenbrenner, 'The Japanese Growth Path: Equilibrium or Disequilibrium', in the *Economic Review* (Tokyo: Hitotsubashi University, May 1970).

19 'Special procurement' expenditure included American military expenditure and the expenditure of American soldiers and civilians in Japan, together with dollar payments in respect of offshore procurement contracts and some other items.

20 M. Hadley, op. cit., pp. 390ff. and passim.

CHAPTER 10

1 This paper was read at an Economic History Seminar at Oxford in October 1977 and was first published in the *Oxford Review of Education*, Vol. 4, No. 1 (1978), under the title of 'Education, Science and the Economic Development of Japan'.

2　W. W. Lockwood (ed.), *The State and Economic Enterprise in Japan* (Princeton University Press, 1965), pp. 34–5. Professor Dore himself evidently regards these figures as very broad estimates—see his article 'The Importance of Educational Traditions: Japan and Elsewhere', in *Pacific Affairs*, Vol. 45, No. 4, (Winter 1972–73), p. 491. They may be on the high side.

3　At the time of the Restoration, it is estimated, there were between 7500 and 11,000 *terakoya*. The larger business houses ran schools in the towns for their apprentices; bookkeeping was among the subjects taught.

4　And also the Chinese.

5　G. B. Sansom, *The Western World and Japan* (The Cresset Press, 1950), p. 111.

6　Carmen Blacker, *The Japanese Enlightenment* (Cambridge University Press, 1964), pp. 18–19 and passim, One must not exaggerate the contrast between the Chinese and the European attitudes to nature. Blake, Wordsworth and Coleridge were worlds away from those who, like Bacon, advocated 'putting nature on the rack'.

7　Disdain for scientific studies was not confined to Asians. In academic and ecclesiastical circles in Europe down to recent times, there were many in full agreement with Bossuet who, when speaking of scientific studies, asserted that it was not consonant with the dignity of a bishop to meddle in such things!

8　G. B. Sansom, op. cit., p. 480.

9　This subject has been dealt with by many authors, for example, G. B. Sansom, op. cit., pp. 476–93; S. Okuma, *Fifty Years of New Japan* (London: Smith Elder, 1909), Vol. 2, pp. 113–92; Syed Ross Masood, *Japan and Its Educational System* (Hyderabad-Deccan: Government Central Press, 1923), passim, as well as by R. P. Dore, loc. cit.

10　Lionel Trilling, *Matthew Arnold* (Allen & Unwin, 1955), p. 385.

11　Described in much detail by Syed Ross Masood, op. cit., pp. 314–39.

12　W. W. Lockwood, (ed.), op. cit., pp. 109–10.

13　Large by the standards of the time, 10,000 spindles (K. Seki, *The Cotton Industry of Japan* (Tokyo: Japan Society for the Promotion of Science, 1956), pp. 15–16).

14　At that time 'factories' were defined as workplaces employing ten persons or more.

15　Source: *Japan-Manchukuo Year Book* (1936).

16　In addition to this expenditure, the government spent heavily on officials and students sent abroad to acquire Western knowledge (see K. Emi, *Government Fiscal Activity and Economic Growth in Japan* (Tokyo: Kinokuniya, 1963), p. 122).

17　K. Emi, op. cit., pp. 114–31.

18　Royalty payments in connection with licences for American and European patents and 'knowhow' remain one of the chief items of Japan's 'invisibles'.

19　J. Hirschmeier, and T. Yui, op. cit., p. 254.

20　Adapted from a table in M. Shinohara, 'Growth and Long Swings in the Japanese Economy', in *Hitotsubashi Journal of Economics* (Tokyo), Vol. 2, No. 1, p. 76.

CHAPTER 11

1 This paper was presented to a Conference of the British Association for Japanese Studies held at St Anthony's College, Oxford in April 1977. It was published in the *Proceedings* of the Association, edited by Gordon Daniels and Peter Lowe, Vol. 2, Part 1 (1977) (University of Sheffield, Centre for Japanese Studies). It was originally entitled 'Britain's Perception of Japan's Postwar Prospects'.

2 This became the Far Eastern Commission after the Moscow Agreement of 27 September 1945. Its members were Australia, Canada, China, France, India, the Netherlands, New Zealand, The Philippine Commonwealth, United Kingdom, United States and the USSR. For a history of the Commission, see G. H. Blakeslee, *The Far Eastern Commission, A Study in International Cooperation 1945–1952* (Washington, DC: Department of State Publications 5138, Far Eastern Series 60, 1953).

3 There was also a German section of EIPS.

4 Ernest Bevin, Foreign Secretary, 1945–51; Sir Stafford Cripps, President of the Board of Trade, 1945–47.

5 The Institute of Pacific Relations Conference, Kyoto (27 September – 8 October 1954).

6 The EIPS paper on Japanese agriculture and the system of land tenure seems to have exerted a considerable influence on the policy of land reform, according to R. W. Buckley, 'British Diplomacy and the Allied Control of Japan, 1945–46', in *Proceedings of the British Association for Japanese Studies*, Vol. 2, Part 1 (1977), p. 183.

7 E.W. Pauley, *Report on Japanese Reparations to the President of the United States, November 1945 to April 1946* (Washington, DC: Department of State Publication, 3174, 1948).

8 'The Concentration of Economic Control in Japan', in the *Economic Journal*, Vol. XLVII (1937), pp. 270–86. This article appears as Chapter 3 in this book.

9 Before the Second World War Viscount Kanō was head of the Yokohama Specie Bank's offices in London and Toronto. After Japan's surrender he became Vice-Director of the War Settlement Liaison Office and later President of the Hakodate Dock Company.

10 The Foreign Secretary always referred to the *Zaibatsu* as the 'Zooboots', not out of any intention to disparage them, but simply in accordance with his free-and-easy pronunciation of all foreign names—or even English ones.

List of the Author's Published Works

[An asterisk indicates articles and papers included wholly or in part either in *British Industry and Economic Policy* or in the present volume of the author's collected papers.]

BOOKS

Modern Japan and Its Problems (Allen and Unwin, 1928)

The Industrial Development of Birmingham and the Black Country, 1860–1927, (Longmans, 1929; reprinted, Frank Cass, 1966)

British Industries and Their Organisation (Longmans, 1933, fifth edition, 1970)

Japan: The Hungry Guest (Allen and Unwin, 1938)

Japanese Industry: Its Recent Development and Present Condition (New York: Institute of Pacific Relations, 1940)

A Short Economic History of Modern Japan (Allen and Unwin, 1946; third edition, 1972)

Japan's Economic Recovery (Oxford University Press, 1958); reissued after revision and enlargement as *Japan's Economic Expansion* (Oxford University Press, 1965)

The Structure of Industry in Britain: A Study in Economic Change (Longmans, 1961; third edition, 1970)

Japan as a Market and Source of Supply (Pergamon Press, 1967)

Monopoly and Restrictive Practices (Allen and Unwin, 1968)

British Industry and Economic Policy (Macmillan, 1979)

BOOKS IN JOINT AUTHORSHIP

[In collaboration with E.B. Schumpeter (ed.), E.F. Penrose and M.S. Gordon]

The Industrialisation of Japan and Manchukuo, 1930–1940 (New York: Macmillan Co., 1940)

[In collaboration with A.G. Donnithorne]

Western Enterprise in Far Eastern Economic Development: China and Japan (Allen and Unwin, 1954)

Western Enterprise in Indonesia and Malaya (Allen and Unwin, 1957)

PAMPHLETS AND SEPARATELY PUBLISHED PAPERS

Japan's Banking System, Chronicle Reprints No. 8 (Kobe: Japan Chronicle, 1924)

The British Motor Industry, Special Memorandum, No. 18 (London and Cambridge: Economic Service, June 1926)

British Industry. British Life and Thought Series (Longmans, for British Council, 1944; revised edition, 1949)

*Economic Thought and Industrial Policy, H.K. Lewis (for University College London, 1948)

Economic Fact and Fantasy: A Rejoinder to Galbraith's Reith Lectures. (Occasional Paper, Institute of Economic Affairs, 1967; second edition, 1969)

Japan and the Crisis in International Finance (Economic Research Council, 1972)

The Price of Prosperity: Lessons from Japan [in collaboration with Chiaki Nishiyama], Hobart Paper, 58 (Institute of Economic Affairs, 1974). (Enlarged version issued in Japanese by Kodansha, Tokyo, 1975)

The British Disease, Hobart Paper 67 (Institute of Economic Affairs, 1976; second edition, 1979)

How Japan Competes, Hobart Paper 81 (Institute of Economic Affairs, 1978)

ARTICLES, PAPERS AND CONTRIBUTIONS TO PUBLISHED WORKS

*'An Eighteenth Century Combination in the Copper Mining Industry', in the *Economic Journal* (March 1923)

'A Recent Challenge to the Gold Standard' (A review article on J.M. Keynes, *A Tract on Monetary Reform*), in *Nagoya Koto Shogyo Gakko Economic Journal*, No. 2 (1924)

*'The Recent Currency and Exchange Policy of Japan', in the *Economic Journal* (March 1925)

*'Industrial Changes in the Midlands', in *The Nation and Athenaeum* (26 February 1927)

*'Methods of Industrial Organisation in the West Midlands, 1860–1927', in *Economic History* (January 1929)

'The Population Problem in Japan', in *Economica* (June 1926)

*'Labour Transference and the Unemployment Problem', in the *Economic Journal* (June 1930)

*'The Last Decade in Japan', in *Economic History* (January 1933)

'Japan's Economic Position and Prospects', in *Geography* (June 1934)

*'Economic Thought and Contemporary Economic Policy', in the *Sociological Review* (July 1934)

'The Political and Economic Position of Japan', in *International Affairs* (July–August 1934)

*'The Concentration of Economic Control in Japan', in the *Economic Journal* (March 1937)

*'Recent Changes in the Organisation of the Japanese Cotton Industry', in the *Proceedings of Manchester Statistical Society* (March 1937)

*'State Intervention in Industry', in the *Quarterly Review* (October 1937)

'L'Université de Liverpool', in *L'Enseignement Economique en France et à l'Etranger.* (Cinquantenaire de la Revue d'Economie Politique, 1887–1937, Part II, Paris, 1937)

*'An Aspect of Industrial Reorganisation', in the *Economic Journal* (June–September, 1945)

'Economic Instability and the Unemployment Problem'. Three supplementary chapters to W.J. Ashley, *The Economic Organisation of England* (Longmans, 1948)

*'The Efficiency of British Industry', in the *Westminster Bank Review* (August 1948)

*'Economic Progress, Retrospect and Prospect', in the *Economic Journal* (September 1950)

'The Concentration of Production Policy', in D.N. Chester (ed.), *Lessons of the British War Economy* (Cambridge University Press, 1951)

*'The Outlook for British Industry', in the *Westminster Bank Review* (August 1952)

*'A Note on Monopoly and Economic Progress', in *Economica* (November 1953)

'Monopoly and Competition in the United Kingdom', in E.H. Chamberlin (ed.), *Monopoly and Competition and Their Regulation* (Macmillan, 1954)

*'Western Enterprise in the Far East', in *International Affairs* (July 1954)

'Industrial Production and Productivity in Japan', in the *Westminster Bank Review* (August 1955)

'Industry and Finance in Present-Day Japan', in the *Bankers' Magazine* (June 1955)

'The Present Economic Situation in Japan', in *International Affairs* (July 1955)

'The British Economy', in R. Frei (ed.), *Economic Systems of the West* (Basel: Kyklos-Verlag, 1957)

Revised version of above issued as 'The British Economy', in Calvin B. Hoover, *Economic Systems of the Commonwealth*, Chapter 3 (Duke University Press, 1962)

'The Economic Map of the World: Population, Commerce and Industry', in the *New Cambridge Modern History*, Vol. XII, Chapter 2 (Cambridge University Press, 1960)

*'The Causes of Japan's Economic Growth', in *The Three Banks' Review* (September 1962)

'Factors in Japan's Economic Growth', in C.D. Cowan (ed.), *The Economic Development of China and Japan*, Chapter 7 (Allen and Unwin, 1964)

'The Industrialisation of the Far East', in the *Cambridge Economic History of Europe*, Vol. VI, Chapter 10 (Cambridge University Press, 1965)

*'The Economic Outlook—A Long Period of "Stop"', in *British Industry*, Confederation of British Industry (January 1965)

*'Japan's Economic Problems and Prospects', in *The Three Banks' Review* (December 1967)

*'The Public and Cooperative Sectors in Japan', in *Annals of Public and Cooperative Economy* (Liège, April–June 1968)

'Japan's Place in Trade Strategy', in Hugh Corbet, *Trade Structure and the Asian-Pacific Region*, Part II (Allen and Unwin, 1970)

*'The State and Private Enterprise', in the *Economic Review* (Tokyo: Hitotsubashi University, May 1970)

*'Government Policy towards Competition and Monopoly', in Society of Business Economists, *Changes in the Industrial Structure of the UK*, (April 1970)

*'Competition and Mergers', in *Mergers, Take-overs and The Structure of Industry* I.E.A. Readings No. 10 (Institute of Economic Affairs, 1973)

Contributions to *Chambers Encyclopaedia*, (1973): 'Industry and Trade, State Regulation of'. (Vol VII); 'Japan: Economic Factors' (Vol VIII); 'Rationalisation of Industry' (Vol XI)

*'Why Japan has Prospered', in *Lloyds Bank Review* (January 1974)

*'A Critical Appraisal of Galbraith's Thinking', in *Der Streit um die Gesellschaftsordnung* (Zurich: Schulthess Polygraphischer Verlag, 1975)

*'Advice from Economists-Forty-Five Years Ago', *The Three Banks' Review* (June 1975)

*'Britain's Perception of Japan's Post-War Economic Prospects', in the *Proceedings of the British Association for Japanese Studies*, Vol. 2, Part 1, Chapter 9. (Sheffield: Centre for Japanese Studies, 1977)

*'Education, Science and the Economic Development of Japan', in the *Oxford Review of Education*, Vol. 4, No. 1 (1978)

'Industrial Policy and Comparative Economic Performance: Britain and Japan', in Sheila Marriner (ed.), *Studies in Business, Economic and Accounting History* (Liverpool University Press, 1978)

Index

210